NETWORK PROGRAMMING
FOR THE MICROSOFT
.NET FRAMEWORK

Anthony Jones
Jim Ohlund
Lance Olson

Microsoft
.net

PUBLISHED BY
Microsoft Press
A Division of Microsoft Corporation
One Microsoft Way
Redmond, Washington 98052-6399

Copyright © 2004 by Anthony Jones, Jim Ohlund, Lance Olson

Library of Congress Cataloging-in-Publication Data
Jones, Anthony, 1973-
    Network Programming for the Microsoft .NET Framework / Anthony Jones, Jim Ohlund,
Lance Olson.
        p. cm.
    Includes index.
    ISBN 0-7356-1959-X
    1. Internet programming.   2. Computer networks.   3. Microsoft .NET Framework.   I.
Ohlund, Jim, 1966-   II. Olson, Lance, 1971-   III. Title.

    QA76.625.J655   2003
    005.2'768--dc22   2003060748

Printed and bound in the United States of America.

1 2 3 4 5 6 7 8 9   QWE   8 7 6 5 4 3

Distributed in Canada by H.B. Fenn and Company Ltd.

A CIP catalogue record for this book is available from the British Library.

Microsoft Press books are available through booksellers and distributors worldwide. For further information about international editions, contact your local Microsoft Corporation office or contact Microsoft Press International directly at fax (425) 936-7329. Visit our Web site at www.microsoft.com/mspress. Send comments to *mspinput@microsoft.com*.

Acquisitions Editor: Danielle Bird Voeller
Project Editor: Denise Bankaitis
Technical Editor: Jim Fuchs

Body Part No. X10-00043

For my loving wife, Genevieve, thanks for your patience and understanding.
—A.J.

For Samantha
—J.O.

With love for my wife, Julie, and my children, Caleb, Meg, and Kate.
—L.O.

Contents

Acknowledgments

We would like to thank the following individuals for their generous contributions to the making of this book. Very special thanks go out to Tatiana Shubin for providing many of the Visual Basic .NET code samples throughout this book. Her samples appear in text form and are also downloadable from the book's Web site. We would also like to thank the following people for their technical reviews and edits of many of the chapters: Kit George, Manish Godse, Arthur Bierer, Adarsh Khare, Chad Mumford, Erik Olson, Mauro Ottaviani, Brad Abrams, Yasser Shohoud, and Alexei Vopilov.

And finally, we would like to thank the people at Microsoft Press for their efforts to ensure that this would be a great book: program manager Danielle Voeller Bird, technical editor Jim Fuchs, project editor Denise Bankaitis, copyeditors Brenda Pittsley and Holly Viola, desktop publisher Elizabeth Hansford, electronic artist Michael Kloepfer, and indexer Bill Meyers.

Introduction

Welcome to *Network Programming for the Microsoft .NET Framework*! The Microsoft .NET Framework exposes many powerful networking APIs, such as Winsock and Hypertext Transfer Protocol (HTTP), in a simple, easy-to-use, and consistent manner without sacrificing performance. Several technologies that have no counterparts in the unmanaged arena are also exposed, including remoting and serialization. This book examines these technologies, as well as the network-related classes exposed by the .NET Framework.

Information in this book applies to version 1.0 and version 1.1 of the .NET Framework. Features exclusive to version 1.1 are noted in the text. To best explain these features, many of which are significant, the code samples associated with the text were developed using Microsoft Visual Studio .NET 2003, which is based on version 1.1 of the .NET Framework. The project files will not compile under earlier versions of Visual Studio; however, it's relatively simple to create a new project file and simply add the code files.

How to Use This Book

This book is divided into three sections, which are:

- General Concepts
- Using the Network
- Advanced Concepts

The first section contains five chapters dedicated to introducing basic concepts. Chapter 1 provides an overview of the .NET Framework, discusses the goals of the Framework and the Common Language Runtime (CLR), and introduces the *System.Net* namespace. The different application models are also discussed.

Chapter 2 looks at the common I/O architecture of the .NET Framework, which includes streams, readers, and writers. Many of the classes covered here provide a common interface by using streams for performing network transactions.

Chapter 3 is dedicated to threading and the asynchronous I/O pattern. These two concepts are vital for writing scalable, robust network applications with the .NET Framework. The asynchronous I/O pattern is the common method for performing asynchronous operations on streams and on Web and socket requests, as discussed in subsequent chapters.

Chapter 4 covers serialization, which is a powerful mechanism for transferring arbitrary data on a stream. This chapter discusses the different serialization methods (binary, XML, and SOAP) and the classes used to access this functionality.

Chapter 5 is devoted to universal resource identifiers (URIs). We define URIs, discuss how they are used, and introduce the *Uri* class for parsing and manipulating them. URIs are an integral part of many networking topics covered in this book.

The book's second section delves into the network classes that move data. Chapter 6 launches the discussion with an overview of the *System.Net* namespace that provides the classes dedicated to network communication.

Chapter 7 introduces the Domain Name System (DNS) and the .NET Framework class for accessing DNS. The code samples that are provided resolve names to their protocol address.

Chapters 8 and 9 are devoted to the *Socket* class, which offers the functionality of the unmanaged Winsock API. Chapter 8 covers socket basics and the client side of socket connections, while Chapter 9 discusses socket servers. These chapters also introduce topics such as datagram sockets, IP multicasting, and raw sockets.

Chapter 10 covers the Web-related classes used to retrieve HTTP content. This chapter offers an introduction to HTTP concepts and describes the Web classes in detail.

The book's final section is devoted to advanced networking concepts. Chapter 11 covers XML Web services and describes how XML Web services work within the context of the different layers of the .NET Framework.

Chapter 12 turns to .NET remoting and transports, explaining how to write your own transport and how a transport plugs into the remoting architecture.

Next, Chapter 13 covers network security, including information on code access security, encryption technology, and protocol behaviors that can affect an application's security and robustness.

Chapter 14 is devoted to performance issues and designing and developing applications with performance and scalability in mind. This chapter covers how to manage local machine resources and network resources. It further includes Web classes and how the configurable options affect overall performance.

Finally, Chapter 15 introduces new technologies under development for release in the next major version of the .NET Framework.

How to Use the Code Samples

Each chapter includes code samples that illustrate the principles and technologies discussed in the chapter. Code snippets are in C# and/or Visual Basic. The complete samples are available at *www.microsoft.com/mspress/books/6446.asp*. To download the sample files, click the Companion Content link in the More Information menu on the right side of the page. This action loads the Companion Content page, which includes a link for downloading the sample files. To install the sample files, click the Download The Book's Sample Files link and follow the instructions in the setup program. You'll need to agree to the license agreement that is presented in order to copy the files to your hard disk. By default, the files will be copied to [My Documents]\Microsoft Press\.NET Network Programming, but you will be given an opportunity to change the destination folder during the installation. A menu item ".NET Network Programming" will be created under "Microsoft Press" in your list of All Programs.

System Requirements

The code samples require the .NET Framework version 1.1 to run. The Framework can be installed on Microsoft Windows 98 or later. The code projects were developed with Microsoft Visual Studio .NET 2003 to run as is, but for those projects that don't specifically use version 1.1 features, the sample code can be used under Microsoft Visual Studio .NET 2002 if a new project is created.

For more information about the .NET Framework version 1.1, including a link to the download site, visit *http://msdn.microsoft.com/library /default.asp?url=/library/en-us/dnnetdep/html/redistdeploy.asp*.

Corrections, Comments, and Help

Every effort has been made to ensure the accuracy of this book and the sample files. Should an error be reported, corrections will be provided at the following Web site: *www.microsoft.com/mspress/support/*.

If you have problems, comments, or ideas regarding this book, please send them to Microsoft Press. You can contact Microsoft Press by sending e-mail to: mspinput@microsoft.com. Or you can send postal mail to:

Microsoft Press
Attn: *Network Programming for the Microsoft .NET Framework* Editor
One Microsoft Way
Redmond, WA 98052-6399

Part I

General Concepts

Network Programming with the Microsoft .NET Framework

Welcome to network programming with the Microsoft Windows .NET Framework. The .NET Framework is a platform for distributed computing that enables developers to create powerful network-aware applications with a new level of simplicity and interoperability. In this book, we'll cover the details you need to know to get the most out of your distributed development efforts as you target this new platform. This text is intended to cover a range of network development scenarios, from writing your first socket-based application to developing high performance n-tier Web applications.

Before we get too far into the network-specific elements, it's important to understand the basic principles behind the creation of the .NET Framework. This chapter will walk you through the basics of the .NET Framework and the common language runtime (CLR), with a particular focus on the network-related elements.

We'll start with an overview of the CLR, the execution environment on which the .NET Framework is based. Next we'll explain the overall goals behind the .NET Framework and define some key terms that will be used in this book. Then we'll go over the *System.**-level namespaces, including a look at each of the common models that can be used to create different types of applications such as Microsoft ASP.NET, Windows Forms, Windows Services, and console-based applications. Code examples that demonstrate a basic network application in the context of each application model are included. With the groundwork in place, the remaining portion of this chapter introduces the elements of the .NET Framework most commonly involved in network programming. You'll see that these pieces represent a layered, cohesive stack, as shown in Figure 1-1. The information you get from reading this book will be applicable regardless of the level at which you interface with the .NET Framework.

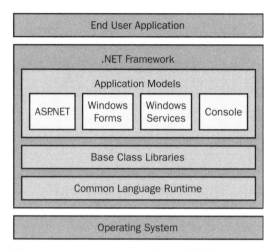

Figure 1-1   An overview of the .NET Framework and related components

Throughout the course of this chapter, we'll be referring to Figure 1-1 as we talk about the different components that make up the .NET Framework and its related components, such as the CLR.

Common Language Runtime

The .NET Framework includes a set of classes that run on top of an execution environment called the CLR. The CLR enables the following key benefits:

■   **Multilanguage support**   True to its name, the CLR is a runtime-execution environment that provides a common set of features across many different languages. Coupled with the .NET Framework classes, developers can write code in the language of their choice and not have to worry about using a different framework of classes. This arrangement is especially useful in a mixed-language environment in which some developers are coding in one language, such as C++, and others are coding in a different language, such as Microsoft

Visual Basic. For example, you don't have to learn a different way to open a file just because a project is better suited to a different programming language.

- **Code access security**   The CLR provides a means of protecting important resources on the system such as the hard disk, the network, or the user interface. Code access security in the CLR protects these resources by inspecting code as it's running and only allowing the code to access a resource if it has *permission*. Administrators and users can decide what permissions they're willing to grant to an application based on information associated with that application called *evidence*. For example, an application that is downloaded off an Internet site and runs in a browser might be able to communicate only with the host site from which it came, whereas an application installed on the local machine and run by a user might be able to send messages to other nodes on the network. In this example, the network represents the protected resource, and the location from which the application runs is used to determine the manner in which the application can access the network.

- **Memory management**   Applications written on top of the CLR do not need to explicitly allocate and free system memory. Handling your own memory management can be complex and time consuming. In fact, memory management is one of the most common sources of bugs and security vulnerabilities in today's applications. Without having to worry about memory management, developers are able to be more productive, write more robust code, and focus on solving their own problems.

- **Managed code**   Managed code is code that executes on top of the CLR. It's called *managed* code because the CLR takes care of, or manages, the code's execution, such as requests for system memory and the application of code access security policies.

Why the .NET Framework?

The .NET Framework was designed with one key goal in mind: to increase the productivity of software developers. This goal is accomplished through a number of features that are built into the framework. Understanding these features will help you maximize your development efforts when using the .NET Framework.

Inherent Benefits of Building on Top of the CLR

As previously mentioned, the .NET Framework is built on the CLR, which was done intentionally to guarantee that the classes in the framework could take advantage of the benefits provided by the CLR. The CLR by itself is an impressive feat of software engineering, but it's the broad set of application functionality on top of the CLR known as the .NET Framework that makes it possible for developers to build fully functional applications that enjoy the benefits of the CLR.

Extensive Use of Patterns

One of the critical ways that the .NET Framework makes the development environment productive is by establishing common patterns for a particular development task that are applied across a broad set of functionality. Error handling, for example, is a task that developers must deal with regardless of the type of application programming interfaces (APIs) used. The .NET Framework simplifies this task by defining one general-purpose mechanism for handling errors so that you can learn it once and then apply the pattern across the development of your application. Examples of patterns in the framework include dealing with collections or groups of objects, interacting with system resources, and handling application events.

Broad Windows Platform Support

The .NET Framework is designed to support development across various versions of the Windows operating system, from Windows 98 up to the latest release of the operating system. This common API set across all the major Windows platforms in deployment today reduces the complexity of development when targeting multiple environments.

Class-Based Model

The APIs in the .NET Framework are encapsulated in classes. A class in the framework usually contains members such as properties and methods. Developers can create an instance of a class in the framework and use it to perform tasks that are required by the application. Developers can also extend classes to include additional behaviors or combine them to define new classes. This object-oriented approach offers a familiar model that you can quickly identify with and relate to as you explore the functionality exposed by the framework.

Layered Architecture

The classes that make up the .NET Framework are *layered*, meaning that at the base of the framework are simple types, which are built on and reused by more complex types. The more complex types often provide the ability to perform more significant operations. For example, the socket class provides raw access to the network. The amount of code that you might write when using the socket class to download a file from the Internet might be 50 lines. The HTTP classes in the framework build on top of the socket class and make it easier to perform the same task. For example, the example that downloads a file from the Internet could now be accomplished in 15 lines of code. More generic *URI resolution* classes make it possible to download the same file in one or two lines of code. This layered approach makes it possible to use the classes that are most applicable to the task your application needs to accomplish. Because one layer builds on top of the other, it also makes it possible for an application to use the higher levels to do most of the work without blocking the ability to access the lower levels for maximum control.

.NET Framework Classes

Now that we've covered a bit of the motivation behind the framework, let's take a deeper look at the classes. Classes in the .NET Framework are divided into logical groups called *namespaces*. Most classes in the .NET Framework exist under a top-level namespace known as *System*. The root *System* namespace contains the basic data types in the framework, such as numbers, Booleans, Uniform Resource Identifiers (URI), strings, and objects, the base type from which all other classes in the framework derive. *System* also contains a broad array of second-level namespaces that represent the core functionality in the framework, such as eventing, infrastructure, interfaces, attributes, and exceptions.

System. * Namespaces Overview

There are two general groups of classes in the .NET Framework: general-purpose base class libraries and application model–specific classes. It's useful to understand the difference between the two so that you'll better know when to use classes from each group as you build your application.

General-Purpose Class Libraries

General-purpose class libraries can be useful in almost any context. For example, *System.String* represents an immutable fixed-length string of Unicode characters. String manipulation is useful in a Web-based application that returns

HTML content to the browser, a GUI client application that runs on the end user's computer, or a long-running service that has no graphical representation at all.

Table 1-1 contains *System* namespaces along with a brief description and an indication of whether the namespace represents a general-purpose base class library or is part of a particular application model. Each namespace contains anywhere from 10 to more than 100 classes, depending on the number of lower-level namespaces it contains.

Table 1-1 Second-Level *System* Namespaces[*]

Namespace	Description	Base Class or Application Model
CodeDom	Classes that can be used to reference the structure of a code document	Base
Collections	Contains interfaces and classes that define various collections of objects, such as lists, queues, bit arrays, hash tables, and dictionaries	Base
ComponentModel	Provides classes that are used to implement the run-time behavior of components and controls	Base
Configuration	Provides classes and interfaces that allow you to programmatically access .NET Framework configuration settings and handle errors in configuration files (.config files)	Base
Data	Contains the classes that represent ADO.NET, which enables you to build components that efficiently manage data	Base
Diagnostics	Provides classes that enable you to interact with system processes, event logs, and performance counters	Base
DirectoryServices	Provides easy access to Active Directory directory services from managed code	Base
Drawing	Provides access to GDI+ basic graphics functionality	Base
EnterpriseServices	Provides an important infrastructure for enterprise applications, including access to COM+	Base
Globalization	Contains classes that define culture-related information, including the language; the country/region; the calendars in use; the format patterns for dates, currency, and numbers; and the sort order for strings	Base
IO	Contains types that allow synchronous and asynchronous reading and writing on data streams and files	Base

Table 1-1   Second-Level *System* Namespaces[*]   *(continued)*

Namespace	Description	Base Class or Application Model
Management	Provides access to a rich set of management information and management events about the system, devices, and applications designed for the Windows Management Instrumentation (WMI) infrastructure	Base
Messaging	Provides classes that allow you to connect to, monitor, and administer message queues on the network and send, receive, or peek messages	Base
Net	Provides access to network resources over protocols such as Transmission Control Protocol (TCP), User Datagram Protocol (UDP), and Hypertext Transfer Protocol (HTTP)	Base
Reflection	Contains classes and interfaces that provide a managed view of loaded types, methods, and fields, with the ability to dynamically create and invoke types	Base
Resources	Provides classes and interfaces that allow developers to create, store, and manage various culture-specific resources used in an application	Base
Runtime	Includes a broad set of third-level namespaces such as a Win32 interoperability layer, remoting, and object serialization	Base
Security	Provides the underlying structure of the CLR security system, including base classes for permissions	Base
ServiceProcess	Provides classes that allow you to implement, install, and control Windows service applications	Application model
Text	Contains classes representing ASCII, Unicode, UTF-7, and UTF-8 character encodings; abstract base classes for converting blocks of characters to and from blocks of bytes; and a helper class that manipulates and formats *String* objects without creating intermediate instances of *String*	Base
Threading	Provides classes and interfaces that enable multithreaded programming	Base
Timers	Provides classes that allow you to raise an event on a specified interval	Base
Web	Supplies classes and interfaces that enable the browser/server communication used by ASP.NET	Application model

Table 1-1 Second-Level *System* Namespaces* *(continued)*

Namespace	Description	Base Class or Application Model
Windows.Forms	Contains classes for creating Windows-based applications that take full advantage of the rich user interface features available in the Microsoft Windows operating system	Application model
Xml	Provides standards-based support for processing XML	Base

* Based on the .NET Framework Class Library overview at *http://msdn.microsoft.com/library/default.asp?url=/library/en-us/cpref/html/frlrfSystemNet.asp.*

As you can tell from Table 1-1, the .NET Framework contains a broad set of functionality.

Application Model–Specific Classes

Think of an application model as a set of classes that define a manner in which an application operates. They define the general structure of the application. The following sections provide a brief look at the application models in the .NET Framework.

ASP.NET ASP.NET, contained in the *System.Web* namespace, is designed to make it easy for developers to build real-world Web applications. It offers a rich application environment for building server-side HTTP applications that dynamically create content and send it to a client, such as a browser or a mobile device.

Using ASP.NET and the base class libraries in the framework designed for distributed application development, you can build applications that gather data from multiple back-end or remote sources and present it to the browser in an aggregated format. The following example demonstrates an ASP.NET page that calls an XML-based Web service using the .NET Framework.

This weather service sample application is extremely simple. It takes a postal code as an input parameter and returns the forecast. In this case, it always returns *sunny* unless the zip code supplied is *11111*, in which case it will say *rainy*, as shown in Figure 1-2. The following code listing shows the code for this application:

Weather Service Sample Application—Visual Basic .NET

```vb
<%@ WebService Language="VB" Class="WeatherService" %>

Imports System
Imports System.Web.Services

' This class exposes a Web Service method that
' takes a zip code and returns the forecast
' for that area.
Public Class WeatherService : Inherits WebService

  ' The logic for GetTodaysForecast is limited for the
  ' purposes of this example to check for
  ' zip = 11111 and return "rainy" if it matches,
  ' otherwise it will return "sunny".
<WebMethod()> Public Function GetTodaysForecast(zip As System.String) As
    System.String

        Dim forecast As String = "sunny"

        If zip = "11111"
            forecast = "rainy"
        End If

        Return forecast
    End Function
End Class
```

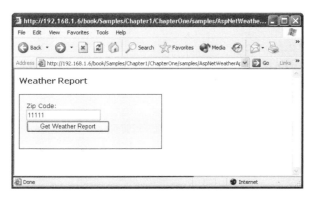

Figure 1-2   ASP.NET weather display page

The ASP.NET weather display page provides a mechanism for entering a postal code into a form and calling the weather service to retrieve and display the forecast, as shown in the following code:

ASP.NET Weather Display Page—C#

```
<%@ Import Namespace="weatherservice" %>
<html>
<script language="C#" runat="server">
  string zipcode = "11111";
  public void Submit_Click(Object sender, EventArgs E)
  {
     try
     {
        // Get the zip code from the form
        zipcode = ZipCode.Text;
     }
     catch (Exception) { /* ignored */ }
        // Create the weather service that will return the forecast
        WeatherService weatherService = new WeatherService();
        // Set the display with the result of GetTodaysForecast
        Result.Text = "Today's forecast is: <b>" +
           weatherService.GetTodaysForecast(zipcode) + "</b>.";
  }
</script>

<body style="font: 10pt verdana">
  <h4>Weather Report </h4>
  <form runat="server">

  <div style="padding:15,15,15,15;background-color:beige;
    width:300;border-color:black;border-width:1;
    border-style:solid">

    Zip Code: <br>
      <asp:TextBox id="ZipCode" Text="11111" runat="server"/><br>

    <input type="submit" id="Add" value="Get Weather Report"
     OnServerClick="Submit_Click" runat="server">
    <p>
    <asp:Label id="Result" runat="server"/>
  </div>
  </form>
</body>
</html>
```

OK, so we just called a pretty basic service on a form that ran on the local machine. "What is so cool about that?" you might ask. Well, on its own, it isn't too exciting. Now consider the possibility that the weather service resides on the Internet rather than on the local machine and is connected to live weather feeds from around the world. The programming model for calling the "ultimate weather service" in this scenario would be exactly the same as the sample you just saw.

Windows Forms   Windows Forms, contained in the *System.Windows.Forms* namespace, is a broad set of classes that enable rapid development of rich client applications.

Using Windows Forms in conjunction with the networking technologies in the .NET Framework, you can create smart end-user applications that interact with other sources of information over the network and present them to the user. An e-mail client, the browser, and music/video players are all examples of rich client applications that use the network.

The following sample demonstrates a Windows Forms application that's used to take a URL from the user, resolve it, and display the resulting HTML in a text box, as shown in Figure 1-3.

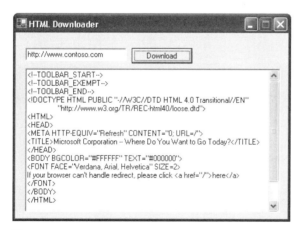

Figure 1-3   Windows Forms–based HTML downloader

HtmlDownloadForm—Visual Basic .NET

```
' This method is called when the user clicks on the download button
Private Sub btnDownload_Click(ByVal sender As System.Object, _
    ByVal e As System.EventArgs) Handles btnDownload.Click

    ' Set the wait cursor so the user knows that the application
    ' is going to do something
    Cursor = Cursors.WaitCursor

    ' The WebClient class can be used to quickly upload/download data
    Dim client As New WebClient()

    ' The call to DownloadData is placed in a Try block because there is
    ' a reasonable chance that it will throw an exception.
    Try
        ' Call DownloadData passing in the URL that was entered into
        ' the UI
        ' Return the byte array back into the content variable.
        Dim content = client.DownloadData(Me.txtUrl.Text)

        ' Use the ASCII encoder to convert the byte array to a string
        ' that can be displayed.
        Me.txtDisplay.Text = Encoding.ASCII.GetString(content)

    Catch ex As Exception
        ' Display the exception if there is one
        MsgBox(ex.ToString)
    End Try
    ' Reset the cursor to normal because the operation is finished.
    Cursor = Cursors.Default
End Sub
```

Windows Services   Windows Services are available through the *System.Service-Process* namespace. The *System.ServiceProcess* classes enable you to create long-running executable applications that run in their own session commonly known as a *service*.

Windows Services are extremely useful for performing routine operations. For example, using Windows Services and the networking classes, you can write an application that checks to see if portions of your Web site are responsive. You can also use services in conjunction with other application models to move data around on scheduled intervals. For example, an ASP.NET page might be rendered using local data that's updated every five minutes through execution of a Windows Service. The following sample demonstrates a Windows Service that downloads a particular file every five minutes.

Windows Service File Downloader—Visual Basic .NET

```vbnet
' This method is called once the service time has gone off
Private Sub tmrDownloadTimer_Elapsed(ByVal sender As System.Object, _
    ByVal e As System.Timers.ElapsedEventArgs) _
    Handles tmrDownloadTimer.Elapsed

        ' Wrap in a try/catch block as this call could fail
        Try
            ' WebClient provides methods for performing basic
            ' network operations such as resolving a URI.
            Dim client As New WebClient()

            ' Downloads the specified URL and saves it to a file
            ' Note that you may want to specify a path for the file
            ' rather than saving it to the default directory
            client.DownloadFile("http://www.contoso.com", _
                "downloadfile.htm")

        Catch ex As Exception

            ' In case it fails, write an exception to the download file
            Dim writer As New StreamWriter("downloadfile.htm")
            writer.Write("The following error occurred. " + ex.ToString())
            writer.Close()

        End Try

        ' Disable download timer
        Me.tmrDownloadTimer.Enabled = False

    End Sub
```

Console   The console is accessible through the *System.Console* class, which is the most basic application model in the .NET Framework. Although the model is quite simple, the console is still an extremely powerful application environment. Many developers prefer the console to other application models because of its inherent simplicity.

The console is a great place for network applications. The most common types of network applications in the console are utility applications that perform some discrete set of functions related to the network. For example, you might want to use a console-based application that sends PING requests to a supplied IP address to determine if a particular node is available on the network. Or you might want a console application that downloads a set of files to make a local backup on demand. *Web crawlers* that download pages on the Internet or an intranet and follow the links are also often written as console applications. Console applications offer a great laboratory in which to develop network logic that can later be moved into a more complex application environment.

The following sample demonstrates a console application that prompts the user for input that's used to resolve a URL and store its contents to a file, as shown in Figure 1-4.

Figure 1-4   Console-based file downloader

Console-Based File Downloader—Visual Basic .NET

```
' This application prompts the console for
' a URL to be downloaded and a file name.  It then
' resolves the URL and stores its contents in the
' specified file.
Module FileDownloader
    Sub Main()
        Dim address As String
        Dim fileName As String
        Dim client As New WebClient()

        ' Prompt for the URL to download
        Console.Write("Enter the HTTP address of the file to download:")
        address = Console.ReadLine

        ' Prompt for the name of the file to be saved
        Console.Write("Enter the file name to save this file as:")
        fileName = Console.ReadLine

        Try
            ' DownloadFile will download the URL supplied in address
            ' and save it to the file specified in fileName
            client.DownloadFile(address, fileName)

        Catch e As Exception
            Console.WriteLine(e.ToString())
        End Try
    End Sub
End Module
```

Common .NET Framework–Based Network Application Elements

Of the namespaces listed in Table 1-1, three base class namespaces focus explicitly on enabling you to develop rich networking scenarios: *System.Net*, *System.Runtime.Remoting*, and *System.Web.Services*. A number of other classes and patterns in the .NET Framework are often useful when it comes to developing applications that interact with the network. This section provides a brief overview of the elements that will be covered in this book and describes why they are often used by network developers.

Input/Output Through Streams

Applications interacting with the network, or with any other resource for that matter, usually need to accomplish one or more of the following:

■ Read input data for the purpose of further processing

■ Write output data for the purpose of further processing by some external entity or by the same application at a later time

The pattern in the .NET Framework for reading and writing data is known as the *Stream pattern*. As you'll see in Chapter 2, the Stream pattern is an incredibly powerful element in the framework because once you learn it, you'll know how to make your application interact with nearly any type of resource available to the system on which it's running.

Threading and Asynchronous APIs

One commonality among network applications is that they tend to perform tasks that can often be time consuming. Sure, the data can be moving around the world at speeds that are baffling, but even 500 milliseconds can turn into a long delay if not properly handled by the application. Applications must go to great lengths to always act responsively to user input. Have you ever used an application that seemed to freeze or hang as it requested information over the network? If so, you know that this can be a very frustrating experience. The .NET Framework supports two key concepts that, when used properly, help to eliminate the frustration caused by an unresponsive application that's waiting on the network. These concepts are threading and the asynchronous API pattern.

The threading support in the framework makes it easy to perform expensive network operations on a thread other than the main thread of execution, which leaves the main thread free to respond to user input in the case of client applications. For server applications, threading can be fine-tuned to maximize hardware utilization and improve the experience of the client interacting with the server.

The .NET Framework also includes a model for calling methods asynchronously. This option gives you many of the same benefits as threading in that you can make a method call on the main thread of execution and quickly return even if the call is one that would block for a long time if called synchronously. The trick comes in the fact that when you make that asynchronous call, a *callback* method is supplied. The framework then processes the call on another thread and calls your callback once the work is done. The big difference between the asynchronous pattern and using the threading support directly is that the framework and the underlying CLR thread pool will take care of threading semantics for you in the asynchronous case. All the classes that support asynchronous execution calls follow this common pattern, so if you learn the pattern for one class, you will have learned it for the whole framework. Chapter 3 will walk you through the details behind both of these important elements of the framework.

Serialization

Serialization is the process by which objects are converted from instance format to a serial or stream format that can be sent across the network. Deserialization is the process of converting that same serialized object back into an instance. Serialization can occur through different formats. For example, binary and SOAP are two formats supported by the .NET Framework. Serialization can also involve different transports. For example, using the .NET Framework, a serialized object can be sent from one machine to another over TCP or over HTTP. Both the format and the transport used can have a significant impact on the ability of one node to interoperate with another. Serialization is a key part of building network applications because it forms the basis by which objects are moved from one application instance to another. Chapter 4 will provide you with an in-depth understanding of the core concepts behind serialization and will demonstrate how to best use it in your applications.

System.Uri

Many applications that use the network do so because they want to access resources. To facilitate the naming of resources, the International Engineering Task Force (IETF) created a standard called the URI. URIs are a critical part of network application development because they enable developers to create names for resources that are globally unique. They also enable applications to decouple a resource on the network from the protocol that is used to retrieve that resource. URIs in the .NET Framework are represented by the *System.Uri* class. Chapter 5 will introduce you to the most common uses of the URI in the .NET Framework and will provide details on key behaviors in *System.Uri*, such as URI comparison, parsing logic, and best practices.

System.Net

System.Net contains the core networking classes that make up the base transport layer for the .NET Framework. The *System.Net* namespace includes classes for working with sockets, TCP, UDP, and higher level protocols such as HTTP and File Transfer Protocol (FTP). Chapter 6 introduces the elements of the *System.Net* namespace and shows how they can be used to build compelling network applications. Chapters 7, 8, and 9 will tell you all that you need to know about using sockets and the Domain Name System (DNS) in the .NET Framework. Chapter 10 covers the details behind the *System.Net* HTTP implementation.

System.Web.Services

The *System.Web.Services* namespace contains classes for creating and consuming Web services. Web services are a set of APIs that enable developers to expose a set of functionality to Web users over the SOAP protocol. Using Web services, you can build applications that interact and interoperate with other nodes on the network and scale to Internet proportions. Chapter 11 demonstrates how the Web services implementation in the .NET Framework is layered on top of other technologies covered in this book and how this information can be useful when building your own or consuming other services. Chapter 11 will include the details behind some of the most common network scenarios, such as calling a Web service from inside ASP.NET in the most scalable way, modifying HTTP headers on a Web service call, and fine-tuning the connection limit and other transport-related properties when consuming a service.

System.Runtime.Remoting

System.Runtime.Remoting contains a framework for creating and executing objects in a distributed manner. It has an extensible architecture that lets you plug in just about any element of the stack, from the transport used to manipulate the object to the payload serialization format with which it is represented.

Chapter 12 describes the elements of the .NET Remoting architecture that relate to the network and demonstrates how they can be modified and extended to get the most out of .NET Remoting.

Security

Security is critical in a networked world. When designing a networked application, developers must constantly be aware of security because most network programs are made interesting by the data or users that are interacting with them. If either of those elements is compromised, the application becomes less useful at best and highly dangerous at worst. The .NET Framework and the underlying CLR were designed from the ground up with network security in mind. In Chapter 13, we'll talk about the most common elements of security, such as authentication, authorization, and encryption and how they factor in with the network-related classes in the framework.

Performance

Network applications often include requirements for high performance. Interactive client applications must remain snappy as the user interacts with resources over the network. Server-side content applications need to perform well to serve the maximum number of clients possible in a timely fashion. Network performance can be a complex and challenging space. The .NET Framework does quite a bit to simplify the process of writing high-performance network applications; however, a few key factors should be considered when writing a network application with the .NET Framework to ensure that you get the most out of your client, server, peer, and the network that they use to interact. Chapter 14 covers network performance, including a set of best practices that will help to fine-tune your network applications.

More to Come

Because the .NET Framework is in active development, Microsoft is working on a number of new components related to distributed programming. In Chapter 15, we'll take a brief look at a number of the exciting trends in network development that are driving this work and discuss ways in which your applications can take advantage of these trends to provide a better user experience. We'll also point out some related areas where we expect to see more support in the framework to help your applications get the most out of the network.

Summary

We've now gone through an overview of the .NET Framework and the CLR. We've talked about the motivating factors behind these technologies and the key benefits that they provide. Finally, we've discussed the elements contained within the .NET Framework that are most applicable to network development scenarios. Hopefully, by now you'll agree that you can build just about any type of network application using the .NET Framework. In the chapters ahead, we'll be going through the specifics of exactly how to build the best distributed applications using each of the key technologies that make up network programming for the .NET Framework.

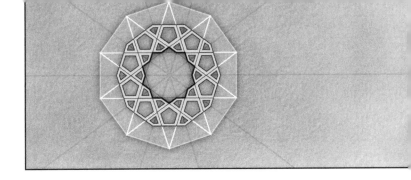

2

Managed I/O: Streams, Readers, and Writers

The Microsoft Windows .NET Framework offers a unified way to access operating system resources such as files, memory, and network resources through the stream I/O pattern. Streams provide a common way to perform I/O operations regardless of the operating system resource. In general, streams allow you to read and write data sequentially to a container (which we call a *backing store*) as if the data is a continuous sequence of bytes where the first byte that's written becomes the first byte to be read, and so on. The container is called a backing store because it will typically hold or store the data that's written to the stream. Figure 2-1 describes a stream as a sheet of paper where the paper represents a backing store that can hold letters of the alphabet. A supplier or writer can write the letters of the alphabet sequentially on the paper. A consumer or reader can eventually read the alphabetic characters from the paper in the order in which they were originally written.

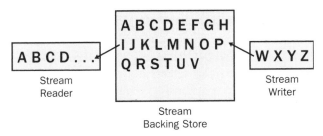

Figure 2-1 The stream I/O process

In this chapter, you'll discover how to perform I/O on files, memory, and networks using stream classes in the .NET Framework. We'll start out describing the *Stream* class that's inherited by several classes that allow you to perform I/O in a common way across different operating system resources. We'll focus mostly on performing I/O on files and network resources because this is a network programming book. Once we have described the core stream classes, we'll talk about other stream classes that interact with the core stream classes. Finally, we'll introduce stream readers and writers that allow you to read and write formatted text and binary data types to streams.

Stream Types

There are two types of streams available: base and composable. *Base streams* are streams that work directly with a backing store such as a file. *Composable streams*, on the other hand, are streams that operate on top of other streams. Composable streams by their nature have constructors that accept a stream as a parameter, whereas base streams do not. Therefore, a composable stream relies on the base stream you provide as input. For example, you can have a stream that handles encryption and decryption of data. If you want to write encrypted data to a file, you can write to a composable encryption stream that must call a base stream that's capable of writing the data from the encryption stream to a file. You can layer as many composable streams as you want on top of one another until you reach a base stream.

Figure 2-2 shows a stream relationship diagram that describes how base streams and composable streams interact with one another. At the top of the diagram, you'll see stream readers and writers that are essentially classes specifically designed to read or write formatted data to a stream. Stream readers and writers are described later in the chapter, and you'll find that they make stream programming easier because they allow you to work with data using a friendlier format, such as strings. It's important to note that the readers and writers can interact with either composable streams or base streams to perform I/O. The composable stream box shows that a composable stream must interact with a base stream to perform I/O on a system resource. A composable stream can also interact with another composable stream. The dashed line between the composable and base stream boxes illustrate this interaction. The base stream box shows that base streams are the only interfaces that actually interact directly with system resources.

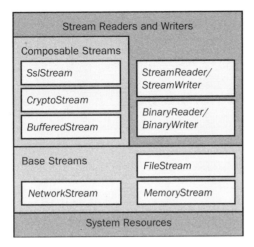

Figure 2-2   Stream relationship diagram

Stream Class

The foundation for managed I/O in the .NET Framework is the *Stream* class. The *Stream* class is an abstract class that must be inherited to create either a base stream or a composable stream. The *Stream* class provides simple common methods to read and write data directly to a store, such as base streams, or to another stream, such as composable streams.

Basic Operations

Once you have successfully created a stream, you can begin performing I/O operations. Table 2-1 describes the main operations that are generally available in all stream classes to handle I/O. Depending on the stream at hand, it will not be possible to implement all operations for various technical reasons. If a stream does not handle a particular method, generally it will throw a *NotSupported-Exception* from the *System* namespace.

Table 2-1   Basic Stream Methods

Method	Description
BeginRead	Allows data to be read asynchronously from a data store
BeginWrite	Allows data to be written asynchronously to a data store
Close	Closes a stream for further I/O operations and releases any operating system resources associated with a stream

Table 2-1   Basic Stream Methods   *(continued)*

Method	Description
EndRead	Completes asynchronous read operations started from *BeginRead*
EndWrite	Completes asynchronous write operations started from *BeginWrite*
Flush	Forces any buffered data associated with a stream to be written to the backing store
Read	Allows one or more data bytes to be read from a backing store
ReadByte	Allows one byte to be read from a backing store
Seek	Allows the *Position* property of the stream to be set
SetLength	Allows the size of the backing store in bytes to be controlled
Write	Allows bytes to be written to a backing store
WriteByte	Allows one byte to be written to a backing store

Common Properties

Stream classes also have several properties that help streams work with a backing store. Table 2-2 describes the available properties.

Table 2-2   Basic Stream Properties

Property	Description
CanRead	Determines if the stream can be read
CanSeek	Determines if the stream allows you to change the *Position* property
CanWrite	Determines if the stream can be written to
Length	Reports the size in bytes of the backing store
Position	Controls the location in a stream where the next byte will be read or written to a backing store

Reading and writing data to stream classes is handled using byte-type arrays. This method is fine if you're developing an application that simply deals with data in binary form. Later in this chapter, we'll present stream reader and writer classes that allow you to read and write text data or other binary data types. For our discussions of the stream, we'll stick to reading and writing data in byte-type form.

Synchronous and Asynchronous I/O

Our discussion of performing I/O with streams in this chapter centers on handling synchronous I/O patterns where the *Read* or *Write* stream methods will block until the I/O operation is completed with the system resource. Depending on the resource, blocking can be very limiting to your application, especially if you need to service something else, such as the user interface of your application, and are stuck waiting all day to read data from a system resource such as a network. The .NET Framework also allows you to perform I/O asynchronously. The next chapter will describe threading and the asynchronous I/O pattern, where you can use the *BeginRead*, *EndRead*, *BeginWrite*, and *EndWrite* methods to avoid blocking on I/O operations. When performing I/O on streams, you should choose between either synchronous or asynchronous I/O patterns and never mix the two styles.

Base Streams

Base streams are stream classes that perform I/O directly with operating system resources such as files, memory, and network resources. In the .NET Framework version 1, only three base streams are available: *FileStream*, *MemoryStream*, and *NetworkStream*.

> **Note**   In the .NET Framework version 2, there are plans to include a new serial base stream that will enable you to communicate with serial devices such as COM ports or even USB serial devices.

File Stream

One of the most practical uses for streams is reading and writing data to files. The .NET Framework provides the *FileStream* class that is specifically designed to work with file I/O. Working with files involves creating a file or opening an existing file, reading and writing data to the file, and eventually closing the file from read and write operations.

> **Note** Later in this chapter, we'll discuss how stream readers and writers can also allow you to read or write data to a file without having to create a file stream. Readers and writers have constructors that take a path identifying a file and internally create a file stream. Unless you need more granular control of file I/O, it's often a good idea to use readers/writers for accessing files without having to explicitly create file streams.

Creating or Opening a File

Before you can begin reading or writing data to a file, you must create a new file or open an existing file. To do so, you must supply file location information to the *FileStream* constructor method. Another static class in the *System.IO* namespace named *File* is also capable of creating a file stream and performing other file management tasks. For simplicity, we only show how to create a new file using the *FileStream* constructor. The following code fragment shows how to create a new file named Jim.dat in your current working directory and set the access control for the file to read and write:

C#

```csharp
FileStream MyFileStream = null;
try
{
    MyFileStream = new FileStream(".\\Jim.dat", FileMode.Create,
        FileAccess.ReadWrite);
}
catch (Exception e)
{
    Console.WriteLine(
        "Failed to create file with the following error: "
        + e.Message);
}
finally
{
    MyFileStream.Close();
}
```

Visual Basic .NET

```
Dim MyFileStream As FileStream
Try
    'Open the file
    MyFileStream = New FileStream(
        ".\Jim.dat", FileMode.Create, FileAccess.ReadWrite)
Catch e As Exception
    Console.WriteLine(
        "Failed to create/open file stream with error: " _
        + e.Message)
Finally
    MyFileStream.Close()
End Try
```

It's important to note that many other prototypes for the *FileStream* constructor enable more control for gaining access to a file. Two main parameters featured in each prototype control file creation: *FileMode* and *FileAccess*. *FileMode* is an enumeration that determines how a file is created. For our sample code, we use the *Create* enumeration flag that causes the system to create a new file if one does not already exist; otherwise, the flag overwrites an existing file. The other enumeration, *FileAccess*, determines if your application can read or write to the file. For our sample code, we've decided to do both.

Reading or Writing to a File

Files are normally constructed as one of two types: text or binary. Text files typically contain printable ASCII and Unicode characters that can normally be viewed using a text reader such as Notepad in Windows. Some examples of text files can be Readme.txt files or even XML files. Binary files, on the other hand, are files that usually contain an ordered set of bytes that are typically not printable. The order (or sequence) of the bytes in a binary file is important to the application that uses the file. An example of a binary file is an MP3 audio file, where bytes are arranged in a sequence to represent encoded audio information. The sequence (or ordering) of bytes in an MP3 file must be ordered in a well-defined way so that an application such as Windows Media Player can play back the audio information correctly. If you try to view a binary file using a text viewer such as Notepad, you'll most likely see a bunch of garbled characters because many of the bytes will typically not be printable ASCII or Unicode characters.

The basic *FileStream* class allows you to read and write data as an array of bytes. As mentioned earlier, we'll present stream reader and writer classes that allow you to read and write formatted text data or other binary data types to a stream. Using the *FileStream* object *MyFileStream* that we created earlier in the chapter, we can begin writing byte-type data to a newly created file. The following code fragment shows how you can write 10 bytes to a file.

C#

```csharp
byte [] MyByteArray = new byte[10];

for (int i = 0; i < MyByteArray.Length; i++)
{
    MyByteArray[i] = 1;
}
try
{
    MyFileStream.Write(MyByteArray, 0, MyByteArray.Length);
}
catch (Exception e)
{
    Console.WriteLine("Write failed with error: " + e.Message);
}
```

Visual Basic .NET

```vbnet
Dim MyByteArray(10) As Byte
Dim i As Short
For i = MyByteArray.GetLowerBound(0) _
    To MyByteArray.GetUpperBound(0) - 1

    MyByteArray(i) = 1
Next

Try
    MyFileStream.Write(MyByteArray, 0, _
        MyByteArray.GetUpperBound(0))
Catch e As Exception
    Console.WriteLine("Write failed with error: " + e.Message)
End Try
```

Once bytes are written to a file, you can continue writing additional bytes or start reading the bytes that are already written. As you write bytes to a file, *FileStream* maintains a stream *Position* property that knows where the last byte was written to the stream or read from the stream. The *Position* property can be manipulated directly by setting it to a value offset position in the file, or you can call the *Seek* method to change the position. The following code fragment demonstrates how to set the position to the beginning of the file using the *Seek* method on *MyFileStream*:

C#

```csharp
// Code fragment using C#
try
{
    MyFileStream.Seek(0, SeekOrigin.Begin);
}
```

```
catch (Exception e)
{
    Console.WriteLine("Seek failed with error: " + e.Message);
}
```

Visual Basic .NET

```
Try
    MyFileStream.Seek(0, SeekOrigin.Begin)
Catch e As Exception
    Console.WriteLine("Seek failed with error: " + e.Message)
End Try
```

Once the position is set and there are bytes that follow the position, you can begin reading bytes from the file. Reading bytes is simple because all you have to do is call the *FileStream*'s *Read* method using a byte array to receive a sequence of bytes from where the stream *Position* is set. When *Read* completes successfully, it will return the number of bytes read. It's important to note that *Read* might return less bytes than you requested and the buffer you supply might not be filled. This normally happens when you reach the end of a file stream. When you reach the end of the file stream and try to read more bytes, *Read* will return zero. The following code fragment describes how to read a file stream one byte at a time until you reach the end of the file:

C#

```
byte [] MyReadBuffer = new byte[1];

while(true)
{
    int BytesRead;

    try
    {
    BytesRead = MyFileStream.Read(
        MyReadBuffer, 0, MyReadBuffer.Length);
    }
    catch (Exception e)
    {
        Console.WriteLine("Read failed with error: " +
            e.Message);
        break;
    }

    if (BytesRead == 0)
    {
        Console.WriteLine(
            "No more bytes to read - reached end of stream");
        break;
    }
}
```

```
    Console.WriteLine("Read byte -> " + _
        MyReadBuffer[0].ToString());
}
```

Visual Basic .NET

```
Dim MyReadBuffer(1) As Byte

While True
    Dim BytesRead As Integer

    Try
        BytesRead = MyFileStream.Read(
        MyReadBuffer, 0, MyReadBuffer.GetUpperBound(0))
    Catch e As Exception
        Console.WriteLine("Read failed with error: " + _
            e.Message)
        Exit While
    End Try

    If BytesRead = 0 Then
        Console.WriteLine("No more bytes to read")
        Exit While
    End If

    Console.WriteLine("Read byte -> " + _
        MyReadBuffer(0).ToString())
End While
```

> **Note** When reading and writing data to a *FileStream*, I/O is buffered, which means that data is read and written to a file in the most efficient manner possible. For example, if your application is designed to write data in small chunks using many *Write* calls, the data written will be collected to memory flushed to the actual disk mechanism at some point. Later in this chapter, we'll talk about a composable stream that provides buffering capabilities to make stream I/O more efficient. However, because the *FileStream* class provides buffering already, there's no point in using another buffering mechanism above this class.

Closing a File

When all reading and writing to a file is complete, you should close the *FileStream* to release operating system resources related to the file being manipulated. To close the *FileStream*, simply call the *Close* method. If you try to read or write to the file after calling *Close*, all methods will fail. We demonstrated how to call *Close* in the *try-catch-finally* programming block earlier in this chapter when we showed how to create a file stream.

The companion material includes a sample named FileStreamSample that demonstrates how to read and write to a file using the same principles learned so far in the code fragments in this section.

Memory Stream

Memory streams, which perform I/O on memory resources, are another type of base stream. Memory streams are very similar to file streams, except that data is read and written to a memory buffer rather than to a file on a disk. You might even be wondering why there's a memory stream class in the first place, especially when you can allocate memory from an application and write directly to a data buffer. From the standpoint of reading and writing data to memory, a memory stream isn't much different from a buffer. One benefit in having memory accessible in the form of a stream is that streams are composable, meaning that you can build one on top of the other very easily, as mentioned earlier. For example, you can have a memory stream that's layered below a composable encryption stream that's layered below a composable compression stream, so at the end of the day, your application is writing compressed encrypted data to memory using one consistent I/O pattern.

Creating a Memory Stream

The *MemoryStream* class allows you to create a memory stream with a memory buffer as a backing store of a fixed size or of a dynamic size. The *MemoryStream* constructor features several prototypes that allow you to pass in a fixed byte-type array buffer that the stream internally uses as a backing store to read and write data. Otherwise, you can specify a size in bytes where the stream will dynamically allocate and manage a buffer for you. The following code fragment creates a memory stream that does not specify a memory size. In this case, the stream will automatically allocate memory as needed as data bytes are written to the stream. Initially, the backing store is set to zero bytes.

C#

```csharp
// Code fragment using C#
MemoryStream MyMemoryStream = null;
try
{
    MyMemoryStream = new MemoryStream();
}
catch (Exception e)
{
    Console.WriteLine(
        "Failed to create a memory stream with error: "
        + e.Message);
    return;
}
finally
{
    MyMemoryStream.Close();
}
```

Visual Basic .NET

```vbnet
Dim MyMemoryStream As System.IO.MemoryStream
Try
    MyMemoryStream = New System.IO.MemoryStream()
Catch e As Exception
    Console.WriteLine("Failed to create a memory " & _
        "stream with error: " + e.Message)
Finally
    MyMemoryStream.Close()
End Try
```

Handling Memory Stream I/O

Reading and writing to a *MemoryStream* is just like handling I/O in a *FileStream*, as described earlier, except that if you create a memory stream with a fixed buffer, you might experience an *IOException* if you attempt to write more bytes than the buffer can handle. Another important item worth mentioning is that it's important to call *Close* on a dynamically allocated memory stream. *Close* effectively releases the memory associated with the stream, and the data written there is no longer available. The companion material includes a sample named MemoryStreamSample that demonstrates how to read and write data bytes to a dynamically allocated and managed memory stream. As the sample runs, it will monitor how many bytes are actually allocated to the dynamic backing store as bytes are read and written using a property unique to the *MemoryStream* class named *Capacity*.

Network Stream

Network streams allow you to communicate between processes over a network or even on the same computer. Network streams rely on the *Sockets* class from the *System.Net* namespace as a backing store to communicate from one socket to another, and any application can create one or more sockets to communicate. Network streams require stream-oriented sockets to form a backing store and work only with connection-oriented network protocols such as TCP/IP. Network streams do not work with datagram-based network protocols such as User Datagram Protocol (UDP). Stream-oriented sockets form a virtual connection between two socket pairs to transmit and receive data in sequential order. One of the most popular stream-oriented sockets is one that communicates over the TCP/IP protocol. There are many other ways that sockets can be created and controlled, which is the topic of discussion in Chapter 12. Utilizing network streams requires a complete understanding of how to set up a stream-oriented connected socket pair. For our discussion of network streams, we'll present only TCP/IP sockets. In this chapter, we'll gloss over the details of creating and setting up a stream-oriented socket connection, and the code fragment in this section will assume that a valid socket connection exists.

Compared to file and memory streams, sockets behave quite differently as a backing store. Stream-oriented connected sockets are bidirectional, which means that there are two communication paths within the connected socket pairs. If you write data to Socket A, you will be able to read the same data only on a peer—Socket B. Figure 2-3 shows bidirectional flow by writing the letters of the alphabet in order from Socket A and receiving the letters on Socket B. In the other direction, we write the numbers 1 through 3 from Socket B and they are read from Socket A. You will not be able to read the data you originally wrote to Socket A from the same socket. The same behavior is true if you write data to Socket B where you'll be required to read the data on Socket A.

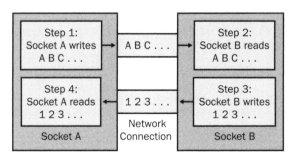

Figure 2-3   Bidirectional stream-oriented connected sockets

Another major difference in a network stream as compared to other streams is that a network stream doesn't maintain the stream *Position* property, which means that you can't call *Seek* or change the *Position* of the stream. When a network stream reads data from a *Socket*, the data becomes consumed and is no longer available to be read again. Therefore, the network stream is unable to maintain the *Position* pointer. For example, in Figure 2-3 on step 2, Socket B can read the A B C characters only one time. Once the characters are read, the characters get removed from the stream. Therefore, if you try to change the *Position* property or call *Seek*, you'll get a *NotSupportedException*.

Creating a Network Stream

Creating a network stream requires having a socket connection established with another socket before you create the network stream to perform I/O. If your socket is not connected, the *NetworkStream* constructor will raise an *Argument-Exception*. Also, your socket must be running in blocking mode, which is the default behavior when you create a socket. If your socket is non-blocking, an *IOException* will be raised. For more information about blocking and non-blocking sockets, see Chapter 8. The following code fragment demonstrates how to create a network stream on top of a socket named *MySocket*:

C#

```
Socket  MySocket;
// Assume we have a connected socket already created.
NetworkStream MyNetworkStream;

try
{
    // Setup a network stream on a connected Socket
    MyNetworkStream = new NetworkStream(MySocket, true);
}
catch (Exception e)
{
    Console.WriteLine("Failed to create network stream " +
        "with error: " + e.Message);
}
finally
{
    MyNetworkStream.Close();
}
```

Visual Basic .NET

```
Dim MySocket As Socket

' Assume we have a connected Socket already created.
Dim MyNetworkStream As System.Net.Sockets.NetworkStream
```

```
Try
    ' Setup a network stream on the client Socket
    MyNetworkStream = New System.Net.Sockets.NetworkStream(
    MySocket, True)
Catch e As Exception
    Console.WriteLine("Failed to create a network stream " & _
        "with error: " + e.Message)
Finally
    MyNetworkStream.Close()
End Try
```

The *NetworkStream* constructor features a useful parameter named *owns-Socket* that allows the network stream to own the underlying socket. When this parameter is *true*, *NetworkStream*'s *Close* method will release the resources of the network stream and close the underlying socket in one call. When the *ownsSocket* parameter is *false*, the underlying socket will stay open for more communication. Your application will have to close the socket at a later point.

Handling Network I/O

As we mentioned earlier, reading and writing to a network stream is a lot different from performing I/O with file and memory streams because network streams use sockets as a backing store. Sockets are bidirectional—as you write data on a socket, you can't receive the same data on the same socket. Also, as you read a socket, the I/O operation can block until the peer socket writes data on your socket or until the peer closes the network stream. Additionally, write operations can block if the peer socket does not read data. When reading data from a network stream, you have to check how many bytes are read into your data buffer supplied to the *Read* operation. If the number of bytes is zero, the peer socket has closed down the communication stream. The following code fragment demonstrates how to read bytes from a network stream named *MyNetworkStream* that we created earlier:

C#

```
try
{
int BytesRead = 0;
byte [] ReadBuffer = new byte[4096];

    do
    {
        BytesRead = MyNetworkStream.Read(
            ReadBuffer, 0, ReadBuffer.Length);

        Console.WriteLine("We read " + BytesRead.ToString()
            + " bytes from a peer socket.");
    }
```

```
    while (BytesRead > 0);
}
catch (Exception e)
{
    Console.WriteLine(
        "Reading a network stream failed with error: "
        + e.Message);
}
```

Visual Basic .NET

```
Try
    Dim BytesRead as Integer
    BytesRead = 0

    Dim ReadBuffer(4096) As Byte

    Do
        BytesRead = MyNetworkStream.Read(ReadBuffer, 0,
            ReadBuffer.GetUpperBound(0))
            Console.WriteLine("We read " + BytesRead.ToString() +
            " bytes from a peer socket.")
    Loop While BytesRead > 0
Catch e As Exception
    Console.WriteLine("Reading a network stream failed " & _
        "with error: " + e.Message)
End Try
```

Writing to a network stream is very straightforward. The only thing you have to worry about is a peer closing a connection because the *Write* operation will raise an *IOException* indicating that the peer is no longer available to receive the data that was written. The following code fragment shows how to write to the *MyNetworkStream* network stream described earlier:

C#

```
// Assume we have a buffer with 1024 bytes
try
{
    MyNetworkStream.Write(Buffer, 0, Buffer.Length);
}
catch (Exception e)
{
    Console.WriteLine(
        "Failed to write to network stream with error: "
        + e.Message);
}
```

Visual Basic .NET

```
Try
    MyNetworkStream.Write(Buffer, 0, Buffer.GetUpperBound(0))

Catch e As Exception
    Console.WriteLine(
        "Failed to write to network stream with error: "
        + e.Message)
End Try
```

Once all I/O has completed on a network stream, it's important to call the *Close* method to free any resources associated with the network stream. Also, if the network stream owns the underlying socket, calling *Close* will free up socket network resources associated with the network stream.

The companion material contains two network stream samples called Sender and Receiver that enable you to send data bytes from the Sender to the Receiver application across a network or even on the same machine. The Receiver application is designed to listen for a network stream connection and receive data as it arrives. The Sender application is designed to connect to the Receiver application's network stream and send data bytes to the Receiver.

Composable Streams

Composable stream classes are streams that can perform I/O on top of another underlying stream. It's important to understand that the underlying stream can be a base stream or even another composable stream. As we mentioned earlier, composable streams have constructors that accept a stream as a parameter. This is a powerful idea because you can layer I/O techniques for reading data from and writing data to resources. For example, if you want to encrypt some data and save it to a file, you could simply open a base stream—*FileStream*—followed by a composable stream—*CryptoStream*—and then begin writing encrypted data to a file, as shown in Figure 2-4. In the .NET Framework version 1, only two composable streams are available: *BufferedStream* and *CryptoStream*.

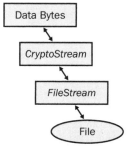

Figure 2-4   Layering one stream on top of another stream

> **Note**   In the .NET Framework version 2, there are plans to include a new composable stream to handle Secure Sockets Layer (SSL) communications over a stream. This new stream potentially will allow you to use streams to communicate to an SSL server over a network by layering an SSL-composable stream over a network stream.

BufferedStream Class

BufferedStream is an interesting class that's designed to improve I/O performance when either reading or writing to another stream. This composable stream can be very useful, especially if your application performs I/O by reading or writing data in very small amounts. The class maintains an internal buffer to cache or collect the data, and at some point it will automatically flush data to the next stream or hold data until your application is ready to read from the stream.

By default, the *BufferedStream* class maintains a buffer of 4096 bytes. You can override the default by specifying any size buffer through the constructor, depending on your application's needs. The buffer can be used only for read or write operations, but not for both at the same time. If your application alternates between *Read* and *Write* calls continuously, the buffer will not be used very effectively. So, if you're developing an application that makes a series of either *Read* or *Write* calls using small amounts of data, the *BufferedStream* class can potentially improve I/O performance with operating system resources.

In the BufferedStreamSample directory of the companion material, we revised the C# version of our network stream Sender application to include a *BufferedStream*. The new buffered stream sample is named Sender. If you run the Sender application to communicate with the network stream Receiver sample application mentioned earlier in this chapter, you'll find that fewer I/O calls are made on the receiver compared to using the non-buffered network stream Sender application. Less calls are made because the buffered stream Sender application gathers the data and transmits the data in one big block over the network.

CryptoStream Class

The *CryptoStream* class is another composable stream that enables an application to encrypt and decrypt data to and from another stream. This class is located in the *System.Security.Cryptography* namespace. To use this class effectively, you need to understand cryptography, which is beyond the scope of this book. However, we'll take a moment here to explain how to encrypt data using a cryptographic algorithm. One book that might be helpful in fully understanding cryptography is *Applied Cryptography: Protocols, Algorithms, and Source Code in C, Second Edition* by Bruce Schneier (John Wiley & Sons, 1995).

In cryptography, two different techniques are used to encrypt and decrypt data: symmetric and asymmetric cryptography. Symmetric methods use a *secret key* to encode and decode data. Asymmetric methods use a *public key* to encode data and a *private key* to decode data. Symmetric cryptography is one of the oldest forms of cryptography, so for our sample code, we'll use the well-known symmetric algorithm Data Encryption Standard (DES). Many other algorithms are available in the .NET Framework to support both symmetric and asymmetric techniques. Table 2-3 describes the available cryptography algorithms.

Table 2-3   Available Cryptography Algorithms

Algorithm	Technique
Digital Signature Algorithm (DSA)	Asymmetric
RSA Security	Asymmetric
Data Encryption Standard (DES)	Symmetric
"Rivest's Cipher" (RC2)	Symmetric
Rijndael	Symmetric
Triple Data Encryption Standard (TripleDES)	Symmetric

The following code fragment shows how to set up a *CryptoStream* that can write encrypted data to a *FileStream* using the DES algorithm. For simplicity, we made up a secret key that's a combination of the variables *DESKey* and *DESInitializationVector* to show how stream encryption can be accomplished using the DES algorithm.

C#

```
// Make up a secret key to be used by DES to encrypt data
byte [] DESKey = {200, 5, 78, 232, 9, 6, 0, 4};
byte [] DESInitializationVector = {9, 9, 9};

//
// Let's create a Symmetric crypto stream using the
// DES algorithm to encode all the bytes written to
// the file Jim.
//
CryptoStream MyStreamEncrypter;
```

```
try
{
    DES DESAlgorithm = new DESCryptoServiceProvider();

    MyStreamEncrypter = new CryptoStream(MyFileStream,
        DESAlgorithm.CreateEncryptor(DESKey,
        DESInitializationVector),
        CryptoStreamMode.Write);
}
catch (Exception e)
{
    Console.WriteLine(
        "Failed to create DES CryptoStream with error: "
        + e.Message);
}
finally
{
    MyStreamEncypter.Close();
}
```

Visual Basic .NET

```
'
' Let's create a private key that will be used to encrypt
' and decrypt the data stored in the file Jim.
'
Dim DESKey() As Byte = {200, 5, 78, 232, 9, 6, 0, 4}

Dim DESInitializationVector() As Byte =
    {0, 1, 2, 3, 4, 5, 6, 7, 8, 9}


'
' Let's create a Symmetric crypto stream using the
' DES algorithm to encode all the bytes written to
' the file Jim.
'
Dim MyStreamEncrypter As CryptoStream

Try
    Dim DESAlgorithm As DES
    DESAlgorithm = New DESCryptoServiceProvider()

    'Dim MyStreamEncrypter As CryptoStream
    MyStreamEncrypter = New CryptoStream(MyFileStream, _
        DESAlgorithm.CreateEncryptor(DESKey, _
        DESInitializationVector), CryptoStreamMode.Write)
```

```
Catch e As Exception
    Console.WriteLine( _
        "Failed to create DES Symmetric CryptoStream " & _
        "with error: " + e.Message)
Finally
    MyStreamEncrypter.Close()
End Try
```

The *CryptoStream* class supports reading and writing data to the stream; however, you can't perform both operations at the same time. During *Crypto-Stream* creation, you have to specify whether your stream will read or write data by using the *CryptoStreamMode* parameter. The *CryptoStream* class also does not support seeking, so you can't change the *Position* property or call the *Seek* method to read or write to another section of a stream.

In the companion material, we have provided a CyptoStreamSample application that demonstrates how to use a *CryptoStream* with a *FileStream* to encrypt data and send it to a file.

Readers and Writers

Stream readers and writers provide a convenient way to read and write text and binary data types to streams. You might have noticed in our discussions so far that stream *Read* and *Write* methods perform I/O using byte-type data arrays. Using byte-type arrays to read and write data makes stream classes inconvenient, especially when you're writing text because your application has to spend a great deal of time converting data types to byte arrays. There are two reader classes—*StreamReader* and *BinaryReader*—and two writer classes—*StreamWriter* and *BinaryWriter*—that make handling I/O on streams a snap.

StreamReader and *StreamWriter*

The best way to read and write character-based data to a stream is by using the *StreamReader* and *StreamWriter* classes. Both classes are based on the abstract classes *TextReader* and *TextWriter* that enable you to read and write a sequence of characters.

These classes also allow you to read and write characters in different character encoding formats, such as ASCII or Universal Character Set (UCS). Many UCS Transformation Formats (UTF) are available, such as an 8-bit encoding form called UTF-8. Table 2-4 describes the available encoding techniques supported by the *StreamReader* and *StreamWriter* classes. By default, these reader/writer classes use UTF-8 encoding and decoding. However, you can specify other techniques through one of the constructor methods.

Table 2-4   Encoding/Decoding Techniques for Stream Readers/Writers

Technique	Description
ASCII	Unicode characters are encoded/decoded as 7-bit ASCII characters
Big-endian Unicode	Unicode characters are encoded/decoded in big-endian byte form
Unicode	Unicode characters are encoded/decoded as UTF-16 characters
UTF-7	Unicode characters are encoded/decoded as UTF-7 characters
UTF-8	Unicode characters are encoded/decoded as UTF-8 characters

The most useful methods in the *StreamWriter* class are *Write* and *Write-Line*, which come from the *TextWriter* class. The only difference between the two methods is that *WriteLine* places a carriage return followed by a line feed at the end of the text and *Write* does not. Both methods have many prototypes and allow you to read and write many numerical data types and strings as text to a stream. For example, the following code fragment shows how to write a simple character string to a file stream:

C#

```
StreamWriter MyStreamWriter = new StreamWriter(MyFileStream);

MyStreamWriter.WriteLine("Using stream writers is great!");
```

Visual Basic .NET

```
Dim MyStreamWriter As StreamWriter
MyStreamWriter = New StreamWriter(MyFileStream)
MyStreamWriter.WriteLine("Using stream writers is great!")
```

In the *StreamReader* class, there's a *Read* method that allows you to read a single character or a specified number of characters from a stream. There's also a *ReadLine* method that allows you to read a line of text into a string. Finally, there's a *ReadToEnd* method that will read the entire contents of the stream and return a string. *ReadToEnd* is great for downloading a small text file over a network stream. In the companion material samples, we have a sample named TextIO that demonstrates how to read and write text to files using stream readers and writers.

BinaryReader and *BinaryWriter*

The *BinaryReader* and *BinaryWriter* stream classes allow you to read and write specific data types to a stream in binary form, which means that the data types are read and written as they're represented in computer memory. For example, you can write an object of type *Int32* and the *BinaryWriter* will write a 4-byte signed integer to a stream and advance the *Position* property of the stream by four bytes. We have a downloadable sample named BinaryIO that demonstrates how to read and write data types using binary readers and writers.

Summary

Streams provide a common and very simple way to perform I/O on operating system resources in the .NET Framework. It doesn't matter if you're writing to a network or a file; the I/O technique is fundamentally the same. In addition, you can layer a stream on top of another stream to make I/O operations even more powerful. Our discussions so far have described streams using the synchronous I/O patterns in which calls to perform I/O will block until the I/O operation is complete. In the next chapter, we'll present threading and the asynchronous pattern in the .NET Framework. We'll show you how to perform I/O operations asynchronously that will enable you to develop greater, more flexible applications.

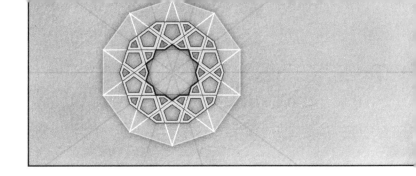

3

Threading and the Asynchronous Pattern

In the last chapter, we saw how blocking I/O is performed on different streams, including network streams. However, blocking I/O is problematic because the I/O calls might do exactly what their name implies—block for an unknown amount of time. If an application does anything besides I/O operations, such as servicing a user interface, calling a blocking method will freeze the user interface and provide for a bad user experience. You can solve this problem with the Microsoft Windows .NET Framework concurrent programming model by using threads or by using the asynchronous programming pattern.

Threads allow you to have one or more execution points in a program that can operate at the same time. When using threads, a thread can be spawned to perform any blocking I/O operations while your main application is freed to do other tasks, such as service the user interface. When a new thread is created, it begins executing from a method within your application. This method then executes all other threads in the application in parallel, including the main application thread.

The asynchronous programming pattern, on the other hand, allows many of the classes in the .NET Framework to perform operations concurrently. With the asynchronous programming pattern, you can post operations such as a read or write to be asynchronously handled by the underlying class object, and the object will signal the application when the operation has completed. This way, the application can post a number of operations concurrently, which will not block, and your main application can perform other actions such as updating the user interface and responding to user events.

This chapter introduces threads and the asynchronous pattern, which can enable you to design great networking applications. First we'll describe the threading concept by showing how to create and manage threads to perform concurrent programming in an application where one or more threads can execute code while your main program continues to execute. Then we'll describe thread synchronization concepts that are important to understand when using threads because of their concurrent programming behavior. Finally, after threads are described, we'll talk about the asynchronous programming pattern that's common to many classes in the .NET Framework and is similar in concept to the threading model.

Threading

Threading is a programming technique that permits two or more programming execution points (a place in your code) to run in an application at the same time. Threading is great because you can develop a single application that can do multiple things at the same time. For example, in Chapter 2, we described how to perform I/O over a network using synchronous programming techniques where your application could service only reading or writing data on a network and nothing else. But what if you want your application to handle several connections at the same time? Threading can help by allowing you to have multiple execution points in your code to service multiple connections in parallel. One thing to note is that you should be cautious about using too many threads to service connections, which we'll discuss later in the chapter. Figure 3-1 demonstrates threading pictorially by describing a generic application having three threads that write data to a file, read data from a network, and update a screen.

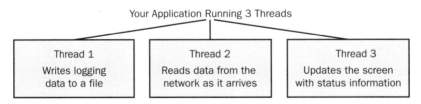

Your Application Running 3 Threads

Thread 1	Thread 2	Thread 3
Writes logging data to a file	Reads data from the network as it arrives	Updates the screen with status information

Figure 3-1 An application running three threads

The .NET Framework provides a *Thread* class in the *System.Threading* namespace that allows you to create and manage threads in your application.

Creating a Thread

Creating a thread is simple. All you have to do is create a thread object using the *System.Threading.Thread* class and pass a delegate method to the *Thread* constructor that will be called when the thread starts running. A delegate method can be any method that does not take a parameter and does not return a value. The following code fragment demonstrates one possible way to develop a delegate method:

C#

```
void MyThreadMethod()
{
    // Do something useful here
}
```

Visual Basic .NET

```
Shared Sub MyThreadMethod()
    ' Do something useful here
End Sub
```

Once a delegate method is defined, you can create a thread. Creating a thread requires that you identify a delegate method to the *Thread* class constructor. A special class named *ThreadStart* allows you to define a delegate method to a thread. Once the delegate method is defined, you simply pass a *ThreadStart* object to the *Thread* constructor. The following code fragment shows how to define a *ThreadStart* delegate method using the *MyThread-Method* method mentioned above and create a thread:

C#

```
Thread MyThread = null;
try
{
    ThreadStart ThreadMethod = new ThreadStart(MyThreadMethod);
    MyThread = new Thread(ThreadMethod);
}
catch (Exception e)
{
    Console.WriteLine("Failed to create thread with error: "
        + e.Message);
}
```

Visual Basic .NET

```
Dim MyThread As Thread = Nothing

Try
    Dim ThreadMethod As ThreadStart = _
        New ThreadStart(AddressOf MyThreadMethod)
    MyThread = New Thread(ThreadMethod)

Catch e As Exception
    Console.WriteLine("Failed to create thread with error: " _
        + e.Message)
End Try
```

Once you've successfully created a thread, you can begin controlling how the thread operates within your program. When the thread is created, nothing actually happens from your application's point of view; therefore, you're required to call the thread's *Start* method to get the thread running. Calling *Start* actually tells the operating system to begin scheduling your thread for processing. The following code fragment demonstrates how to start a thread using the *MyThread* object created earlier:

C#

```
try
{
    MyThread.Start();
}
catch (Exception e)
{
    Console.WriteLine("The thread failed to start with error: "
        + e.Message);
}
```

Visual Basic .NET

```
Try
    MyThread.Start()

Catch e As Exception
    Console.WriteLine("The thread failed to start with error: " _
        + e.Message)
End Try
```

Once the thread is started, your delegate method will begin to run. A thread can be started only once. If you try to start the thread twice, a *ThreadStateException* will be raised, indicating that the thread can't be started twice. Also, when the thread delegate method completes, you can't restart the thread; if you try to, an exception will be raised.

Your application is allowed to run only a finite number of threads at the same time. If you try to start a thread while too many threads are running, *Start* will throw an *OutOfMemoryException*. You might be wondering how many threads can start running in your application. It depends on operating system resources such as memory. In general, it's a bad practice to run too many threads at the same time because scheduling threads for execution takes up operating system resources such as the computer processor and memory. It's important to realize that a computer processor can actually service only one thread at a time, and when two threads are running, the operating system is switching control from one to the other. Operating system thread scheduling gives the application the illusion that each thread is running at the same time. If the application is running on a multiprocessor machine, the operating system can truly execute multiple threads at the same time. It's important to understand that threading does not increase the amount of computing you can do in your application, but instead, it allows you to create more dynamic applications that can interact better with multiple resources at the same time instead of just doing one thing at a time.

> **Note**   The .NET Framework features code access security for many of the managed classes in the .NET Framework. However, threads can't be controlled by code access security features in the .NET Framework version 1. A control flag for threads can be accessed by using the *System.Security.Permissions.SecurityPermissionFlag.ControlThread* permission from the *System.Security.Permissions.SecurityPermission* class. However, although the control flag exists, the security permission flag does not have any effect on controlling threads from a security zone.

Controlling a Thread

A thread has several operating states that identify its current operating status. Table 3-1 describes the available states. Several *Thread* class methods—*Abort*, *Suspend*, *Interrupt*, and *Resume*—control thread execution inside your program. Each of these methods can change the operating state of your thread.

Table 3-1 Thread Operating States

State	Description
AbortRequested	Indicates that the *Abort* method has been called on the thread
Running	Indicates that the thread has been started and is running
Stopped	Indicates that the thread has terminated because the delegate method completed or has been interrupted by the *Interrupt* method
Suspended	Indicates that the thread has stopped processing because of the *Suspend* method but is not terminated
SuspendRequested	Indicates that the *Suspend* method has been called on the thread
Unstarted	Indicates that the thread has been created but not started
WaitSleepJoin	Indicates that the thread's delegate method has called either *Sleep* or *Wait* on a resource or has called *Join* to wait on another thread

Abort

The *Abort* method is designed to stop a thread from running in a controllable, well-defined manner. *Abort* causes a special *ThreadAbortException* to be immediately raised in the thread delegate method and is the best way to stop a thread dead in its tracks. If your thread delegate does not catch the exception, the thread is automatically stopped and the thread state changes to *Stopped*. If the delegate catches the exception, the delegate has an opportunity to cancel the abort request by calling the static *ResetAbort* method of the *Thread* class within the delegate *catch* block. When *ResetAbort* is called, the delegate might continue processing outside the originating *try/catch* block that caught the exception. The following code fragment shows how to catch the *ThreadAbortException* in a delegate method. We also placed comments that describe how you can cancel the abort operation using the *ResetAbort* method.

C#

```
public static void MyThreadMethod()
{
    try
    {
        // Do something useful here
    }
    catch (ThreadAbortException e)
    {
        Console.WriteLine("Caught thread abort exception: "
            + e.Message);
```

```
                // We could call Thread.ResetAbort here, and the delegate will
                // continue processing after this try - catch block.
        }
}
```

Visual Basic .NET

```
Shared Sub MyThreadMethod()
    Try
        ' Do something useful here

    Catch e As ThreadAbortException
        Console.WriteLine("Caught thread abort exception: " _
            + e.Message)

        ' We could call Thread.ResetAbort here, and the delegate will
        ' continue processing after this try - catch block.
    End Try

End Sub
```

Suspend, *Interrupt*, and *Resume*

Another possible way you can stop a thread from running is by calling *Suspend* or *Interrupt*. *Suspend* is different from *Abort* because with *Suspend*, your thread delegate method only pauses and does not experience an exception. Calling *Suspend* will immediately suspend a thread from running and allows you to continue running the thread at a later time by calling *Resume*.

Calling *Interrupt* on a thread will also suspend a thread from running, but only if the delegate routine calls the *Monitor.Wait*, *Thread.Sleep*, or *Thread.Join* method during processing. If the delegate routine never calls one of these methods, the thread will not be interrupted. If your thread does get interrupted and you need to get the thread running again, you'll have to call the *Resume* method.

Finishing a Thread

When your thread starts running after calling *Start*, it runs by default in the foreground, meaning that your main program will wait for your thread to complete before the main program can exit. This wait is great because your main program will not have to make special code to wait on one or more threads to complete, especially if your threads are doing something critical in your application such as saving important data to a file. If you don't want the main program to wait for your thread to complete, you can change the *Thread* class property *IsBackground* from the default Boolean value *false* to the value *true*.

When the value is *true*, your thread will run in the background. If the main program exits while your thread is running in the background, the common language runtime will automatically invoke the *Abort* method on your thread when the main program exits. If your thread is not doing something critical to your application, running a thread in the background is advisable.

If you need to know when a thread has completed or if you want to wait on a thread to complete, you can call *Join*. *Join* is designed to wait on a thread until the thread completes, or it can wait for a specified amount of time until the time expires or the thread completes.

There is a simple downloadable thread sample named ThreadSample that demonstrates how to create and run a thread that's designed to update a shared variable named *m_SomeNumber* in the delegate method. The main program prints the shared variable in one-second intervals 10 times, showing how the shared variable has been changed by the delegate method.

Windows Forms I/O Problem Using Threading

As we have discussed so far in this chapter, we highly recommend using threads to perform blocking operations asynchronously, which enables you to develop applications that provide a much better experience for the user. This recommendation is especially true when working with Windows Forms. Rather than have the form freeze up while you're waiting on a blocking call, everything in the user's screen remains nice and responsive.

When working with threads while developing a Windows Forms application, there's a good chance that you might want to perform I/O on a Windows Form control such as a text box while running a thread delegate method. Doing so presents an I/O problem because the form is designed to process I/O within a Windows Form thread while your delegate method runs in another thread. For a Windows Form to handle I/O correctly, you must allow the Windows Form thread to coordinate (or marshal) the I/O calls. The form processes these calls sequentially, so you should not write directly to the form from another thread.

To allow a Windows Form to coordinate I/O, a special method is available in the forms (*System.Windows.Forms.Form*) object named *Control.Invoke* that's designed to marshal the I/O calls for a forms thread. *Control.Invoke* accepts a delegate method as a parameter and will run your delegate method from within the Windows Forms thread to coordinate I/O. The following programming steps can help you successfully use

Invoke to coordinate I/O from a thread. This code assumes that the delegate methods are defined within your form class, so we can easily reference form objects using the *this* object.

1. Define a method that will write a string message to your form. The following method is designed to send a message to a text box in a Windows Form:

```
public void MyTextBoxWriter(string MessageToWrite)
{
    this.StatusBox.Text = MessageToWrite;
    this.StatusBox.Show();
}
```

2. Define a delegate method description for the method in step 1.

```
public delegate void myDelegateMethod(string TextMessage);
```

3. Declare an instance of your form writer method as a delegate.

```
myDelegateMethod FormWriterMethod = new
    myDelegateMethod(MyTextBoxWriter);
```

4. Call your forms *Control.Invoke* method from any thread in your application to marshal the delegate to the forms thread to perform I/O. Because the delegate method is designed to take a string as a parameter, we have to set up an argument array with a string as the first element and pass it to *Invoke*.

```
object [] args = new object[1];
args[0] = "This is a test";

this.Invoke(FormWriterMethod, args);
```

Additionally, there is an asynchronous version of *Invoke* named *BeginInvoke* and a results method named *EndInvoke* that will allow you to perform *Invoke* using the .NET Framework asynchronous pattern. The .NET Framework asynchronous pattern design is discussed in the "Asynchronous Pattern" section later in this chapter.

On the downloadable chapter samples page, we have provided a Windows application named WinNetworkIO that demonstrates how to develop a client network stream application that uses threads and updates a Windows Form with I/O from the network using the form *Invoke* method.

Using Thread Pools

The .NET Framework offers another way to use threading for running short program tasks by using the *System.Threading.ThreadPool* class. Thread pools are
designed to create and maintain a pool of running threads that service delegate
methods from a queue. The idea is to conserve the thread creation and deletion
process when you are performing many small tasks asynchronously. The
ThreadPool class is statically defined and is available to your application without instantiation.

To queue up a task to a thread pool, you have to define a *WaitCallback*
delegate method. A *WaitCallback* delegate method is similar to the *ThreadStart*
delegate method we described earlier, except that *WaitCallback* accepts a *State*
parameter that allows you to pass state information to your thread when it's
queued to the thread pool. The *State* parameter allows you to pass any object
type, such as a string or even an integer, into your delegate method, which is
convenient because you can pass objects that might be needed during the asynchronous operation. The following code fragment demonstrates how to create
a *WaitCallback* delegate method. In the method, we expect an integer type to
be passed in the *State* parameter.

C#

```
void MyThreadPoolMethod(object State)
{
    // Assume an integer type was passed to the
    // state object parameter.

    int g = (int) State;

    // Do something useful here
}
```

Visual Basic .NET

```
Shared Sub MyThreadPoolMethod(ByVal State As Object)

    ' Assume an integer type was passed to the
    ' state object parameter.
    Dim g As Integer = State

    ' Do something useful here

End Sub
```

Once your *WaitCallback* method is defined, you can queue it up to the
thread pool using the statically defined *ThreadPool.QueueUserWorkItem*
method. The following code fragment demonstrates how to identify a thread

pool callback method and queue it up to the thread pool. We pass an integer value of *4* to the *State* parameter that will be received in the callback method.

C#

```
WaitCallback CallbackMethod = new WaitCallback(MyThreadPoolMethod);
ThreadPool.QueueUserWorkItem(CallbackMethod, 4);
```

Visual Basic .NET

```
Dim CallbackMethod As WaitCallback = _
    New WaitCallback(AddressOf MyThreadPoolMethod)
ThreadPool.QueueUserWorkItem(CallbackMethod, 4)
```

Your application can queue as many tasks as you want to the thread pool queue. By default, the thread pool can run up to 25 threads per processor. It's important that your *WaitCallback* method does not block and does not take too much time to process while using one of the thread pool threads. If your method does block or takes too long to process, you'll consume a thread in the pool and make it unavailable to process other *WaitCallback* methods in the queue. If all the threads in the thread pool are busy or are blocked, the thread pool queue will continue to grow until a thread becomes available to handle the next request in the queue. As the thread pool grows, it will consume memory from your application. If the thread pool grows too large, your application can run out of memory.

Threads used in the thread pool run in the background. As we described earlier in the chapter, background threads can terminate when the main program exits. The *ThreadPool* class design will not allow thread pool worker threads to run in the foreground. If your main program exits while thread pool threads are running, any executing *WaitCallback* methods will not run to completion, which can be bad if you have a *WaitCallback* method doing something critical such as saving data to a file. One possible way to ensure that thread pool *WaitCallback* methods run to completion before the main program exits is by using events to synchronize the main application thread with any thread pool threads running critical *WaitCallback* methods.

Using Events to Synchronize Threads

Events are special objects that are designed to help you synchronize thread activities. Events can be defined and instantiated by using the *AutoResetEvent* and *ManualResetEvent* classes. Both classes allow you to define events to synchronize thread activities. Event objects have two operating states: signaled and non-signaled. Threads in your application can either wait on event objects to become signaled or signal an event object changing the operating state from non-signaled to signaled. For example, assume that you have two threads named A and B, respectively. Thread A can wait on a non-signaled event object until thread B signals the event object, indicating that thread B is finished doing something important. The *AutoResetEvent* class is designed to automatically reset an event from the signaled to the non-signaled state when a thread has finished waiting for the event to become signaled. The *ManualResetEvent* class, on the other hand, requires your application to reset the state from signaled to non-signaled after waiting has occurred.

The following code fragment demonstrates how to develop a thread pool *WaitCallback* method named *MyThreadPoolMethodWithAnEvent* that's designed to coordinate the completion of the callback method with the calling application by using a *ManualResetEvent* object. The *WaitCallback* method accepts a *ManualResetEvent* object in the *State* parameter. When *MyThread-PoolMethodWithAnEvent* completes, it signals the passed-in manual reset event object using the event object's *Set* method.

C#

```
void MyThreadPoolMethodWithAnEvent(object State)
{
    // Assume a manual reset event object was passed
    // in the State parameter
    ManualResetEvent MRE = (ManualResetEvent) State;

    // Do something useful here

    // Signal the manual reset event object when the callback routine
    // is finished
    MRE.Set();
}
```

Visual Basic .NET

```
Shared Sub MyThreadPoolMethod(ByVal State As Object)

    ' Assume a manual reset event object was passed
    ' in the State parameter
    Dim MRE As ManualResetEvent = CType(State, ManualResetEvent)

    ' Do something useful here

    ' Signal the manual reset event object when the callback routine
    ' is finished
    MRE.Set()
End Sub
```

Once *WaitCallback* is defined, the main program thread can wait for the manual reset event handle to be signaled, indicating that the *WaitCallback* routine has completed its work.

The following code fragment shows how to set up the manual reset event handle for the *MyThreadPoolMethodWithAnEvent* callback routine. The code waits on the *ManualResetEvent* handle to become signaled by using the *WaitHandle.WaitAll* method. The *WaitHandle.WaitAll* method can wait on one or more handles to become signaled before the method returns. In this code, we only wait on one handle to become signaled.

C#

```
WaitCallback CallbackMethod =
    new WaitCallback(MyThreadPoolMethodWithAnEvent);

// Create an array of wait handle objects to wait on
WaitHandle []WaitHandleArray = new WaitHandle[1];

// Assign a manual reset event object to the array
WaitHandleArray[0] = new ManualResetEvent(false);

// Pass the manual reset event object to the wait callback method
ThreadPool.QueueUserWorkItem(CallbackMethod, WaitHandleArray[0]);

// Wait for the callback method to complete
WaitHandle.WaitAll(WaitHandleArray);
```

Visual Basic .NET

```
Dim CallbackMethod As WaitCallback = _
    New WaitCallback(AddressOf MyThreadPoolMethod)

' Create an array of wait handle objects to wait on
Dim WaitHandleArray(1) As WaitHandle

' Assign a manual reset event object to the array
WaitHandleArray(0) = New ManualResetEvent(False)

' Pass the manual reset event object to the wait callback method
ThreadPool.QueueUserWorkItem(CallbackMethod, WaitHandleArray(0))

' Wait for the callback method to complete
WaitHandle.WaitAll(WaitHandleArray)
```

If you have more than one *WaitCallback* routine running in the thread pool, you can expand *WaitHandleArray* to manage multiple event objects at the same time.

Designing Critical Sections in Your Code

When your application uses multiple threads, there's a good chance that you'll have a section of code or even multiple sections of code that read or write something to an object that is shared by multiple running threads. For example, your application might be writing to a shared byte array buffer or even to a shared integer variable. If your application is designed to modify and reference a shared object from multiple threads, you'll have to coordinate access to the shared object and design a critical section of code. There are two useful classes, *Monitor* and *Interlocked*, that can help you coordinate access to objects in your code.

Monitor

The .NET Framework provides a useful class named *Monitor* in the *System.Threading* namespace that enables you to synchronize access to objects that are shared by multiple code paths. *Monitor* enables you to design a critical section in your code where you can access and modify an object without having other threads access your object at the same time. This critical section is important because you might have a group of variables that get updated in one thread while another thread might access your variables but expects a complete update before it reads the variables.

To use *Monitor* effectively, you have to acquire a monitor lock to an arbitrary object such as the object you're trying to protect by taking the following steps:

1.   Call *Monitor.Enter* using some object to acquire a monitor lock.

2.   Update or access your shared object safely.

3.   Call *Monitor.Exit* to release the monitor lock on the object.

The following code fragment demonstrates these steps using a byte array object named *Buffer*. The code uses the shared *Buffer* object as a monitor lock and also updates the shared *Buffer* object safely between the *Enter* and *Exit* calls.

C#

```
byte [] Buffer = new byte[32];

Monitor.Enter(Buffer);

for (int i = 0; i < Buffer.Length; i++)
{
    Buffer[i] = 1;
}

Monitor.Exit(Buffer);
```

Visual Basic .NET

```
Shared m_Buffer(32) As Byte

Monitor.Enter(Buffer)

Dim i As Integer
For i = 0 To Buffer.GetUpperBound(0) - 1
    Buffer(i) = 1
Next

Monitor.Exit(Buffer)
```

When multiple threads call *Enter* using the same object to acquire a monitor lock, only one thread will have *Enter* complete and the other threads will block on the *Enter* call. The thread that has *Enter* complete acquires a monitor lock on the object that was passed to *Enter*. Once the thread has completed work on the shared object at hand, it must release the monitor lock by calling *Exit*. Once the monitor lock is released, other threads can attempt to acquire a monitor lock on the object at hand.

A downloadable code sample named CriticalSection demonstrates these principles on how to use the *Monitor* class to protect a shared buffer by defining critical sections of code that access the same byte array buffer object.

Interlocked

The .NET Framework also features another useful class named *Interlocked* that can help you increment and decrement shared integer variables and perform safe atomic assignments of shared objects safely from multiple threads. *Interlocked* features two methods: *Increment* and *Decrement*. *Increment* adds 1 to an integer, and *Decrement* subtracts 1 from an integer. For example, the following code fragment shows how you can safely increment and decrement an integer by 1:

C#

```
int i=5;

Interlocked.Increment(ref i);
Interlocked.Decrement(ref i);
```

Visual Basic .NET

```
Dim i as Integer

Interlocked.Increment(i)
Interlocked.Decrement(i)
```

Interlocked also lets you perform safe atomic assignment of object values by using the *Exchange* method. For example, assume that you have two objects named A and B, and you want to safely copy the contents of object B into object A. *Exchange* lets you pass in as parameters two objects of the same type and copies the content of the second parameter safely into the first parameter. For example, the following code fragment shows how to exchange two integer values safely:

C#

```
int A = 65
int B = 88

Interlocked.Exchange(ref A, B);
```

Visual Basic .NET

```
Dim A as Integer
Dim B as Integer

A = 65
B = 88

Interlocked.Exchange(A, B)
```

When the code fragment runs, A will contain the contents of B. The nice thing about the *Interlocked* class is that you can safely perform operations that modify variables with very little code.

Asynchronous Pattern

Now that you have an understanding of how to use threads to perform tasks asynchronously, we'll present another way you can perform tasks asynchronously by using the asynchronous pattern that's available in many of the classes in the .NET Framework. The asynchronous pattern is designed around methods that can potentially block when they perform their operation. Methods that block typically take a long time to perform a task such as writing data to a file or reading data from a network.

Classes that are designed to use the asynchronous pattern for methods that block have a *BeginXXX* method to start a task and an *EndXXX* method that completes a task. The *XXX* portion represents an actual name of the blocking task in the class. For example, in the *FileStream* class, the *Write* method can potentially block when writing data to a file. The *FileStream* class has *Begin-Write* and *EndWrite* counterpart methods that use the asynchronous pattern to prevent blocking on an I/O operation.

> **Note**   You should not mix the use of asynchronous calls with synchronous calls from the same instance of a class in the .NET Framework. For example, do not attempt to perform a *FileStream Read* synchronous operation while a *FileStream BeginRead* asynchronous operation is running. Doing so can cause unpredictable behavior in the class at hand.

To use the asynchronous pattern, you must call the *BeginXXX* method and supply a delegate callback method to the *BeginXXX* call. When *BeginXXX* is called, it will complete immediately and the class at hand will run the *XXX* operation in parallel, which means that your calling application (or calling thread) is free to continue processing other code. Each .NET Framework class internally handles asynchronous processing using threads and other operating system asynchronous mechanisms. The main point to remember here is that all the classes that use the asynchronous pattern do so with the same design from your application's point of view. When an asynchronous operation completes, your supplied delegate method is invoked to process the completed task results. Inside your delegate method, you have to call the *EndXXX* counterpart method to retrieve the completed task results.

> **Note**   When your application performs an asynchronous *BeginXXX* call, you should not call the *EndXXX* counterpart method using the *IAsyncResult* value returned from *BeginXXX* while the call is running asynchronously. If you do so, your *EndXXX* call will block until the *BeginXXX* has completed. When your *BeginXXX* delegate method finally calls *EndXXX* after the asynchronous operation is completed, an *InvalidOperationException* will be thrown on the delegate's *EndXXX* call.

For example, let's describe how to process a *Read* call asynchronously from the *NetworkStream* class using the asynchronous pattern. We chose *Read* because it will typically block when you wait for data to arrive on a network stream. To call *Read* asynchronously, you must call *BeginRead* and supply an asynchronous delegate method named *AsyncCallback* that will be invoked when the *BeginRead* operation completes. An *AsyncCallback* method is similar to a thread delegate method, as described earlier in the chapter. However, *AsyncCallback* requires you to supply an *IAsyncResult* interface that's used to retrieve the results of a completed asynchronous operation. The following code fragment demonstrates how to design an *AsyncCallback* method that handles the completion of a *BeginRead* asynchronous operation from the *Network-Stream* class we described in Chapter 2.

C#

```csharp
void ProcessReceiveResults(IAsyncResult AsyncResult)
{
    NetworkStream NS = (NetworkStream) AsyncResult.AsyncState;

    try
    {
        int BytesRead = 0;

        BytesRead = NS.EndRead(AsyncResult);

        if (BytesRead == 0)
        {
            NS.Close();
            return;
        }
    }
    catch (Exception e)
    {
        Console.WriteLine("Failed to read network stream with error: "
            + e.Message);
        NS.Close();
    }
}
```

Visual Basic .NET

```vbnet
Shared Sub ProcessReceiveResults(ByVal AsyncResult As IAsyncResult)
    Dim NS As NetworkStream = AsyncResult.AsyncState

    Try
        Dim BytesRead As Integer = 0

        BytesRead = NS.EndRead(AsyncResult)

        If (BytesRead = 0) Then
            NS.Close()
            Exit Sub
        End If
```

```
Catch e As Exception
    Console.WriteLine("Failed to read network stream with error: " _
        + e.Message)

    NS.Close()
End Try
End Sub
```

The *AsyncResult* parameter is an input parameter that receives an *IAsync-Result* object that you have to pass to the *EndRead* counterpart method. (Alternatively, you can use the *IAsyncResult* object that's returned from the originating *BeginRead* call.) Also, *IAsyncResult* contains an important member variable named *AsyncState* that contains the state parameter that was passed in the originating *BeginRead* call. Typically, you'll use the state parameter to pass information that's related to the asynchronous call *BeginXXX*. For example, in the preceding code fragment, we demonstrated how to pass an instance of the *NetworkStream* class to the delegate.

Once your delegate method is defined, you can start the asynchronous operation using the delegate method. The following code fragment demonstrates how to use the *ProcessReceiveResults* delegate to handle the asynchronous result of a *BeginRead* operation on a network stream:

C#

```
AsyncCallback AsyncReceiveCallback =
    new AsyncCallback(ProcessReceiveResults);

MyNetworkStream.BeginRead(Buffer, 0, Buffer.Length,
    AsyncReceiveCallback, MyNetworkStream);
```

Visual Basic .NET

```
AsyncReceiveCallback As AsyncCallback = _
    New AsyncCallback(AddressOf ProcessReceiveResults)

MyNetworkStream.BeginRead(Buffer, 0, Buffer.Length,
    AsyncReceiveCallback, Me)
```

When a *BeginXXX* starter method is called, it will complete immediately and return an *IAsyncResult* object. Your calling program might call the *EndXXX* counterpart method on the returned *IAsyncResult*. If the asynchronous operation has not completed, the *EndXXX* method will block until the operation has completed. Typically, most applications will handle the completed results in the delegate method instead of in the calling program thread. As you can see in the previous code fragment, we did not retrieve the returned *IAsyncResult* from the *BeginRead* call. Instead, we allowed our *ProcessReceiveResults* delegate method to handle the completed results.

In this chapter's downloadable samples, we provide two samples, Async-NetworkIO and ThreadNetworkIO, that are revisions of the network stream server sample found in Chapter 2. These revised servers are designed to handle multiple network connections and demonstrate how to use the *NetworkStream* class to perform network I/O asynchronously. AsyncNetworkIO uses the asynchronous pattern, and ThreadNetworkIO uses threads. The original network stream server sample accepted only one connection and processed I/O synchronously on only one connection. Because these applications process I/O asynchronously, they are now capable of handling multiple network connections at the same time.

Summary

This chapter introduced two important concepts useful in network programming: threading and the asynchronous pattern. These asynchronous programming techniques allow you to design more flexible applications so that you can do multiple things at the same time in one application. This flexibility is important because you can develop a networking application that can service a user interface while it processes I/O on a network, which makes the user experience much better. Many of the remaining chapter discussions and samples will use these asynchronous programming techniques.

4

Serialization

Serialization is the process of packaging data structures into a format that can be easily transported. Typically, an instance of a class in one process is taken and sent to another process over some kind of streaming mechanism such that the remote process can reconstruct an instance of the same class with the same member values. This chapter will discuss the process of serialization as well as the different types of serialization available.

Serialization is a very powerful and useful mechanism for sharing data. If you've ever had to send all the properties or data or both associated with a data structure to another process, say on another machine, you're familiar with the difficulty. The challenge is that a class or other data structure can reference memory and pointers that are valid only in the context of the current process. Implementing your own scheme for packaging complex structures can be extremely cumbersome, especially if the members are variable-length arrays or arbitrary string values. Fortunately, the Microsoft Windows .NET Framework offers built-in support for serialization.

> **Note** In our scenario, we transport the structure across process boundaries, but with the .NET Framework, serialization can occur over application domains. An application domain can be a process boundary, but it can also be an application running in a "sandbox" in a process with other applications. Application domains will be covered in more detail in Chapter 12.

In the .NET Framework, objects are serialized onto a stream and deserialized from a stream. As we saw in Chapter 2, a stream can take many forms—network, memory, file, and so on. In this chapter, we'll concentrate on the process of serialization and deserialization and not the medium over which it is transported. Before getting into the details of serialization, we'll first look at the different formats that data can be serialized into. Then we'll have a detailed discussion of each type of serialization.

Serialization Formats

There are three major formats of serialization available: binary, XML, and SOAP. The most obvious difference between these formats is the physical output of the serialization process and, of course, the source format from which the object is deserialized. Binary serialization produces a non-printable sequence of byte-oriented data that represents the source object. For example, if a class is binary serialized to a file, the file contents might look like the following code, where the left side contains the raw hex and the right side contains the printable characters (with a dot indicating a non-printable character):

```
00 01 00 00 00 FF FF FF-FF 01 00 00 00 00 00 00   ...............
00 0C 02 00 00 00 3D 73-69 6D 70 6C 65 2C 20 56   ......=simple, V
65 72 73 69 6F 6E 3D 30-2E 30 2E 30 2E 30 2C 20   ersion=0.0.0.0,
43 75 6C 74 75 72 65 3D-6E 65 75 74 72 61 6C 2C   Culture=neutral,
20 50 75 62 6C 69 63 4B-65 79 54 6F 6B 65 6E 3D    PublicKeyToken=
6E 75 6C 6C 05 01 00 00-00 24 53 69 6D 70 6C 65   null.....$Simple
42 69 6E 61 72 79 53 65-72 6C 69 61 7A 61 74 69   BinarySerliazati
6F 6E 2E 4D 79 42 61 73-69 63 44 61 74 61 03 00   on.MyBasicData..
00 00 09 49 6E 74 46 69-65 6C 64 31 0C 53 74 72   ...IntField1.Str
69 6E 67 46 69 65 6C 64-31 09 49 6E 74 46 69 65   ingField1.IntFie
6C 64 32 00 01 00 08 08-02 00 00 00 2A 04 00 00   ld2.........*...
06 03 00 00 00 0F 42 61-73 69 63 20 44 61 74 61   ......Basic Data
20 49 6E 66 6F 38 06 00-00 0B                      Info8....
```

Another characteristic of binary serialization is that it retains type information within the generated data stream, which means that when the object is deserialized, the re-created object is an exact copy of the original.

The advantage of binary serialization is that the resulting serialized stream is very compact, and the disadvantage is that a binary stream is not very portable. As you'll see later in this section, the difference in the serialized size between binary and the other serialization methods can be great, which can have considerable impact if the data is being serialized to the network. If both the producer and the consumer of the binary stream use the .NET Framework, portability won't be an issue. However, if the application needs to send a serialized object to an application running on a different operating system, portability issues are likely because possible differences in byte ordering and data type sizes could introduce compatibility problems.

XML serialization, on the other hand, is all about standards and portability. When a class is serialized to XML, a character stream is created that's formatted according to the XML language standard. XML is an incredibly flexible markup language used to describe arbitrary data. The element tags used to describe the data are specific to the data itself. The following is an example of valid XML data:

```
<?xml version="1.0"?>
<MyBasicData xmlns:xsd="http://www.w3.org/2001/XMLSchema"
        xmlns:xsi="http://www.w3.org/2001/XMLSchema-instance">
  <IntField1>1234</IntField1>
  <StringField1>Hello World</StringField1>
</MyBasicData>
```

The element tags in this example are *MyBasicData*, *IntField1*, and *StringField1*. Because XML allows arbitrary element names, they could be named something completely different. Of course, if XML is being used to exchange information, the producer and the consumer need to agree on a set of standard element tags to describe the data. As you can see in the previous example, the serialized XML does not contain any type information unless the element tags chosen somehow describe the data type of the element value. For example, there's no indication whether the element value *1234* is an integer or a string.

As mentioned, XML is ideal when portability is an issue. Also, because many services today use XML to describe data, it's easy to write code that outputs XML in a specified format that can be used by other entities. The portability and interoperability gains do come with a cost: the generated XML stream is significantly larger than the equivalent binary serialized stream, and XML serialization does not retain type information. Table 4-1 compares the size of the serialized object for both binary and XML serialization in the .NET Framework version 1.

Table 4-1   Serialization Efficiency Comparison

Serialization Class	Type	Class Size (Bytes)	Field Count	Serialized Size (Bytes)
BinaryFormatter	binary	24	3	202
XmlSerializer	XML	24	3	745
BinaryFormatter	binary	4020	3 (array)	4213
XmlSerializer	XML	4020	3 (array)	16827

The class size column indicates the size of all member properties of the class. Field count indicates the number of properties contained in the class, and the serialized size column indicates the size of the resulting serialized object in bytes. Note that the second pair of entries is a class with three fields of which one is a 1000-element array. As you can see, for binary serialization, there's roughly a 180-byte fixed overhead for serialization regardless of the original class size. On the other hand, with XML serialization, the serialized data size is not directly tied to the field count or the class size because the XML element names generated depend on how the class is defined. We'll discuss the *Binary-Formatter* and *XmlSerializer* classes in the next two sections.

The last serialization type is a protocol based on XML called SOAP, which is a standard method for describing, discovering, and invoking methods. The XML language itself imposes no restrictions on how to describe the *meaning* of the data; it only defines the format and sequence of the tags that describe the data. The SOAP specification defines the set of common element tags and properties to describe data. The SOAP specification can be found at *http://www.w3.org/TR/SOAP*.

Although the SOAP protocol is transport-independent, meaning that it can be sent over a number of different transport protocols, SOAP is typically transported over the HTTP protocol in version 1 of the .NET Framework and is an integral part of XML-based Web services, which are covered in greater detail in Chapter 12. The following code listing shows a class serialized to the SOAP protocol:

```
<SOAP-ENV:Envelope xmlns:xsi="http://www.w3.org/2001/XMLSchema-instance"
    xmlns:xsd="http://www.w3.org/2001/XMLSchema" xmlns:SOAP-
    ENC="http://schemas.xmlsoap.org/soap/encoding/" xmlns:SOAP-
    ENV="http://schemas.xmlsoap.org/soap/envelope/"
    xmlns:clr="http://schemas.microsoft.com/soap/encoding/clr/1.0" SOAP-
    ENV:encodingStyle="http://schemas.xmlsoap.org/soap/encoding/">
<SOAP-ENV:Body>
        <a1:MyBasicData id="ref-1"
        xmlns:a1="http://schemas.microsoft.com/clr/nsassem/SimpleBinarySeriali
        zation/simple%2C%20Version%3D0.0.0.0%2C%20Culture%3Dneutral%2C%20Publ
        icKeyToken%3Dnull">
        <IntField1>999</IntField1>
        <StringField1 id="ref-3">Hello World</StringField1>
        <IntField2>1492</IntField2>
    </a1:MyBasicData>
</SOAP-ENV:Body>
</SOAP-ENV:Envelope>
```

Now it's time to get into the details of serialization, and we'll start with binary serialization.

Binary Serialization

As mentioned earlier, binary serialization takes a class and packages it onto a stream as a series of bytes that can be rebuilt into an exact copy of the object at the destination. For binary serialization to work, both the serializer and deserializer must have access to the assembly that contains the definition for the object. The .NET Framework offers considerable flexibility in controlling how data is serialized. Before an object can be binary serialized, it must be marked as such by adding the *Serializable* attribute to the class, as shown here:

C#

```
[Serializable]
public class MyBasicData
{
    public int    IntField1;
    public string StringField;
    private int   IntField2;
}
```

Visual Basic .NET

```
<Serializable()> _
Class MyBasicData
    Public IntField1 as Integer
    Public StringField1 as String
    Private IntField2 as Integer
End Class
```

Each class that is to be serialized requires the *Serializable* attribute, which means that classes derived from a serializable class must also have the *Serializable* attribute set for them to be serialized. Likewise, if a class contains instances of other classes as members, those too must be marked with the *Serializable* attribute for the entire structure to be packaged. If an error is encountered during serialization or deserialization, the *System.Runtime.Serialization.SerializationException* exception is thrown.

The next step is to create an instance of the formatter, which will perform the work of serializing the class. In the case of binary serialization, a binary formatter object is created that implements the *IFormatter* interface. After the object is created, the *Serialize* method is invoked on a valid stream with the object to be serialized. The *BinaryFormatter* class is part of the *System.Runtime.Serialization.Formatters.Binary* namespace. The following C# code illustrates serializing a simple class (defined earlier) to a file stream.

C#

```
FileStream    fileStream;
MyBasicData  myData = new MyBasicData()
FileStream    binFileStream;
IFormatter    binFormatter = new BinaryFormatter();

binFileStream = new FileStream(  // Open a file stream to write to
    "Binary_Serialization.bin",
    FileMode.Create,
    FileAccess.Write,
    FileShare.None
    );
try
{
    binFormatter.Serialize( binFileStream, myData );  // Serialize it
    binFileStream.Close();
}
catch (System.Runtime.Serialization.SerializationException err )
{
    Console.WriteLine("Error occurred during serialization: " + err.Message);
}
```

Visual Basic .NET

```
Dim myData as MyBasicData = new MyBasicData()
Dim binFileStream as FileStream
Dim binFormatter as IFormatter = new BinaryFormatter()

binFileStream = new FileStream( _
    "Binary_Serialization.bin", _
    FileMode.Create, _
    FileAccess.Write, _
    FileShare.None _
    )
Try
    binFormatter.Serialize( binFileStream, myData )
    binFileStream.Close()
Catch err as System.Runtime.Serialization.SerializationException
    Console.WriteLine("Error occurred during serialization: " + err.Message)
End Try
```

This code serializes an instance of the *MyBasicData* class to a file. The basic steps are

1. Create an instance of the serializable class that's to be serialized.

2. Create the stream on which the data is to be serialized.

3. Create the binary formatter.

4. Serialize the object to the stream.

Once the object is serialized to a binary stream, the following code will deserialize the object:

C#

```
FileStream     binFileStream;
IFormatter     binFormatter;
MyBasicData    myData;

binFileStream = new FileStream(
    "Binary_Serialization.bin",
    FileMode.Open,
    FileAccess.Read,
    FileShare.Read
    );
binFormatter = new BinaryFormatter();
try {
    myData = (MyBasicData) binFormatter.Deserialize( binFileStream );
}
catch ( System.Runtime.Serialization.SerializationException err )
{
    Console.WriteLine("An error occurred during deserialization: {0}",
        err.Message);
}
```

Visual Basic .NET

```
Dim binFileStream as FileStream
Dim binFormatter as IFormatter
Dim myData as MyBasicData

binFileStream = new FileStream( _
    "Binary_Serialization.bin", _
    FileMode.Open, _
    FileAccess.Read, _
    FileShare.Read _
    )
binFormatter = new BinaryFormatter()
Try
    myData = binFormatter.Deserialize( binFileStream )
Catch err as System.Runtime.Serialization.SerializationException
    Condole.WriteLine("An error occurred during deserialization: {0}", _
        err.Message)
End Try
```

To summarize the binary deserialization process:

1.   Open the file stream where the serialized object is contained.

2.   Create an instance of the binary formatter.

3.   Call the *Deserialize* method on the formatter with the stream as an argument.

If an error occurs while serializing or deserializing the data, the exception *SerializationException* is thrown. This exception typically occurs during deserialization if the data on the stream does not match a valid serialized object header. For example, while serializing the object, if the text string *hello* is written to the *FileStream* before the serialized object, and on deserialization, those 5 bytes are not consumed beforehand, the deserialization method will encounter the invalid header, which is the string.

As you can see, the binary serialization process is simple, straightforward, and powerful. Imagine having a class that represents some data set such as a customer database. The entire set of customers (for example, multiple instances of the customer class) can be serialized to a file using a file stream or even transmitted across the network using a network stream.

Controlling Binary Serialization

In the previous code sample, the entire class was serialized to the data stream. There could be a situation in which you do not want all the class data serialized. For example, it would not be a good idea to serialize the password data contained in a class that describes a user account (at the very least, not in clear text). There are two methods for controlling how data is binary serialized: selectively serializing class properties by adding an additional attribute, and implementing a custom serialization interface. If the issue is that only certain fields should be serialized, the attribute *NonSerialized* can be placed before each field not to be serialized. The following class definition illustrates this method:

```
[Serializable]
public class MySelectiveData
{
    public int      UserId;
    public string   UserName;
    [NonSerialized] private string Password;
}
```

In this class definition, the *Password* element is marked as *NonSerialized*, which means that this field will not be packaged for transport over a stream when the *Serialize* method is invoked.

If exact control over how serialization and deserialization occurs is required, the process can be further customized by having the class implement the *ISerializable* interface. This method is useful when certain marshaled data is no longer valid in the process where deserialization takes place. For example, if a serializable class contains a reference to the local IP address and is then marshaled to a process on a different machine, it might be desirable to have the local IP field reflect the current machine. If a class implements a distributed service, which can reside on any machine in the network, the class representing this service can be serialized to another machine for load balancing purposes and would need to update the local IP information to re-create sockets to handle client requests.

For a class to implement the *ISerializable* interface, it must implement the following two methods:

```
public virtual void GetObjectData(SerializationInfo info,
    StreamingContext context );
protected  MyObjectConstructor ( SerializationInfo info,
    StreamingContext context );
```

The *GetObjectData* method is used in the serialization process. Each field that is to be serialized is assigned a value name in the *SerializationInfo* object, which is achieved by calling the *AddValue* method of *SerializationInfo* with the value name and the field. The second required method is a constructor for the class, which is called when the object is deserialized. This constructor retrieves the serialized field values and initializes the member properties to values that are meaningful in the current context. The following code illustrates custom serialization:

C#

```
[Serializable]
public class MyCustomData : ISerializable
{
    public int       IntField1;
    public string    StringField1;
    public IPAddress LocalAddress;

    // Default constructor
    public MyCustomData()
    {
        IntField1 = 1234;
        StringField1 = "Initialize Data";
        LocalAddress = IPAddress.Any;
    }
    // Called in the serialization process
    public virtual void GetObjectData(
```

```
            SerializationInfo info,
            StreamingContext context
            )
        {
            info.AddValue( "IntField1", IntField1 );
            info.AddValue( "whatever", StringField1 );
            info.AddValue( "LocalIP",  LocalAddress );
        }
        // Constructor used in the deserialization process
        protected MyCustomData( SerializationInfo info, StreamingContext context )
        {
            IPHostEntry ipHost = Dns.GetHostByName( "localhost" );
            IPAddress   resolveAddress;

            // Retrieve the value of LocalAddress
            try
            {
                ipHost = Dns.GetHostByName("localhost");
                if ( ipHost.AddressList.Length > 0
                    resolveAddress = ipHost.AddressList[0];
                else
                    resolveAddress = IPAddress.Loopback;
            }
            catch ( SocketException err )
            {
                Console.WriteLine("Unable to resolve localhost; using loopback");
                resolveAddress = IPAddress.Loopback;
            }
            IntField1 = info.GetInt32( "IntField1" );
            StringField1 = info.GetString( "whatever" );
            LocalAddress = resolveAddress;
        }
    }
```

Visual Basic .NET

```
<Serializable()> _
Public Class MyCustomData Implements ISerializable
    Public IntField1 As Integer
    Public StringField1 As String
    <NonSerialized()> Public LocalAddress As IPAddress

    ' Default constructor
    Public Sub New()
        IntField1 = 1234
        StringField1 = "Initialize Data"
        LocalAddress = IPAddress.Any
    End Sub
```

```
' Called in the serialization process
Sub GetObjectData( _
    ByVal info As SerializationInfo, _
    ByVal context As StreamingContext _
    ) _
    Implements ISerializable.GetObjectData

    info.AddValue("IntField1", IntField1)
    info.AddValue("whatever", StringField1)
End Sub

' Constructor used in the deserialization process
Private Sub New( _
    ByVal info As SerializationInfo, _
    ByVal c As StreamingContext _
    )
    Dim ipHost As IPHostEntry

    IntField1 = info.GetInt32("IntField1")
    StringField1 = info.GetString("whatever")

    ' Retrieve the value of LocalAddress
    Try
        ipHost = Dns.GetHostByName(Dns.GetHostName())
        If (ipHost.AddressList.Length > 0) Then
            LocalAddress = ipHost.AddressList(0)
        Else
            LocalAddress = IPAddress.Loopback
        End If
    Catch err As System.Net.Sockets.SocketException
        Console.WriteLine("Unable to resolve localhost; using loopback")
        LocalAddress = IPAddress.Loopback
    End Try
End Sub
End Class
```

In this example, the *GetObjectData* method assigns values to each property that is to be serialized. As you can see, the string values assigned can be arbitrary values, and all the *GetObjectData* method needs to do is assign a value to each property that is to be serialized.

The constructor for the class takes *SerializationInfo* and *Streaming-Context* objects for parameters. In the preceding example, the constructor retrieves the stored values for *IntField1* as well as *StringField1*. Because the *LocalAddress* field might not have meaning at the destination process, the custom constructor resolves the current host name and assigns the first *IPAddress* resolved to the member field. If the DNS lookup fails, the Internet Protocol version 4 (IPv4) loopback address is assigned.

The binsoapserial.cs sample illustrates the methods of binary serialization covered earlier. You can find this program in the companion content in the folder Chap04\binary_and_soap\simple\cs. The sample is also available in Microsoft Visual Basic .NET under the vb.net directory. The sample illustrates three ways to serialize different classes: a simple class, a class with the *Non-Serialized* attribute, and a class that implements the *ISerializable* interface. See the sample for a complete description of its usage.

A more advanced serialization sample that serializes data over a TCP socket connection is located in the folder Chap04\binary_and_soap\socket. Again, there are C# and Visual Basic .NET subfolders (named cs and vb.net).

XML Serialization

XML serialization differs from binary serialization in two ways. First, the types of data that can be serialized are limited. Second, type information is not serialized with the data, which means that there's no guarantee that the serialized object will be deserialized to the same object type. The following list describes the item types that can be serialized using XML serialization:

- Public fields and read/write properties of public classes (read-only properties will not be serialized)

- Classes implementing *ICollection* and *IEnumerable*

- *XmlElement* objects

- *XmlNode* objects

- *DataSet* objects

- Classes with default constructors

Before getting into too much detail, let's take a quick look at a simple XML serialization sample. The following code fragment is the class definition to be serialized:

C#

```
public class MyXmlSimpleData
{
    public int      IntField;
    public string   StringField;
    public DateTime CurrentDate;
    private int     PrivateField;
    public MyXmlSimpleData()
    {
        IntField = 1234;
```

```
        StringField = "Xml Simple Serialization";
        CurrentDate = DateTime.Today;
        PrivateField = 333;
    }
}
```

Visual Basic .NET

```
Public Class MyXmlSimpleData
    Public IntField as Integer
    Public StringField as String
    Public CurrentDate as DateTime
    Private PrivateField as Integer
    Public Sub New()
        IntField = 1234
        StringField = "Xml Simple Serialization"
        CurrentDate = DateTime.Today
        PrivateField = 333
    End Sub
End Class
```

First notice that no special attribute tags are required to indicate that this class can be serialized, as is the case with binary serialization. The process of serializing the class is extremely simple, as the following code illustrates:

C#

```
MyXmlSimpleData  xmlData;
XmlSerializer    xmlDataSerializer;
StreamWriter     streamFileWriter;

xmlData = new MyXmlSimpleData();
xmlDataSerializer = new XmlSerializer( typeof( MyXmlSimpleData ) );
streamFileWriter = new StreamWriter( "simple.xml" );
xmlDataSerializer.Serialize( streamFileWriter, xmlData );
```

Visual Basic .NET

```
Dim xmlData as MyXmlSimpleData
Dim xmlDataSerializer as XmlSerializer
Dim streamFileWriter as StreamWriter

xmlData = new MyXmlSimpleData()
xmlDataSerializer = new XmlSerializer( GetType( MyXmlSimpleData ) )
streamFileWriter = new StreamWriter( "simple.xml" )
xmlDataSerializer.Serialize( streamFileWriter, xmlData )
```

In this example, an instance of the *MyXmlSimpleData* class is instantiated first and then *XmlSerializer* is created, which requires the data type of the class to be serialized—in this case, *MyXmlSimpleData*. In the next step, the stream is created, which is a simple file. Finally, the object is serialized to the stream. Once the object is serialized to the stream, the following code will deserialize it:

C#

```
MyXmlSimpleData xmlData;
XmlSerializer    xmlDataSerializer;
FileStream       xmlFileStream;

xmlDataSerializer = new XmlSerializer( typeof( MyXmlSimpleData ) );
xmlFileStream = new FileStream( "simple.xml", FileMode.Open );
xmlData = (MyXmlSimpleData) xmlDataSerializer.Deserialize( xmlFileStream );
```

Visual Basic .NET

```
Dim xmlData as MyXmlSimpleData
Dim xmlDataSerializer as XmlSerializer
Dim xmlFileStream as FileStream

xmlDataSerializer = new XmlSerializer( GetType( MyXmlSimpleData ) )
xmlFileStream = new FileStream( "simple.xml", FileMode.Open )
xmlData = xmlDataSerializer.Deserialize( xmlFileStream )
```

The steps are very similar to the serialization process shown earlier. The difference is that we don't instantiate an instance of *MyXmlSimpleData* because we're retrieving it from the stream, and the *Deserialize* method is called instead with the data stream.

After serializing the object to the stream, which in this case is a file, you can take a look at the resulting XML. The following code is the XML generated for the preceding class. Notice that only the public properties are included— that is, there's no *PrivateField* entry. Also notice that there's no type information—just the values for each field.

```
<?xml version="1.0" encoding="utf-8" ?>
  <MyXmlSimpleData xmlns:xsd="http://www.w3.org/2001/XMLSchema"
       xmlns:xsi="http://www.w3.org/2001/XMLSchema-instance">
      <IntField>1234</IntField>
      <StringField>Xml Serialization Sample</StringField>
      <CurrentDate>2003-02-09T00:00:00.0000000-08:00</CurrentDate>
  </MyXmlSimpleData>
```

Controlling XML Serialization

As is the case with binary serialization, XML serialization involves attributes that control how a class is serialized using the *XmlSerializer* formatter. One such attribute is the *XmlElement* attribute. Each attribute contains any number of constructors as well as properties that can be assigned in the attribute applied to a class or a class member. For example, in the following code snippet, the *XmlElement* attribute is used to rename the *IntField1* property from the default value of *IntField1* to *Integer_Field*:

C#

```
public class MyRenamedXmlData
{
    [ XmlElement( ElementName = "Integer_Field" ) ]
    public int IntField1;
}
```

Visual Basic .NET

```
Public Class MyRenamedXmlData
    <XmlElement("Integer_Field")> _
    Public IntField1 as Integer
End Class
```

As mentioned, the *XmlElement* attribute is just one of many attributes that can be applied to a class definition that affects the generated XML. Table 4-2 lists the different attributes that can be applied to classes and class members. Notice that when specifying an attribute within a class definition, the last *Attribute* text is left off. For example, in the preceding code snippet, we specified *XmlElement* instead of *XmlElementAttribute*. Also, within the parentheses following each XML attribute, any public properties exposed by that attribute class can be set. In this example, *ElementName* is a property of the *XmlElementAttribute* class. The Visual Basic .NET syntax is slightly different. First, instead of square brackets, angled brackets denote the attribute, and second, the property is passed to the constructor for the *XmlElementAttribute* class.

Table 4-2   XML Attributes

Attribute	Description
XmlAnyAttributeAttribute	Indicates that all XML attributes unknown to the schema should be placed in an array of *XmlAttribute* objects on deserialization
XmlAnyElementAtribute	Indicates that all XML elements unknown to the schema should be placed in an array of *XmlElement* objects on deserialization
XmlArrayAttribute	Controls properties of an array

Table 4-2 XML Attributes   *(continued)*

Attribute	Description
XmlArrayItemAttribute	Controls individual elements within an array
XmlAttributeAttribute	Indicates that the class should be serialized as an XML attribute
XmlChoiceIdentifierAttribute	Indicates that the member can be described by an enumerated list
XmlElementAttribute	Indicates that the member will be serialized as an XML element
XmlEnumAttribute	Controls the element name of an enumeration member
XmlIgnoreAttribute	Indicates that the member should be ignored when serialized
XmlIncludeAttribute	Indicates that the class should be included when generating schemas
XmlNamespaceDeclarationsAttribute	Indicates that a property, parameter, return value, or class member contains a prefix associated with namespaces used within the XML document
XmlRootAttribute	Indicates a class, a structure, an enumeration, or an interface as the root element of the XML document
XmlTextAttribute	Indicates that the member should be serialized as XML text
XmlTypeAttribute	Controls the name and namespace of the XML type

Although we won't get into the specifics of every attribute that can possibly be applied to a class, the xmlserial.cs sample illustrates several XML attributes. You can find this program in the companion content in the folder Chap04\xml\cs. Again, a Visual Basic .NET version of the same program is available under the vb.net folder. For a full description of each attribute and its properties, consult the Platform SDK or the .NET Framework SDK.

Overriding XML Serialization

As we saw in the previous section, the XML generated in the serialization process can be modified by applying attributes. However, what if you have a situation in which you need to generate multiple XML streams? Let's say, for instance, that in the *MyRenamedXmlData* class, the property name for *IntField1* needed to be different depending on the consumer of the serialized XML. In this case, applying an attribute would not suffice because the applied attribute is always used when using the default XML serializer. You need to override the default XML serialization.

The process of overriding the default XML serialization requires the following steps:

1. Create one or more XML attributes (such as those listed in Table 4-2) that apply to one element within the class to serialize. Remember that these attributes are actually classes with properties and methods.

2. Create an instance of the *XmlAttributes* class that each XML attribute created in step 1 is added to.

3. Create an instance of the *XmlAttributeOverrides* class that applies the *XmlAttributes* class to a specified class property or method.

The following code illustrates overriding the default XML serialization process by implementing the custom serialization in the *OverrideSerialization* method:

C#

```
public class MyXmlOverrideSample
{
    public int       IntField1;
    public DateTime CurrentDate;

    public void OverrideSerialization( FileStream fileStream )
    {
        XmlElementAttribute    xmlElementAttribute = new XmlElementAttribute();
        XmlAttributes          xmlAttributes = new XmlAttributes();
        XmlAttributeOverrides xmlAttributeOverrides = new
            XmlAttributeOverrides();
        XmlSerializer xmlSerializer = null;

        xmlElementAttribute.ElementName =
            "Override_Integer_Field_Numero_Uno";
        xmlAttributes.XmlElements.Add( xmlElementAttribute );
        xmlAttributeOverrides.Add( typeof(MyXmlOverrideSample),
            "IntField1", xmlAttributes );
        xmlSerializer = new XmlSerializer( typeof(MyXmlOverrideSample),
            xmlAttributesOverride );
        xmlSerializer.Serialize( filesStream, this );
    }
}
```

Visual Basic .NET

```
Public Class MyXmlOverrideSample
    Public IntField1 as Integer
    Public CurrentDate as DateTime

    Public Sub OverrideSerialization( fileDataStream as Filestream )
        Dim xmlElementAttr as XmlElementAttribute = new XmlElementAttribute()
        Dim xmlAttr as XmlAttributes = new XmlAttributes()
        Dim xmlOverrides as XmlAttributeOverrides = new _
            XmlAttributeOverrides()
        Dim xmlDataSerializer as XmlSerializer

        xmlElementAttr.ElementName = "Override_Integer_Field_Numbero_Uno"
        xmlAttr.XmlElements.Add( xmlElementAttr )
        xmlOverrides.Add( GetType(MyXmlOverrideSample), "IntField1", _
            xmlAttr)
        xmlDataSerializer = new XmlSerializer(GetType(MyXmlOverrideSample), _
            xmlOverrides)
        xmlDataSerializer.Serializer( fileDataStream, this )
    End Sub
End Class
```

This example shows a method that serializes the class to a stream but changes the XML element name for the *IntField1* member to *Override_Integer_Field_Numero_Uno*. Note that when the object is serialized, the remaining properties that were not overridden are serialized as expected.

As we mentioned, the xmlserial.cs and xmlserial.vb samples provide code that performs XML serialization on a variety of classes: a simple class, one with XML attributes applied, and one that overrides serialization. See the sample for the complete code listing.

SOAP Serialization

As we mentioned earlier, SOAP is a standard based on XML for describing properties and methods. SOAP is used by Web services as well as .NET Remoting precisely for these abilities. In this sense, SOAP serialization is similar to remote procedure calls (RPCs) but is mainly concerned with standardizing message passing. SOAP provides a standard of describing these *remote* procedures and properties. The *IFormatter* interface described in the "Binary Serialization" section earlier in this chapter offers a way of generating SOAP messages by creating an instance of the *SoapFormatter* class.

You follow the same guidelines to use *SoapFormatter* as you do to use *BinaryFormatter*, as described in the "Binary Serialization" section. The only difference is that the *IFormatter* instance used is a *SoapFormatter*—that is, the class being serialized as well as any inherited classes must have the *Serializable* attribute set. The assembly containing the serialized object definition must be available at both the source and the destination. The serialized stream can also be customized in the same way by adding the *NonSerialized* attribute or by implementing the *ISerializable* interface, as you saw earlier. The following code serializes an object with the *SoapFormatter*:

C#

```
// Using the MyBasicData class defined earlier
MyBasicData  basicData = new MyBasicData();
IFormatter   soapFormatter = new SoapFormatter();
FileStream   fileStream;

fileStream = new FileStream(
    "soapformatter.xml",
    FileMode.Create,
    FileAccess.Write,
    FileShare.None
    );
soapFormatter.Serialize( fileStream, basicData);
```

Visual Basic .NET

```
Dim basicData as MyBasicData = new MyBasicData()
Dim soapFormatter as IFormatter = new SoapFormatter()
Dim fileDataStream as FileStream

fileDataStream = new FileStream( _
    "soapformatter.cml", _
    FileMode.Create, _
    FileAccess.Write, _
    FileShare.None _
)
soapFormatter.Serialize( fileDataStream, basicData )
```

As we've seen with the previous serialization types, there is always a way to customize the serialization output. For SOAP serialization using the *Soap-Formatter* class, it is the same as for the binary formatter—either the *NonSeri-alizable* attribute can be applied to class properties or the class to be serialized can implement the *ISerializable* interface.

To see *SoapFormatter* in action, take a look at the binsoapserial.cs or bin-soapserial.vb sample. *SoapFormatter* is illustrated in this sample because it is a type of *IFormatter* and the rules for controlling SOAP serialization are the same as for using the *BinaryFormatter*.

Code Access Security

Both the *BinaryFormatter* and the *SoapFormatter* demand the *SecurityPermissionFlag.SerializationFormatter* permission, which is granted only to applications running in the local machine account. Therefore, if an application running either in the intranet or Internet zone attempts to serialize or deserialize a data stream, an exception will be thrown.

The *XmlSerializer* does not have any inherent security restrictions—that is, it can be accessed from any zone. The only restriction is if the class being serialized has declarative security attributes, in which case an exception is thrown.

Summary

It's evident that serialization is a powerful and very useful mechanism for transporting complex data across processes, regardless of whether they're running on the same machine or across a network. The .NET Framework offers three types of serialization, and each has its advantages. Binary serialization is the easiest of all serializers to use and also produces the most compact data. The XML serializer offers interoperability and portability at the expense of a much larger serialized data size. Finally, serializing to SOAP allows interoperability with SOAP-based services such as .NET Remoting and Web services. The ability to serialize data forms the building blocks for many technologies such as .NET Remoting and Web services, which are covered later in this book.

5

Developing with Uniform Resource Identifiers

As the Web began to take shape, many problems associated with its massive growth arose. Being able to identify objects or resources in a way that avoided conflicts was one key problem for the creators of the Web. These objects were often files such as documents, graphics, or programs. Uniform Resource Identifiers (URIs) were created to solve the problem of unique object identification by specifying a universal set of namespaces that can be used to identify all resources. URIs play a critical role in network development because users often need to either interact with or refer to resources that are represented by URIs.

This chapter covers the components of a URI and introduces you to *System.Uri*, the Microsoft Windows .NET Framework class used to represent a URI. We'll discuss the most common techniques used when manipulating URIs with *System.Uri* and then delve into the aspects that developers often struggle with, such as understanding the escaping logic, comparing URIs, exposing URIs in your application, and working with different URI schemes.

Key Components of a URI

A URI is defined in Request for Comments (RFC) 2396 as a "compact string of characters for identifying an abstract or a physical resource." A URI in general is made up of two parts: the scheme and the scheme-specific part.

In Figure 5-1, you can see that the scheme is often associated with protocols seen on the Web today, where the scheme-specific part identifies the resource. Many scheme-specific parts of a URI also have an authority, a path, and a query, but these parts are not required.

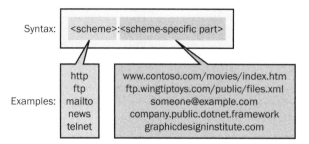

Figure 5-1   Syntax and examples of the required URI parts

In Figure 5-2, you'll notice that the authority is often used to contain what is commonly considered to be the host name or host address. The path might contain file names, and the query is used to specify name/value pairs of information.

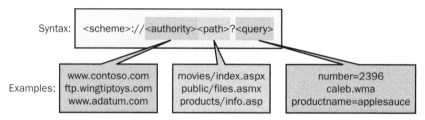

Figure 5-2   Syntax and examples of common (but not required) URI parts

Scheme Component

The scheme determines the logic that's used for parsing and, in cases where possible, for resolving the resource specified in the scheme-specific part. Scheme names are defined in lowercase. However, because URIs are not always machine generated, most applications will accept a scheme in a case-insensitive manner.

Authority Component

The authority component of a URI is defined as the top hierarchical element of the URI that governs the remainder of the namespace defined by the URI. The authority component is often preceded by a double slash (//). For example, consider the following URI:

```
http://www.contoso.com/products/list.aspx?name=soap
```

The authority in this example is *www.contoso.com*, and it's responsible for the remainder of the namespace.

Many schemes designate protocols that include a default port number to be used when resolving the resource. If the port number is omitted from the authority, the default is used. In this example, the default port number for the HTTP protocol is 80. An authority could specify a non-default port number, as follows:

```
http://www.contoso.com:8080/products/list.aspx?name=soap
```

Path Component

The path is used to further identify the resource within the scope of the specified scheme and authority (when an authority is present). The path is often preceded by a single slash (/) and might contain multiple path segments separated by a slash. For example, the following URI contains three path segments:

```
http://www.contoso.com/products/new/list.aspx?name=soap
```

In this example, the segments are *products*, *new*, and *list.aspx*.

> **Tip**   Note that *list.aspx* is a path segment. The general syntax for a URI does not define the notion of a file and an extension. Developers should be careful about making any assumptions based on the notion that a file name and an extension can be reliably parsed from a URI. There's no guarantee that a segment that looks like a file and an extension is not just a directory with a dot in the middle.

Query Component

The query, also called the query string, represents a string of information that's interpreted by the resource. Although the query string is often used to provide information to be interpreted by the resource, developers should be aware of the fact that the query component is considered part of the URI, so its contents can be used to determine the resource that's obtained when the URI is resolved.

Note that some URI schemes, such as HTTP, support the notion of a *fragment*. A fragment is a string of information that's meant to be interpreted by the program resolving the URI and is not considered part of the URI. The fragment is separated from the URI by a crosshatch (#) character. For example, suppose the following URI and fragment are entered into a browser:

```
http://www.contoso.com/products/new/list.htm#newproducts
```

In this example, the *newproducts* fragment might be interpreted by the browser as a bookmark telling it which portion of the page it should display. The resource in this case is represented by *http://www.contoso.com/products*

/new/list.htm. Because the fragment is not part of the URI, its contents are not used to determine the resource that's obtained if the resource can be resolved.

URI Types

You've probably noticed by now that we've been careful to point out that not all resources represented by a URI can be resolved. In fact, there are two principal types of URIs: URLs and URNs. The type that most people are familiar with is the Uniform Resource Locator (URL). A URL is a subset of a URI that identifies a resource by indicating how the resource can be accessed. For example, most of the URIs displayed thus far in this chapter fit into the URL category because you can use them to access a resource. However, URIs can also be used to name things without necessarily describing how they are accessed. In the case where the URI defines a name, it's called a Uniform Resource Name (URN). The benefit of having a URN is that it can be used to identify a resource even after the resource ceases to exist or becomes unavailable. For example, the URI *urn:people:santaclaus* could be used to name Santa Claus, but it does not give us the information necessary to locate him.

The one other type distinction that's important to understand for URIs is that of an *absolute URI* versus a *relative URI*. An absolute URI contains a scheme and a scheme-specific part. So far in this chapter, we've mostly been talking about absolute URIs. It's also possible to have a relative URI, which is a URI reference that's related to some base URI. A relative URI does not contain a scheme. In most cases, a relative URI contains only the path and query components. Because the scheme and the authority are not present, they must be known through some other means. For example, an application downloading an HTML page might find an absolute URI in the document and then find relative links within the embedded HTML. If the absolute URI is not defined in the document, the application might assume that the original URI for the downloaded HTML page is the base URI.

Working with *System.Uri*

System.Uri is the .NET Framework class used to represent a URI. Using the *System.Uri* class, you can validate, parse, combine, and compare URIs. You construct an instance of *System.Uri* by supplying a string representation of the URI in the constructor.

C#

```
try
{
    Uri uri = new Uri("http://www.contoso.com/list.htm#new");
```

```
    Console.WriteLine(uri.ToString());
}
catch(UriFormatException uex)
{
    Console.WriteLine(uex.ToString());
}
```

Visual Basic .NET

```
Try
    Dim uri As New Uri("http://www.contoso.com/list.htm#new")
    Console.WriteLine(uri.ToString)
Catch uex As UriFormatException
    Console.WriteLine(uex.ToString)
End Try
```

The code in this sample constructs a new URI instance and displays the URI to the console. Although constructing a URI is a very simple task, there are a number of things to consider when working with a URI.

Canonicalization

Canonicalization is the process of converting a URI into its simplest form. This process is important because there are multiple ways to express a URI in its raw or string form that ultimately canonicalize into the same URI. Consider the following example:

C#

```
try
{
    // Note the raw URIs are all different
    Uri uriOne = new Uri("http://www.contoso.com/Prod list.htm");
    Uri uriTwo = new Uri("http://www.contoso.com:80/Prod%20list.htm");
    Uri uriThree = new Uri("http://www.contoso.com/Prod%20list.htm");
    // The Canonical representation is the same for all three
    Console.WriteLine("uriOne = " + uriOne.ToString());
    Console.WriteLine("uriTwo = " + uriTwo.ToString());
    Console.WriteLine("uriThree = " + uriThree.ToString());
}
catch(UriFormatException uex)
{
    Console.WriteLine(uex.ToString());
}
```

Visual Basic .NET

```
Try
    ' Note the raw URIs are all different
    Dim uriOne As New Uri("http://www.contoso.com/Prod list.htm")
```

```
    Dim uriTwo As New Uri("http://www.contoso.com:80/Prod%20list.htm")
    Dim uriThree As New Uri("http://www.contoso.com/Prod%20list.htm")
    ' The Canonical representation is the same for all three
    Console.WriteLine("uriOne = " + uriOne.ToString())
    Console.WriteLine("uriTwo = " + uriTwo.ToString())
    Console.WriteLine("uriThree = " + uriThree.ToString())
    Catch uex As UriFormatException
    Console.WriteLine(uex.ToString)
End Try
```

In this example, the space can be either a literal value or an "escaped" form. Also, the *:80* port number can be excluded in the canonical form because it's the default port for the scheme for this URI. The canonical representation of a URI can be obtained by calling the *ToString* method of *System.Uri*.

Comparing URIs

It's often useful to compare two URIs. However, it's important to understand that *System.Uri* compares URIs in their canonical form instead of in their raw form. Consider the following example:

C#

```
try
{
    // Note the raw URIs are different
    Uri uriOne = new Uri("http://www.contoso.com/Prod list.htm");
    Uri uriTwo = new Uri("http://www.contoso.com:80/Prod%20list.htm");

    // Comparison is based on the canonical representation
    // so uriOne and uriTwo will be equal.
    Console.WriteLine(uriOne.Equals(uriTwo));
}
catch(UriFormatException uex)
{
    Console.WriteLine(uex.ToString());
}
```

Visual Basic .NET

```
Try
    ' Note the raw URIs are different
    Dim uriOne As New Uri("http://www.contoso.com/Prod list.htm")
    Dim uriTwo As New Uri("http://www.contoso.com:80/Prod%20list.htm")

    'Comparison is based on the canonical representation
    'so uriOne and uriTwo will be equal.
    Console.WriteLine(uriOne.Equals(uriTwo))
```

```
Catch uex As UriFormatException
    Console.WriteLine(uex.ToString)
End Try
```

Another interesting point to note is that because the fragment isn't considered part of the URI, it's omitted from the URI comparison in *System.Uri*. For example, a comparison of *http://www.contoso.com/Prod list.htm* and *http://www.contoso.com/Prod list.htm#newItems* will return *true* because *#newItems* is ignored.

Working with Schemes

As described earlier in this chapter, the scheme part of a URI is the element at the beginning of the URI that defines how the URI can be parsed and, in the case of a URL, resolved. Most schemes define a scheme-specific part that follows the general guidelines listed earlier in this chapter of having an authority, a path, and (potentially) a query component. However, schemes are not required to follow this pattern. In fact, some schemes define their own logic that does not correspond to these common parts. For example, consider the following URIs:

```
http://www.contoso.com/Prodlist.htm
mailto:cdo@contoso.com?meg=kate
```

The first URI is an example of the HTTP scheme. It defines an authority (*www.contoso.com*) and a path (*Prodlist.htm*). The second URI is an example of the *MAILTO* scheme. *MAILTO* does not define authority and path components. Rather, it defines a *to* component and a *headers* component. In this example, the *to* value is *cdo@contoso.com*, the header name is *meg*, and the header value is *kate*.

In general, *System.Uri* will simply look for the colon to parse the scheme from the scheme-specific part. There is one exception to this rule that developers should understand. Because it's common for URIs of the *file:* scheme to be entered without the scheme, as in *c:\test\test.htm*, *System.Uri* supports the automatic conversion of local paths (*c:\test\test.htm*) to *file:* scheme URIs (*file:///c:/test/test.htm*). So, if you have a single character scheme, the *System.Uri* class will treat it as a *file:* scheme.

System.Uri has an in-depth understanding of a number of the most commonly used schemes so that it can take these special cases into account. The following list represents the schemes understood by *System.Uri* in version 1.1 of the .NET Framework:

■   FILE

■   HTTP

- HTTPS

- FTP

- GOPHER

- MAILTO

- NEWS

- NNTP

- UUID

- TELNET

- LDAP

- SOAP

Although this list is expected to grow over time, the fact that schemes can be defined at any time ensures that there will be cases in which *System.Uri* encounters a scheme that it does not recognize. In those cases, *System.Uri* will fall back to using parsing logic based on the general URI components described at the beginning of this chapter. If that URI scheme follows these general component recommendations, the URI will parse just fine. However, if that unknown scheme has defined its own scheme-specific part that does not follow the common pattern, such as with *MAILTO, System.Uri* does not have a way of knowing how to parse out the components and will throw a *UriFormat-Exception* if it can't map the scheme into the common pattern. For example, consider the following example:

C#

```
try
{
    Console.WriteLine("Unknown scheme general pattern");
    Uri uriUnknown = new Uri("unknown://authority/path?query");
    Console.WriteLine("scheme:" + uriUnknown.Scheme);
    Console.WriteLine("authority:" + uriUnknown.Authority);
    Console.WriteLine("path and query:" + uriUnknown.PathAndQuery);

    Console.WriteLine();

    Console.WriteLine("Unknown scheme that uses a custom pattern");
    Uri uriUnknownCustom = new Uri("unknown:path.authority.query");
    Console.WriteLine("scheme:" + uriUnknownCustom.Scheme);
    Console.WriteLine("authority:" + uriUnknownCustom.Authority);
    Console.WriteLine("path and query:" + uriUnknownCustom.PathAndQuery);

}
```

```
catch(UriFormatException uex)
{
    Console.WriteLine(uex.ToString());
}
```

Visual Basic .NET

```
Try
    Console.WriteLine("Unknown scheme general pattern")
    Dim uriUnknown As New Uri("unknown://authority/path?query")

    Console.WriteLine("scheme:" + uriUnknown.Scheme)
    Console.WriteLine("authority:" + uriUnknown.Authority)
    Console.WriteLine("path and query:" + uriUnknown.PathAndQuery)

    Console.WriteLine()

    Console.WriteLine("Unknown scheme that uses a custom pattern")
    Dim uriUnknownCustom As New Uri("unknown:path.authority.query")

    Console.WriteLine("scheme:" + uriUnknownCustom.Scheme)
    Console.WriteLine("authority:" + uriUnknownCustom.Authority)
    Console.WriteLine("path and query:" + uriUnknownCustom.PathAndQuery)

Catch ex As Exception
    Console.WriteLine(ex.ToString)
End Try
```

This sample outputs the following to the console:

```
Unknown scheme that follows the general pattern
scheme:unknown
authority:authority
path and query:/path?query

Unknown scheme that uses a custom pattern
scheme:unknown
authority:
path and query:path.authority.query
```

In this sample, *System.Uri* is able to correctly parse the unknown scheme that uses the general scheme pattern. However, in the case where the scheme-specific part is based off a custom pattern, the authority is not parsed because the logic for parsing the component parts is not defined.

> **Note** In version 1.1 of the .NET Framework, there's no way to specify custom parsing logic so that a URI scheme that does not follow the general URI pattern and is not known by *System.Uri* can "plug in" and provide its own parsing implementation. This lack of support for custom URI scheme parsing is expected to the change in the next major release of the .NET Framework. In general, if you have to create a new scheme, it's best to follow the general component syntax of *scheme: //authority/path?query* because most URI parsing libraries will understand the scheme.

Parsing Host Names

Although the concept of a host is not explicitly defined as part of the URI, a host name is often referenced as the authority portion of the URI. Therefore, you should consider the following points when dealing with host names in *System.Uri*, especially in the case of HTTP URIs:

- *System.Uri* supports a fully qualified DNS name (FQDN), an IP address, or a machine name as the host name.

- *System.Uri* always converts the host name to lowercase characters as part of parsing the URI.

- Internet Protocol version 6 (IPv6) addresses should be entered inside square brackets for URI construction, for example, *http://[::1]/path*.

- Internet Protocol version 4 (IPv4) addresses can be entered in their conventional dot-separated format, for example, *http://127.0.0.1*.

Using *System.Uri* in Your Application

In the course of developing your application or classes that work with a URI, there are a few key guidelines that you should follow to ensure that your application gets the best performance and security. The *System.Uri* type is extremely valuable when it comes to parsing and validating a URI. However, this functionality comes at a cost and there are cases when it should not be used.

When to Use *System.Uri*

Consider using *System.Uri* in your application whenever you need to parse or validate a URI in any way. Like many things in development, a URI can appear to be very simple on the surface but turn out to be quite complex when you begin to consider all the cases. We've seen that developers who avoid the temptation to write a "simple URI parser" are often rewarded later on in the development cycle when application logic or input assumptions change, causing the simple logic to become much more complex.

A significant cost is associated with constructing an instance of *System.Uri* when compared to that of simply creating a string. Most of this cost is because of the URI validation logic. Because of this cost, it's important that methods in your application that parse a URI and then pass the URI on to any other method should always pass the URI as a *System.Uri* type rather than as a string. This way, you avoid a scenario where the URI is parsed multiple times as it gets converted from a string to a *Uri* instance, back to a string, and back to a *Uri* instance as it moves through the call stack.

When Not to Use *System.Uri*

Because of the cost of construction, *System.Uri* should not be used if you never intend to parse or validate the URI being represented. In these cases, a *String* type should be used to contain the URI.

In version 1.1 of the .NET Framework, *System.Uri* implements the *MarshalByRefObject* interface, which means that passing a *System.Uri* object as a parameter in a remote call will cause the *Uri* instance to be passed by reference rather than by value. Passing the *Uri* instance by reference can lead to unintended circumstances such as having an extremely high performance cost of accessing the properties that you think are local when they are really being remoted to another application that's possibly on another machine. The fact that *System.Uri* implements *MarshalByRefObject* can also lead to a security or functional issue in your code if the application is making decisions based on an assumption that the *Uri* instance is immutable. Because of these reasons, you should avoid passing a URI as part of the signature in a remote procedure call. In cases where you must pass a URI in a remote procedure call, consider passing the URI as a *String* rather than as an instance of *System.Uri*.

> **Note**   It is anticipated that in the next major release of the .NET Framework, *MarshalByRefObject* will be removed from the *System.Uri* signature so that it is always passed in remote calls by value rather than by reference.

Summary

This chapter introduced the Uniform Resource Identifier (URI). We described its purpose, the required parts, and the common components that exist in a URI. This chapter also introduced *System.Uri*, the type used to represent and manipulate a URI in the .NET Framework. Finally we discussed the issues that developers often encounter when working with *System.Uri* and exposing it in the application programming interfaces (APIs) that they develop.

Part II

Using the Network

6

Introduction to *System.Net*

System.Net is the namespace in the Microsoft Windows .NET Framework that contains the core classes intended for building applications that communicate over a network. The types of functionality found in *System.Net* range from access to a raw socket to the ability to upload to and download from resources on the Internet. In addition to providing a language-independent, object-oriented way to access network resources, *System.Net* serves as the communication infrastructure for higher-level, distributed application programming models such as XML-based Web services and .NET Remoting.

Layers of *System.Net*

The *System.Net* classes can be divided into four layers, as depicted in Figure 6-1 and described in the following list.

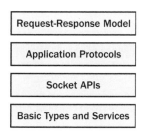

Figure 6-1   The layers of *System.Net*

■ **Basic network types and services**   Fundamental types that are used for working with Internet Protocol (IP) addresses or non-IP network addresses such as Internetwork Packet Exchange (IPX). This layer also includes classes for performing Domain Name System (DNS) resolution.

■ **Socket-level APIs**   A set of managed classes for performing network communication over a socket, such as sending and receiving data between two hosts.

■ **Application protocols**   Classes intended to be used both on the client and on the middle tier. These classes are for protocols layered on top of the socket APIs, such as the Hypertext Transfer Protocol (HTTP) and the File Transfer Protocol (FTP).

■ **Protocol-independent request-response model**   These classes provide a pattern that is used by request-response protocols for resolving Uniform Resource Identifiers (URIs) without requiring the developer to write protocol-specific code.

In this section, we'll walk through each layer and introduce the most commonly used classes for each layer. The layers will be covered in-depth in the following chapters.

Basic Network Types and Services

Figure 6-2 contains the classes that make up the basic types and services included in *System.Net*. In the subsequent sections, we'll look briefly at each of the basic types and services that are made accessible through *System.Net*. Although this section introduces the key types, most of them are covered in-depth in the chapters that follow.

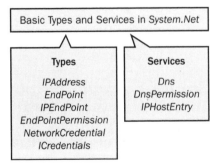

Figure 6-2   Basic types and services provided by *System.Net*

Using IP Addresses

The *IPAddress* type provides a class representation of an IP address. It includes methods that can be used to perform common operations on an IP address, such as parsing the address. The following code shows how you would parse an IP address.

C#

```csharp
static void ParseIPAddress(string addressString)
{
    try
    {
        IPAddress address = IPAddress.Parse(addressString);
        Console.WriteLine("The address is " + address.ToString()
            + " and is of the family "
            + address.AddressFamily.ToString() + ".");
    }
    catch(Exception ex)
    {
        Console.WriteLine("Failure parsing " + addressString + ". " +
            ex.ToString());
    }
}
```

Visual Basic .NET

```vbnet
Sub ParseIPAddress(ByVal addressString As String)
    Try
        Dim address As IPAddress
        address = IPAddress.Parse(addressString)

        Console.WriteLine("The address is " & address.ToString _
            & " and is of the family " & _
            address.AddressFamily.ToString + ".")

    Catch ex As Exception
        Console.WriteLine("Failure parsing" & addressString & _
            ". " & ex.ToString)

    End Try
End Sub
```

Note that if an invalid IP address is specified in this case, *IPAddress* will throw a *FormatException* that should be handled by the application. The *IPAddress* class should be used for validation any time your application receives an IP address as input from a user, a configuration file, or another source. *IPAddress* also provides the ability to determine whether a particular address is a member of the Internet Protocol version 6 (IPv6) or the Internet Protocol version 4 (IPv4) address family. Finally, *IPAddress* contains a number of helper methods and fields, such as *IPAddress.Any*, *IPAddress.IPv6Any*, and *IPAddress.IsLoopback*. The *Any* fields can be used to indicate that the application should bind to a port that listens on all network interfaces of that address family. The *IsLoopback* method can be useful when validating whether a local loopback address is being used. More information regarding IP addressing is found in Chapter 7.

Working with Different Address Families

The *System.Net.EndPoint* class provides developers with a way to access resources through *System.Net* over protocols that belong to different address families that have different semantics at the addressing level. This functionality is useful when you need to write an application that talks over a non-IP protocol, such as AppleTalk, IPX, or infrared. Because IP-based protocols are the most commonly used on today's networks, *System.Net* includes an *IPEndPoint* type in the .NET Framework. In the case of *IPEndPoint*, an end point is defined as an IP address and a port number. The .NET Compact Framework includes an *IrDAEndPoint* implementation of the *EndPoint* class that can be used for communicating with other nodes using infrared technologies. In the case of an *IrDAEndPoint*, an end point is defined as a device ID and a service name. Although most developers will simply work within the confines of the IP address family, this extensibility point is useful because the definition of an end point often varies from one address family to another.

Accessing Protected Resources

System.Net defines an *ICredential* interface and an associated *NetworkCredential* class that provide a means of specifying network credentials, such as a user name and a password in cases where network authentication is required when accessing a resource. These classes are mainly used in the context of the HTTP application protocol classes. However, in an upcoming release of the .NET Framework, their use is likely to be expanded to include other socket-level authentication scenarios as well. The following code demonstrates how you can use the *NetworkCredential* class to authenticate with a remote resource.

C#

```
static void RequestProtectedResource(string resource)
{
    Console.WriteLine("Please enter your user name.");
    string userName = Console.ReadLine();

    Console.WriteLine("Please enter your password.");
    string password = Console.ReadLine();

    WebClient client = new WebClient();
    client.Credentials = new NetworkCredential(userName, password);
    client.DownloadFile(resource, "page.htm");
}
```

Visual Basic .NET

```
Sub RequestProtectedResource(ByVal resource As String)

    Console.WriteLine("Please enter your user name.")
    Dim userName As String
    userName = Console.ReadLine()

    Console.WriteLine("Please enter your password.")
    Dim password As String
    password = Console.ReadLine()

    Dim client As New WebClient
    client.Credentials = New NetworkCredential(userName, password)
    client.DownloadFile(resource, "page.htm")

End Sub
```

> **Note**   Notice that in this code the credentials are obtained by prompting the user to enter them on the command line. *System.Net* also provides a way of using the default credentials of the account under which the application is running. You do so by setting the *Credentials* property on a class equal to *CredentialCache.DefaultCredentials*. Whenever possible, developers should use default credentials instead of prompting the user or reading credentials from some other source because default credentials are obtained through the security systems integrated into the underlying operating system.

Accessing DNS

DNS can be used to represent nodes on the network with human-readable names rather than IP addresses. For example, imagine trying to remember a string of characters such as *www.contoso.com* instead of a series of numbers such as *207.168.24.30*. One feature provided by DNS is the ability to have multiple IP addresses assigned to one host name. You can even have different IP address types (for example, IPv4 and IPv6) assigned to the same host. It's often useful to be able to resolve a name to the list of IP addresses associated with that name.

Access to DNS is enabled and controlled in *System.Net* through the *Dns*, *DnsPermission*, and *IPHostEntry* classes. DNS is covered in more detail in Chapter 7. The following example shows the basic steps involved in resolving a name and outputting the corresponding IP addresses to the console using *System.Net*.

C#

```csharp
static void ResolveName(string name)
{
    try
    {
        IPHostEntry hostInfo = Dns.Resolve(name);
        foreach(IPAddress address in hostInfo.AddressList)
            Console.WriteLine(address.ToString());
    }
    catch(Exception ex)
    {
        Console.WriteLine(ex.ToString());
    }
}
```

Visual Basic .NET

```vbnet
Sub ResolveName(ByVal name As String)
    Try
        Dim hostInfo As IPHostEntry
        hostInfo = Dns.Resolve(name)

        Dim address As IPAddress
        For Each address In hostInfo.AddressList
            Console.WriteLine(address.ToString)
        Next address

    Catch ex As Exception
        Console.WriteLine(ex.ToString)
    End Try
End Sub
```

Using the Socket-Level Classes

The socket-level classes in *System.Net* enable fine-grained control over the way data is read from and written to the network. These classes include access to sockets, a stream pattern for network I/O, and some helper classes that simplify a number of the most common tasks that are desirable when working with this level of the network. Figure 6-3 displays the groups of classes that make up the socket-level APIs for *System.Net*.

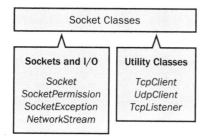

Figure 6-3   Socket-level classes in *System.Net*

Socket Classes

The *System.Net.Sockets* namespace contains a class-based representation of the Windows Sockets model commonly known as Winsock. These classes are particularly focused on a subset of the Winsock model that deals with IP-based protocols such as User Datagram Protocol (UDP) and Transmission Control Protocol (TCP). These classes can be extended to enable other protocols such as NetBIOS and Infrared. The key classes to be aware of at this level are *Socket*, *SocketPermission*, and *SocketException*. The *Socket* class provides the vast majority of the functionality needed to access the network and acts as the gatekeeper for the transition from managed .NET Framework code to the underlying native *Win32* APIs. *SocketException* is used to represent most exceptions that occur within the *Socket* class. The *SocketPermission* class is used to control access to socket-level resources through code access security. These classes are described in more detail in Chapters 8 and 9. The following example demonstrates how to download a Web page using the socket-level classes.

C#

```
static void Main(string[] args)
{
    // Validate the input values
    if(args.Length < 2)
    {
        Console.WriteLine("Expected DownloadWebPage.exe serverName path");
```

```
        Console.WriteLine("Example: DownloadWebPage.exe contoso.com /");
        return;
    }

    string server = args[0];
    string path = args[1];
    int port = 80;

    IPHostEntry host = null;
    IPEndPoint remoteEndPoint = null;
    Socket client = null;

    // Resolve the server name
    try
    {
        host = Dns.GetHostByName(server);
    }
    catch(Exception ex)
    {
        Console.WriteLine(ex.ToString());
        return;
    }

    // Attempt to connect on each address returned from DNS
    // Break out once successfully connected
    foreach(IPAddress address in host.AddressList)
    {
        try
        {
            client = new Socket(address.AddressFamily, SocketType.Stream,
                ProtocolType.Tcp);

            remoteEndPoint = new IPEndPoint(address, port);
            client.Connect(remoteEndPoint);
            break;
        }
        catch(SocketException ex)
        {
            Console.WriteLine(ex.ToString());
        }
    }

    // MakeRequest will issue the HTTP download request
    // and write the server response to the console
    MakeRequest(client, path, server);
    client.Close();
}
```

```
public static void MakeRequest(Socket client, string path, string server)
{
    // Format the HTTP GET request string
    string Get = "GET " + path + " HTTP/1.0\r\nHost: " + server
        + "\r\nConnection: Close\r\n\r\n";

    Byte[] ByteGet = Encoding.ASCII.GetBytes(Get);

    // Send the GET request to the connected server
    client.Send(ByteGet);

    // Create a buffer that is used to read the response
    byte[] responseData = new byte[1024];

    // read the response and save the ASCII data in a string
    int bytesRead = client.Receive(responseData);
    StringBuilder responseString = new StringBuilder();
    while (bytesRead != 0)
    {
        responseString.Append(Encoding.ASCII.GetChars(responseData),
            0, bytesRead);

        bytesRead = client.Receive(responseData);
    }

    // Display the response to the console
    Console.WriteLine(responseString.ToString());
}
```

Visual Basic .NET

```
Sub Main(ByVal args As String())

    ' Validate the input values
    If args.Length < 2 Then
        Console.WriteLine("Expected DownloadWebPage.exe serverName path")
        Console.WriteLine("Example: DownloadWebPage.exe contoso.com /")
        Return
    End If

    Dim server As String = args(0)
    Dim path As String = args(1)
    Dim port As Integer = 80

    Dim host As IPHostEntry
    Dim remoteEndPoint As IPEndPoint
    Dim client As Socket
```

```
    ' Resolve the server name
    Try
        host = Dns.GetHostByName(server)
    Catch ex As Exception
        Console.WriteLine(ex.ToString())
        Return
    End Try

    ' Attempt to connect on each address returned from DNS
    ' Exit out once successfully connected
    For Each address As IPAddress In host.AddressList
        Try
            client = New Socket(address.AddressFamily, _
                SocketType.Stream, ProtocolType.Tcp)

            remoteEndPoint = New IPEndPoint(address, port)
            client.Connect(remoteEndPoint)
            Exit For
        Catch ex As Exception
            Console.WriteLine(ex.ToString())
        End Try
    Next

    ' MakeRequest will issue the HTTP download request
    ' and write the server response to the console
    MakeRequest(client, path, server)
    client.Close()
End Sub

Sub MakeRequest(ByVal client As Socket, ByVal path As String, _
ByVal server As String)

    ' Format the HTTP GET request string
    Dim getString As String = "GET " + path + " HTTP/1.0" + ControlChars.CrLf
    getString += "Host: " + server + ControlChars.CrLf + "Connection: Close"
    getString += ControlChars.CrLf + ControlChars.CrLf

    Dim ByteGet As Byte() = Encoding.ASCII.GetBytes(getString)

    ' Send the GET request to the connected server
    client.Send(ByteGet)

    ' Create a buffer that is used to read the response
    Dim responseData() As Byte = New Byte(1024) {}

    ' Read the response and save the ASCII data in a string
    Dim bytesRead As Integer = client.Receive(responseData)
    Dim responseString As StringBuilder = New StringBuilder
```

```
While bytesRead > 0
    responseString.Append(Encoding.ASCII.GetChars(responseData),
        0, bytesRead)

    bytesRead = client.Receive(responseData)
End While

' Display the response to the console
Console.WriteLine(responseString.ToString())
End Sub
```

You'll notice that the sample for downloading a Web page using sockets is much longer than the code it would take to do the same thing using a higher layer in *System.Net*, such as *WebRequest* or *WebClient*. This additional code is the tradeoff that's often made when you decide to program at the socket level. Your application will have much greater control over the protocol that's emitted, but it does so at the cost of additional code.

Reading and Writing with *NetworkStream*

Although *NetworkStream* isn't a large class, it's extremely useful because it provides a stream-based model for reading and writing data over a network. *NetworkStream* implements the standard methods and properties that you'll find on the base *System.IO.Stream* pattern, as discussed in Chapter 2. You should consider a couple of interesting elements that are specific to this implementation when working with *NetworkStream*. First, a *NetworkStream* instance can be obtained either by constructing one from a socket or by getting one from another class such as one of the socket-level helper classes described in the next section. Second, because *NetworkStream* is based on a TCP connection and does not buffer data, it's not seekable.

> **Note**   You can't set the *Position* property to seek a particular point in the stream. You should be aware of this limitation if you rely on other classes that use the *Stream* type and expect this functionality from the stream.

Using the Socket-Level Helper Classes

The socket-level helper classes include *TcpClient*, *TcpListener*, and *UdpClient*. These classes simplify the most common tasks that an application might perform using the TCP and UDP protocols. The *TcpClient* class is focused on the scenario of connecting to a remote host and getting a stream that can be used to read and write data. The *TcpListener* class is the inverse of *TcpClient*. It provides methods for accepting an incoming socket connection and accessing a stream that's created on top of that connection. The *UdpClient* class contains methods for sending and receiving data over UDP, including *JoinMulticastGroup* and *DropMulticastGroup* for IP multicasting data.

Because the UDP protocol is connectionless, no model is provided for creating a *NetworkStream* on top of it. Without the ability to create a stream, there's little value to having a listener correspondent to the *UdpClient* class because the *UdpClient.Receive* method takes care of receiving data from a remote host.

> **Note**   Because the socket-level helper classes do not include asynchronous methods, applications designed for high-load scenarios should use the *Socket* class instead.

Application Protocols

The application protocols level contains classes designed for resolving specific protocols. Resources that can be resolved using these protocols are most often represented by a URI. In version 1.1 of the .NET Framework, the supported schemes include HTTP, HTTPS, and FILE. In an upcoming release of the .NET Framework, this layer will be enhanced to include FTP protocol support as well. Each of these protocols implements the general request-response pattern that will be described in the next section. Figure 6-4 provides a graphical representation of the key application protocol classes in version 1.1 of *System.Net*.

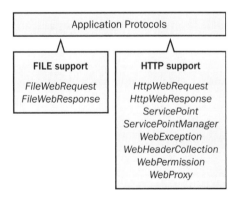

Figure 6-4   Application protocol classes in version 1.1 of *System.Net*

Protocol Support

The HTTP protocol is supported primarily by the *HttpWebRequest* and *HttpWeb-Response* classes in *System.Net*. These classes provide a complete implementation of the HTTP 1.1 and 1 protocols. The feature set includes support for all of the HTTP verbs defined in RFC 2616 as well as custom commands, HTTP pipelining, and chunked uploading and downloading of content. *HttpWebRequest* and *HttpWebResponse* have been designed to work well under situations that require high load and scale. They're also suitable for use both in client application scenarios and n-tier server scenarios. The HTTP support in *System.Net* is described in more detail in Chapter 10. The following example demonstrates how to download a file using the HTTP classes.

C#

```
static void Main()
{
    try
    {
        // Create the request object
        HttpWebRequest request =
            (HttpWebRequest)WebRequest.Create(
            "http://www.contoso.com/file.htm");

        // Optionally, you can set HTTP-specific elements on
        // the request, such as the User-Agent header
        request.UserAgent = "Test Client version 1.0";

        // Issue the request
        HttpWebResponse response = (HttpWebResponse)request.GetResponse();

        // Read the content
        StreamReader reader = new StreamReader(response.GetResponseStream(),
            Encoding.ASCII);

        string content = reader.ReadToEnd();

        // Display the content to the console
        Console.WriteLine(content);

        // Close the response
        response.Close();
    }
    catch(WebException wex)
    {
        Console.WriteLine(wex.ToString());
        // Check the status to see if there might be a response object
        if(wex.Status == WebExceptionStatus.ProtocolError)
```

```
        {
            HttpWebResponse response = (HttpWebResponse)wex.Response;
            Console.WriteLine();
            Console.WriteLine("The protocol error returned was '" +
                response.StatusCode.ToString() + "'.");
            response.Close();
        }
    }
}
```

Visual Basic .NET

```
Sub Main()
    Try
        ' Create the request object
        Dim request As HttpWebRequest = _
            WebRequest.Create("http://www.contoso.com/file.htm")

        ' Optionally, you can set HTTP-specific elements on
        ' the request, such as the User-Agent header
        request.UserAgent = "Test Client version 1.0"

        ' Issue the request
        Dim response As HttpWebResponse = request.GetResponse()

        ' Read the content
        Dim reader As New StreamReader(response.GetResponseStream(), _
            Encoding.ASCII)

        Dim content As String = reader.ReadToEnd()

        ' Display the content to the console
        Console.WriteLine(content)

        ' Close the response
        response.Close()

        Catch wex As WebException
        Console.WriteLine(wex.ToString())
        ' Check the status to see if there might be a response object
        If wex.Status = WebExceptionStatus.ProtocolError Then
            Dim response As HttpWebResponse = wex.Response
            Console.WriteLine()
            Console.WriteLine("The protocol error returned was '" & _
                response.StatusCode.ToString & "'.")

            response.Close()
        End If
    End Try
End Sub
```

HTTP Connection Management

The HTTP protocol layer includes the *ServicePoint* and *ServicePointManager* classes for controlling connection semantics associated with the HTTP requests between an application and a remote host. The *ServicePointManager* class is used to specify settings that apply to all connections made by the application, whereas the *ServicePoint* class provides the ability to change settings on a host-by-host basis. For example, the default connection limit is two connections per application and host pair; however, this limit can be changed on a per-host basis through the *ServicePoint* class or globally for all host connections in the application through the *ServicePointManager* class. Connection semantics can be specified through the *ServicePoint.ConnectionLimit* property or the *ServicePointManager.DefaultConnectionLimit* property. Other interesting features that can be manipulated using the connection management classes include pipelining, certificate authentication, SSL encryption, setting the behavior of the *Expect* HTTP header (by default this behavior is 100-continue), and use of the TCP Nagle algorithm.

HTTP Error Handling

Error handling for HTTP is accomplished using the *WebException* class. *WebException* contains a *Status* property to indicate the reason the *WebException* was thrown. This value is useful because it helps to determine whether a valid *HttpWebResponse* object that can be used to read the response from the server is associated with the *WebException* even though an exception was thrown. For example, an authentication challenge that's not handled successfully by the client will result in a *WebException*. However, it's possible that the server included additional information in the response, so reading the data sent back from the server is still interesting in this case. There are other cases where the *WebException* occurs before the connection to the remote host has been established, such as a name resolution failure. In these cases, no *HttpWebResponse* object is associated with the *WebException*. Because of this model, it's important to always check the *Status* property before accessing the *Response* property on *WebException*.

> **Note**   The *WebException.Status* property should not be confused with the protocol status codes that can be returned by an HTTP server, such as a 401. These codes and their text descriptions can be found on the *HttpWebResponse* property available on *WebException.Response* if the *WebException.Status* property is one that contains a response.

Other commonly used classes at the HTTP level include the *WebProxy* and *GlobalProxySelection* classes for specifying the use of HTTP proxy servers. The *NetworkCredential* and *CredentialCache* classes associate credentials with a request, and the *Cookie* class manipulates HTTP cookies.

File Scheme Support

In addition to HTTP schemes, version 1.1 of the .NET Framework supports resolution of FILE: URIs. This functionality is contained in the *FileWebRequest* and *FileWebResponse* classes. These classes follow the same request-response model as *HttpWebRequest* and *HttpWebResponse*. However, they are fairly thin wrappers over the *File* class found in the *System.IO* namespace. *FileWebRequest* and *FileWebResponse* have been provided for convenience so that developers working with the FILE: URI scheme do not have to use a different model from that used when resolving HTTP URIs.

Request-Response Model

The request-response model in *System.Net* is defined by the *WebRequest* and *WebResponse* classes. These abstract base classes provide an implementation pattern that's used by protocol-specific implementations such as the FILE and HTTP handlers described in the previous section. This common pattern for request-response enables developers to resolve resources containing different URI schemes in a consistent and protocol-independent manner. For example, this common model enables a developer to write the same code to download a resource on an FTP server as that needed to download a resource on an HTTP server. This model is extensible, so third-party implementers can plug in their own protocol handlers as well. There are also a number of helper classes that work with this model and apply to the various supported protocols. Figure 6-5 highlights the request-response model, including the key methods and properties of *WebRequest* and *WebResponse*, as well as the helper classes that work with the model.

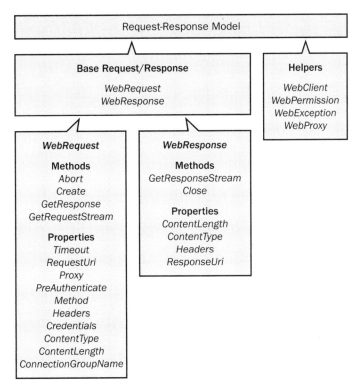

Figure 6-5   The *System.Net* request-response model

Resolving URIs with *WebRequest* and *WebResponse*

The *WebRequest* and *WebResponse* classes contain methods and properties that apply generically across the different supported protocols and enable applications to download and upload data given a specific URI and to specify authentication details, proxy information, and content details such as the type and size of the content. An asynchronous pattern is also provided for any operation that could be blocking on network activity. Extensibility is achieved through the *WebRequest.RegisterPrefix* method or through entries in the *System.Net* section of the application-specific or machine-wide configuration file. The following example demonstrates how to download a file using the request-response model. You'll notice that this example is very similar to the example shown earlier in the section on HTTP, with the exception that this example resolves URIs with differing protocol schemes.

C#

```csharp
static void Main()
{
    ResolveResource("http://www.contoso.com/file.htm");
    ResolveResource("file://c:\\temp\\file.htm");
}

static void ResolveResource(string address)
{
    try
    {
        // Create the request object
        WebRequest request = WebRequest.Create(address);

        // Issue the request
        WebResponse response = request.GetResponse();

        // Read the content
        StreamReader reader = new StreamReader(response.GetResponseStream(),
            Encoding.ASCII);

        string content = reader.ReadToEnd();

        // Display the content to the console
        Console.WriteLine(content);

        // Close the response
        response.Close();
    }
    catch(WebException wex)
    {
        // Display the exception details
        Console.WriteLine(wex.ToString());
    }
}
```

Visual Basic .NET

```vbnet
Sub Main()
    ResolveResource("http://www.contoso.com/file.htm")
    ResolveResource("file://c:\\temp\\file.htm")
End Sub

Sub ResolveResource(ByVal address As String)
    Try
        ' Create the request object
        Dim request As WebRequest = WebRequest.Create(address)
```

```
' Issue the request
Dim response As WebResponse = request.GetResponse()

' Read the content
Dim reader As New StreamReader(response.GetResponseStream(), _
    Encoding.ASCII)

Dim content As String = reader.ReadToEnd()

' Display the content to the console
Console.WriteLine(content)

' Close the response
response.Close()

Catch wex As WebException
    ' Display the exception details
    Console.WriteLine(wex.ToString())
End Try
End Sub
```

Request-Response Model Helper Classes

Request-response model helper classes perform a specific function that's usually common to the different protocols that implement *WebRequest* and *WebResponse*. *WebProxy* and *WebException* are both examples of such helper classes.

Another example of a request-response model helper is the *WebPermission* class. *WebPermission* is used to define code access security privileges for classes that implement the *WebRequest* and *WebResponse* base classes. Privileges that are controlled through *WebPermission* include the ability to access a specific URI, a wildcard set of URIs as supplied by a regular expression, or all URIs as identified by the *System.Security.Permissions.PermissionState* enumeration.

Finally, the *WebClient* class provides a number of task-focused methods that perform operations that are commonly useful to applications that deal with resources on the Web. Here are the operations available as one-line method calls with *WebClient*:

- Download a URI-based resource to memory.

- Download a URI-based resource and save it to a file.

- Given a URI, return a readable stream.

- Given a URI, return a writable stream.

- Upload data from memory to a URI-based resource.

■   Upload data from a file to a URI-based resource.

■   Post a name-value collection to a Web form.

Because the *WebClient* class uses the *WebRequest* and *WebResponse* classes in its implementation, it works with any protocol handler that has been registered into the request-response model. The following code demonstrates a version of the *DownloadWebPage* sample considered in the section on *Web-Request* and *WebResponse* that has been modified to use *WebClient*.

C#

```
static void Main()
{
    ResolveResource("http://www.contoso.com/file.htm");
    ResolveResource("file://c:\\temp\\file.htm");
}

static void ResolveResource(string address)
{
    try
    {
        // Download the content
        WebClient client = new WebClient();
        byte[] contentBytes = client.DownloadData(address);

        // Convert the content bytes to a string
        string content = Encoding.ASCII.GetString(contentBytes);

        // Display the content to the console
        Console.WriteLine(content);
    }
    catch(WebException wex)
    {
        // Display the exception details
        Console.WriteLine(wex.ToString());
    }
}
```

Visual Basic .NET

```
Sub Main()
    ResolveResource("http://www.contoso.com/file.htm")
    ResolveResource("file://c:\\temp\\file.htm")
End Sub

Sub ResolveResource(ByVal address As String)
    Try
        ' Download the content
```

```
        Dim client As New WebClient
        Dim contentBytes() As Byte = client.DownloadData(address)

        ' Convert the content bytes to a string
        Dim content As String = Encoding.ASCII.GetString(contentBytes)

        ' Display the content to the console
        Console.WriteLine(content)

    Catch wex As WebException
        ' Display the exception details
        Console.WriteLine(wex.ToString())
    End Try
End Sub
```

Notice that the networking code in this example has been reduced to two lines, where one of the lines is simply creating the class and the other is performing the download operation. Consider further a comparison of the size of this sample to the socket sample at the beginning of this chapter that performed roughly the same operation of downloading a file. *WebClient* offers the simplest way in *System.Net* to accomplish some of the most common network tasks. Similar to the *UdpClient* and *TcpClient* classes introduced earlier in this chapter, *WebClient* does not contain asynchronous methods. Applications requiring asynchronous functionality should use the *WebRequest* and *WebResponse* classes instead of *WebClient*.

Deciding When to Use *System.Net*

The .NET Framework contains a number of classes that can come into play when building a distributed application. The usage scenarios for these classes range from connecting to a database to calling a method on a remote object, with a significant number of options in between. Given this broad range, it can be difficult to know exactly which set of classes will be best suited to your scenarios. This section briefly covers the most commonly considered options when building a distributed application on the .NET Framework and provides guidance that can help you determine which layer is most appropriate for the needs of your application.

Common Scenarios for Using *System.Net*

Let's begin this exercise by covering the most common scenarios for using the layers in *System.Net*. These scenarios can be divided into the three categories shown on the following page.

- Accessing an existing service or protocol provided by *System.Net*

- Implementing a protocol not provided by *System.Net*

- Extending a higher layer of the stack that uses *System.Net*

Seems pretty easy, right? Well, let's spend a bit more time going through each of the categories to talk about why they make sense.

Accessing an Existing Service or Protocol Provided by *System.Net*

Application services that make sense for *System.Net* are demonstrated in the samples throughout this book. The most common case by far is that of accessing resources that are available on an HTTP server. If your program needs download or upload resources over HTTP or HTTPS, *System.Net* should be an easy choice. Likewise, if your application needs to access the name resolution services available in DNS, *System.Net.Dns* is the best choice. Going forward, FTP and access to other standard protocols will fit into this category as well.

Implementing a Protocol Not Provided by *System.Net*

Perhaps your application needs to interact with a service that supports some well-known protocol that's not supported directly in *System.Net*. For example, consider the Network Time Protocol (NTP). RFC 1305 provides the following description of NTP:

"NTP provides the mechanisms to synchronize time and coordinate time distribution in a large, diverse internet operating at rates from mundane to lightwave."

An application wanting to interact with another service that supports the desired protocol would need to implement the NTP protocol in this example. NTP is layered on top of UDP, which is accessible in *System.Net* through the socket layer classes. The application would then call the socket layer classes to construct a UDP socket and emit the NTP protocol. Other examples that commonly fit well into this category of protocols that are built using the socket-level classes are the Network News Transfer Protocol (NNTP), the Post Office Protocol (POP3), and the Simple Mail Transfer Protocol (SMTP).

Applications might also be implementing a custom protocol that's only well known within a specific organization. Although this approach is discouraged when architecting new applications, it's often required in cases where the new application must interoperate with a legacy system. Often, a good approach in these cases is to use *System.Net* to write the custom protocol that consumes the data from the legacy system and then use a more interoperable solution, such as XML-based Web services, to expose the data or service to other applications within the organization.

Extending a Higher Layer of the Stack That Uses *System.Net*

As we'll discuss at length in Chapters 11 and 12, *System.Net* provides the underlying transport implementation for the Web services and the .NET Remoting technologies in the .NET Framework. Accessing elements of *System.Net* to extend and customize the behavior of these higher layers can be a very useful tool for enhancing the performance, interoperability, scalability, and functionality of your application.

System.Net vs. Web Services or .NET Remoting

The .NET Remoting and Web services technologies in the .NET Framework provide rich and extensible frameworks for accessing objects and services that live outside of your application. In some cases, the boundary between the application and a remote object is simply an application domain. In other cases, it might be across a process, and in other cases, it might be across a network.

It's often much easier for applications to interact at an object level rather than deal directly with protocols. Therefore, it's recommended that applications use the .NET Remoting and Web services wherever possible. Even when the .NET Remoting and Web services are viable options, *System.Net* is a better choice in some cases. For example, suppose that your application needs to download a large amount of data, such as a 10 megabyte (MB) file, and it wants the ability to selectively request portions of that data or the ability to cache the download and retrieve only the portions not downloaded in cases of a failure. In this case, using a Web server and the HTTP layer exposed through *System.Net* might be a more appropriate architecture than exposing the data through a Web service or a .NET Remoting object. The transport and encoding semantics associated with HTTP are more amenable to this scenario than those provided by the higher layers.

It's expected that over time these higher layers will continue to evolve until they are almost always the right choice when you control both the client and the server. However, this transformation will take a significant number of years to achieve. Once we reach that point, *System.Net* will be most useful for extending and enhancing these higher layers and interacting with legacy services to expose them up through the higher layers.

Summary

This chapter introduced the *System.Net* namespace. It described the purpose of the classes in *System.Net* and reviewed its layers of functionality. We reviewed the basic types and services such as address manipulation and interaction with DNS. We discussed the socket-level classes, including *Socket*, *NetworkStream*, and other helper classes. We then walked through the *HttpWebRequest* and *HttpWebResponse* classes, which provide access to the HTTP protocol. Finally, we reviewed the request-response URI resolution pattern and its helpers.

This chapter also covered recommendations on when to use *System.Net* versus the higher-level communication classes provided by Web services and .NET Remoting. Now that we've introduced the classes and their basic purpose, the next five chapters will describe the workings of these classes in much more detail.

7

IP Addressing and DNS

Internet Protocol version 4 (IPv4) is commonly known as the network protocol used on the Internet. IPv4 is widely available on most computer operating systems and can be used on most local area networks (LANs), such as a small network in your office, and on wide area networks (WANs), such as the Internet. With the explosion of computers on the Internet, the limitations of IPv4 are becoming apparent, and as a result, the next generation of Internet Protocol was developed, IP version 6 (IPv6).

When a computer or a device is connected to an IP network, it must obtain at least one or more IP addresses either dynamically or statically for it to communicate over an IP network. Static IPs are configured manually by the administrator of the machine or device, and dynamic IPs are automatically assigned to a computer over a network using one of the following methods: Dynamic Host Configuration Protocol (DHCP) or Router Advertisement (RA). DHCP is commonly used on IPv4 networks, while RA is typically found on IPv6 networks. As you'll see in this chapter, IP addresses are represented in numerical form, which makes it difficult for users to remember a computer or device identification on an IP network. To make addressing more flexible, IP networks typically have a Domain Name System (DNS) available, which allows you to identify machines or devices by a more meaningful, friendly name instead of the difficult-to-remember numerical identification.

In this chapter, we'll describe how computers identify and address one another using the IPv4 and IPv6 protocols. Understanding IP addressing is essential for working with the Microsoft Windows .NET Framework networking classes, which allow you to communicate over IP networks. These classes will be discussed in the next two chapters. The .NET Framework networking classes also support addressing non-IP address-based communications using

Internetwork Packet Exchange (IPX), AppleTalk, Infrared, and so on. However, the focus of this book is only the IP-based classes. Once IP addressing is explained, we'll explain name resolution techniques using DNS through the .NET Framework that can simplify the complexities of IP addressing.

IP Addressing

On IP networks, computers and devices identify one another using numerical IP addresses. As mentioned earlier in this chapter, two versions of IP are in use today: IPv4 and IPv6. The next two sections describe IP address formats in more detail.

IPv4 Protocol

The IPv4 protocol was developed in the mid 1970s as a part of the Advanced Research Project Agency (ARPA) of the United States Department of Defense. Ipv4 has become the de facto standard protocol on the Internet. With IPv4, computers are assigned an address that's represented as a 32-bit quantity, formally known as an *IPv4 address*. All current versions of the Windows operating system support the IPv4 protocol.

IPv4 addresses are typically represented in a dotted decimal format, for example, xxx.xxx.xxx.xxx, where each *xxx* section is an octet (8 bits) of the address and is converted to a decimal number that's separated by a period (dot). An IPv4 address might look like 172.31.28.120. IPv4 addresses are divided into classes that describe the portion of the address assigned to the network and the portion assigned to actual end points (or computers). Table 7-1 lists the different classes.

Table 7-1   IPv4 Address Classes

Class	Network Portion	First Number	Number of End Points
A	8 bits	0 to 127	16,777,216
B	16 bits	128 to 191	65,536
C	24 bits	192 to 223	256
D	n/a	224 to 239	n/a
E	n/a	240 to 255	n/a

All IP addresses that identify individual computer interfaces (also known as *unicast addresses*) can be broken into two parts: the network portion and the host ID. The network portion is the first part of the address, which can be a variable number of bits, and it identifies the specific network a host resides on. The host portion of the address is comprised of the remaining bits in the address and uniquely identifies that computer's interface on the given network. When specifying an IP address, the number of bits indicating the network portion can be appended to the dotted decimal address after a slash mark (/). For example, the address 172.31.28.120/16 indicates that the first 16 bits make up the network portion of the address. This address, followed by the slash, is known as the Classless Interdomain Routing (CIDR) notation, which is equivalent to the netmask. The address 172.31.28.120/16 has an equivalent subnet mask of 255.255.0.0.

The last two entries in Table 7-1 are special classes of IPv4 addresses. Class D addresses are reserved for IPv4 multicasting, and class E addresses are experimental. Also, the following blocks of addresses have been reserved for private use and can't be used by a system on the Internet:

- 10.0.0.0 to 10.255.255.255 (10.0.0.0/8)

- 172.16.0.0 to 172.31.255.255 (172.16.0.0/12)

- 192.168.0.0 to 192.168.255.255 (192.168.0.0/16)

Finally, the loopback address (127.0.0.1) is a special address that refers to the local computer.

To list the IPv4 addresses assigned to a Windows computer, the ipconfig.exe utility on Windows NT, Windows 2000, Windows XP, and Windows Server 2003 will output a list of the IP addresses for all network interfaces on the local computer. For Windows 9x (including Windows Me), the utility for retrieving IPv4 address information is winipcfg.exe.

We've briefly discussed the breakdown of the IPv4 address space, and within these different address classes are three types of IPv4 addresses: unicast, multicast, and broadcast. There are also two other special address types—loopback and wildcard. Table 7-2 lists the different types of IPv4 addresses. The next sections will briefly discuss these different types of IPv4 addresses. For a much more detailed discussion of IPv4 networking and addressing, consult *The Protocols (TCP/IP Illustrated, Volume 1)* by W. Richard Stevens (Addison-Wesley, 1994).

Table 7-2   IPv4 Address Types

Type	Address or Range	Description
Broadcast	255.255.255.255	When data is sent to this address, all computers on the local network will receive it.
Loopback	127.0.0.1	This address represents only the local computer.
Multicast	224.0.0.1 to 239.255.255.255	These are multicast addresses used to send from one source to many recipients.
Unicast	0.0.0.1 to 223.255.255.255	These are unique addresses assigned to a computer's interfaces.
Wildcard	0.0.0.0	Also known as the any address, this address represents all interfaces on the computer.

Although IPv4 addresses are not too large in form, they still can be quite cumbersome to remember when trying to identify computers. Therefore, IP networks can have a DNS service that provides a mapping between a user-friendly name and an IP address. Later in the chapter, we'll show how to use the DNS service to resolve names to addresses.

Unicast Addresses

Unicast addresses are assigned to an individual computer's interface, and only one interface can be assigned that address. If another computer on the network is configured with that address, data will not be delivered correctly. Typically, computers are configured either with a manually assigned IPv4 address or they obtain one from a configuration protocol such as DHCP. If, for some reason, a computer configured to retrieve a DHCP-assigned address can't, the network stack will assign an *autoconfigure* address in the range of 169.254.0.0/16. An autoconfigure address is valid only on the local network link; it is not routable or valid on the Internet.

The IPv4 unicast address space sets aside several regions that are designed for use on isolated networks, that is, networks not connected directly to the Internet (often intranets). The following addresses are reserved for intranet uses:

- 10.0.0.0 to 10.255.255.255 (10.0.0.0/8)
- 172.16.0.0 to 172.31.255.255 (172.16.0.0/12)
- 192.168.0.0 to 192.168.255.255 (192.168.0.0/16)

Other than the fact that these addresses can never appear on the Internet, they follow the same rules as regular unicast addresses, such as only one instance of a given intranet address can be present on the local network. These addresses are routable on the private network.

These private addresses are also used by Network Address Translators (NATs), which are commonly found on routers and Digital Subscriber Line (DSL) modems. These addresses are useful when an Internet service provider (ISP) allows a customer only one global IPv4 address, but the customer has several computers on a home network to connect to the Internet. A NAT assigns each computer on the home network one of the private intranet addresses, and the NAT router is assigned the global IPv4 Internet address. The NAT translates communication to and from the home network computers. NATs are useful in this respect, but they can introduce problems, as we will discuss later.

Wildcard Address

The wildcard address is a special address used when an application wants to receive network traffic on any interface on the computer, which is typically the case for server applications. However, if an application wants to operate on a single interface, it uses the unicast IPv4 address assigned to the interface that it's interested in.

Loopback Address

The loopback address is typically used for interprocess communication. If multiple sockets on the sample computer need to communicate with each other, the loopback address is used to establish a connection within the local machine.

Broadcast Address

The broadcast address is used as a destination address when sending data. When data is sent to the broadcast address, every computer on the local network must process that packet to determine if anyone is waiting for broadcast data. It's considered bad practice to design applications that use broadcast data because every machine on the network must process that message when most machines probably do not care about that data.

Multicast Addresses

Multicast addresses are used by applications that need to send data from a single source to many recipients. Unlike broadcast data, multicasting provides a way for applications to register whether they are interested in data sent to a particular multicast address. Multicasting will be discussed in greater detail in the next chapter.

IPv6 Protocol

The IPv6 protocol is a relatively new protocol aimed to replace the IPv4 protocol; it addresses several key limitations of IPv4. First and foremost, the world is running out of IPv4 addresses, which is leading to a proliferation of NAT techniques where multiple computers can share (or hide behind) a single IP address. The problem with NATs is that they break the end-to-end connectivity experience. As mentioned earlier in this chapter, computers behind a NAT are assigned private addresses. Consider the case where you and your buddy want to start an instant messenger–type application. If both computers are behind a NAT, when you connect to your buddy, all you have is your buddy's private IP address, which is not valid to address over the Internet. To circumvent this problem, a central server (that has a valid non-private IPv4 address) needs to be present to route the traffic accordingly. The good thing about IPv6 is that it was designed with a much larger 128-bit address space, which means that there are plenty of addresses for everyone.

Because IPv6 addresses are much bigger than IPv4 addresses, they are represented in hexadecimal form, such as fe80::240:96ff:fe36:d757, where each hex digit represents 4 bits of the address and each 16-bit chunk of the address is separated by a colon. You'll notice our example address has a double colon, which represents zero compression. If there is a series of 16-bit chunks that are all zero, they can be replaced by the double colon. This compression can occur only once in the address.

The IPv6 address space is hierarchical, which means that high-order bits define the address types shown in Table 7-3. For example, a multicast address always starts with a series of consecutive one bits (or 0xFF when viewed in hex). A hierarchical address space simplifies the protocol routing on networks.

IPv6 addresses and host names can also be registered with DNS so that applications can resolve a host name and receive IPv6 addresses in return. Again, we'll talk more about using DNS to resolve names to IP addresses later in the chapter.

Note that the IPv6 protocol is only available on Windows XP and later. Also, the IPv6 sockets are not accessible from the .NET Framework unless explicitly enabled. To enable the IPv6 protocol, edit the machine.config file under %SYSTEMROOT%\Microsoft.Net\Framework*version*\config, where *version* is the .NET Framework version number in which IPv6 is to be enabled. Versions 1.1.4322 and later support IPv6 sockets. The configuration file is XML based. Search for the ipv6 entry, which looks like this:

```
<!-- <ipv6 enabled="false"/> -->
```

Set the property to *true*, and remove the XML comment tags, <!-- and -->, so that the line looks like this:

```
<ipv6 enabled="true"/>
```

Hopefully, future versions of the .NET Framework will ship with this flag automatically enabled.

The next sections will give a short introduction of the different types of IPv6 addresses. For a comprehensive discussion of the IPv6 protocol, consult *Understanding IPv6* by Joseph Davies (Microsoft Press, 2002).

Table 7-3   IPv6 Address Types

Type	Prefix/Address	Description
Broadcast	n/a	The IPv6 protocol does not support the notion of broadcast data.
Global	001	Address that is globally reachable on the Internet.
Link-local	1111 1110 10	Local address that is not routable but can be used to communicate to other computers on the same network link.
Loopback	::1	Address representing the local computer.
Multicast	1111 1111	Multicast addresses used to send from one source to many recipients.
Site-local	1111 1110 11	Represents addresses that are reachable only in a LAN environment.
Wildcard	::	Also known as the any address; represents all interfaces on the computer.

Unicast Addresses

IPv6 addresses are assigned to interfaces just as the IPv4 protocol addresses are, with a few exceptions. First, a computer with IPv6 installed will have multiple IPv6 unicast addresses assigned to it. By default, all interfaces will be assigned a link-local address regardless of whether a global address is obtained. This address is analogous to the autoconfigure assigned address in IPv4. A link-local address is always prefixed with the hex sequence *FE80*. So, fe80::240:96ff:fe36:d757%4 is an example of a local link address.

One thing to note is the *%4* at the end of the address. The percent sign indicates a scope ID, while the number *4* indicates that this link-local address is on interface number 4. Link-local addresses such as IPv4 autoconfigure addresses are not routable, meaning that they are valid only on that local network link. So, an application connecting to another computer using link-local addresses must specify the local link on which the remote link-local address can be reached. In Figure 7-1, there are two computers on the same link: computer A with the address fe80::1%1 and computer B with fe80::2%2. If computer A needs to connect to B, A substitutes its local interface from which B is reachable as the scope-id in the destination address, which would be fe80::2%1.

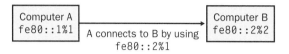

Figure 7-1   Connecting using link-local addresses

An interface will always have a link-local address, and it might also have a site-local address, a global address, or both. A site-local address is analogous to the private address ranges in IPv4 except that all IPv6 site-local addresses begin with the prefix *FEC0*. Site-local addresses are typically used for corporate intranets where traffic should not be routable to the global Internet. There are IPv6 global addresses that are fully routable and valid everywhere.

Site-local and global addresses can either be manually configured or assigned via router advertisements—that is, the network infrastructure can assign the network portion of the address and the local computer will create the host portion from the Media Access Control (MAC) address of the interface. The same CIDR notation is used with IPv6 addresses. For example, a router might advertise a site-local prefix of fec0::/48, meaning that the first 48 bits of the address are the network portion of the 128-bit IPv6 address.

Wildcard Address

The IPv6 wildcard address is a double include, which indicates all zeroes and has the same meaning as in IPv4. An application binds to the wildcard address to listen across all interfaces on the local system.

Loopback Address

The IPv6 loopback address is ::1, which indicates all zeroes except that last bit, which is one. The loopback address indicates the local computer.

Broadcast Address

The IPv6 protocol does not support the notion of a broadcast packet—that is, there's no support for sending a packet that will be received by every computer on the local network. Applications that require this ability should use multicasting because only computers interested in receiving the data would join the same group.

Multicast Addresses

All multicast addresses in IPv6 begin with the prefix *1111 1111* (FF). IPv6 multicasting is very similar to IPv4 multicasting and will be covered in more detail in the next chapter.

DNS

Now that you have a basic understanding of IPv4 and IPv6 addressing, you probably can see that IP addresses are computer friendly but not very user friendly because of their numeric form, which is hard to remember. Imagine trying to browse the Web and having to remember long numerical strings of your favorite Web sites. Most people would much rather go to a Web site by memorizing a friendly name such as *www.microsoft.com* than navigate using a numerically formed IP address. IP networking features DNS, which is designed to associate one or more IP addresses with names and is normally referred to as *DNS name resolution.*

The .NET Framework features a *Dns* class in the *System.Net* namespace that's designed to perform DNS name resolution. The *Dns* class can perform both forward and reverse name lookup to a DNS server. Forward name lookup is resolving a name to one or more IP addresses, and reverse name lookup is resolving an IP address to a name. Forward name lookup is the most common name resolution technique used in network applications. One of the biggest benefits of using forward name lookup is that you can practically ignore the details of IP addressing in your network application.

Forward Name Lookup

The *Dns* class provides the *GetHostByName* and the *Resolve* methods to perform forward DNS name lookup. Both methods accept a string parameter representing a name to look up, and both return an *IPHostEntry* object that will return a list of one or more IPv4 or IPv6 addresses if the name was able to be resolved. Also, the *IPHostEntry* object will return any alias names that can be associated with the originating name. If a name can't be resolved, both methods will throw a *SocketException*. Both methods will also accept an IP address as a string instead of a name and return the address to the *IPHostEntry* object. The behavior of these methods might seem strange, but it's actually convenient because you can develop an application that can address computers by name and by IP address. When your application supplies an IP address, these methods do not actually query DNS; instead, they simply recognize the IP address canonical form and return the address to the *IPHostEntry* object.

An *IPHostEntry* object is designed to contain three pieces of information: *HostName, Aliases,* and *AddressList.* The *HostName* property receives the host name that you're trying to resolve. If you're trying to resolve an IP address, the *HostName* property will receive your IP address. The *Aliases* property will receive an array of alias names if any are returned from a DNS forward name lookup. The DNS service can potentially return alias names for the host you're querying if it's configured to do so. The final property is *AddressList,* which will contain an array of one or more IP addresses if your DNS query succeeds. The following code fragment demonstrates how to use *GetHostByName* to resolve the name *www.microsoft.com* to an IP address:

C#

```
try
{
    IPHostEntry IPHost =
        Dns.GetHostByName("www.microsoft.com");

    // Print out the host name that was queried
    Console.WriteLine("The host name is: " +
        IPHost.HostName.ToString());

    // Print out any aliases that are found
    if (IPHost.Aliases.Length > 0)
    {
        Console.WriteLine("Aliases found are:");
        foreach(string Alias in IPHost.Aliases)
        {
            Console.WriteLine(Alias);
        }
    }

    Console.WriteLine("IP addresses found are:");

    int IPv4Count = 0;
    int IPv6Count = 0;

    // Print out all the IP addresses that are found
    foreach(IPAddress Address in IPHost.AddressList)
    {
        if (Address.AddressFamily ==
            AddressFamily.InterNetwork)
        {
            IPv4Count++;
            Console.WriteLine("IPv4 Address #" +
                IPv4Count.ToString() + " is " +
```

```
                              Address.ToString());
        }
        else if (Address.AddressFamily ==
            AddressFamily.InterNetworkV6)
        {
            IPv6Count++;
            Console.WriteLine("IPv6 Address #" +
                IPv6Count.ToString() + " is " +
                Address.ToString());
        }
    }
}
catch (Exception e)
{
    Console.WriteLine("GetHostByName failed with error: "
        + e.Message);
}
```

Visual Basic .NET

```
Try
    Dim IPHost As IPHostEntry = _
        Dns.GetHostByName("www.microsoft.com")

    ' Print out the host name that was queried
    Console.WriteLine("The primary host name is: " + _
        IPHost.HostName.ToString())

    ' Print out any aliases that are found
    If (IPHost.Aliases.Length > 0) Then
        Console.WriteLine("Aliases found are:")
        Dim CurAlias As String
        For Each CurAlias In IPHost.Aliases
            Console.WriteLine(CurAlias)
        Next
    End If

    Console.WriteLine("IP addresses found are:")

    Dim IPv4Count As Integer = 0
    Dim IPv6Count As Integer = 0

    ' Print out all the IP addresses that are found
    Dim Address As IPAddress

    For Each Address In IPHost.AddressList
        If (Address.AddressFamily = _
            AddressFamily.InterNetwork) Then
```

```
                    IPv4Count += 1
                    Console.WriteLine("IPv4 Address #" + _
                    IPv4Count.ToString() + " is " + _
                    Address.ToString())

                ElseIf (Address.AddressFamily = _
                    AddressFamily.InterNetworkV6) Then
                    IPv6Count += 1
                    Console.WriteLine("IPv6 Address #" + _
                        IPv6Count.ToString() + " is " + _
                        Address.ToString())
                End If

            Next

        Catch e As Exception
            Console.WriteLine( _
            "GetHostByName failed with error: " + _
            e.Message)
        End Try
```

As you can see, *GetHostByName* can potentially return more than one IP address from a DNS query. This behavior is important to understand because your network application should attempt to use the entire array of available addresses one at a time to set up communication over an IP network. In the preceding code fragment, we simply printed out all the IPv4 and IPv6 addresses that are available from a name. When you develop a network client application, your client should walk the *AddressList* using one *IPAddress* at a time to attempt communication over IP. You should try each address returned, regardless of whether it's IPv4 or IPv6. If the communication does not work, you should go to the next item in the list and try again until you run out of addresses. If you do successfully establish communication before exhausting the list, you should stop processing the list and go about performing network communication. The next chapter introduces client network programming using sockets, which requires you to supply an IP address to set up communication. Handling DNS replies properly in a client application will make your client more robust.

DNS queries can potentially take a lot of time to perform in your application. So far, we've shown how to perform forward name lookup using the synchronous *GetHostByName* call. When you call *GetHostByName*, it can block on a name query, which can result in making your application unresponsive. To keep your application from blocking this way, the .NET Framework provides an asynchronous version of forward name lookup that follows the asynchronous pattern described in Chapter 3. In this type of lookup, you use *BeginGetHostByName* and *EndGetHostByName*. The first thing you need to do when performing a forward name lookup DNS query asynchronously is to define a delegate method that handles the asynchronous completion of an asynchronous DNS query, as shown here:

C#

```csharp
void ProcessDnsResults(IAsyncResult ar)
{
    try
    {
        IPHostEntry IPHost = Dns.EndGetHostByName(ar);

        // Process IP information here from the
        //completed DNS query.
    }
    catch (Exception e)
    {
        Console.WriteLine(
            "GetHostByName failed with error: "
            + e.Message);
    }
    finally
    {
        Console.WriteLine("Finished querying DNS.");
    }
}
```

Visual Basic .NET

```vbnet
Shared Sub ProcessDnsResults(ByVal ar As IAsyncResult)
    Try
        Dim IPHost As IPHostEntry = Dns.EndGetHostByName(ar)

        ' Process IP information here from the
        ' completed DNS query.

    Catch e As Exception
        Console.WriteLine( _
            "GetHostByName failed with error: " _
            + e.Message)

    Finally
        Console.WriteLine("Finished querying DNS.")
    End Try
End Sub
```

Once a delegate method is defined, you can use it in the asynchronous call to *BeginGetHostByName*, as follows:

C#

```
AsyncCallback AsyncDnsCallback =
    new AsyncCallback(ProcessDnsResults);

try
{
    Dns.BeginGetHostByName("www.microsoft.com",
        AsyncDnsCallback, null);
}
catch (Exception e)
{
    Console.WriteLine(
        "BeginGetHostByName failed with error: "
        + e.Message);
}
```

Visual Basic .NET

```
Dim AsyncDnsCallback As AsyncCallback = _
    New AsyncCallback(AddressOf ProcessDnsResults)

Try
    Dns.BeginGetHostByName("www.microsoft.com", _
        AsyncDnsCallback, Nothing)

Catch e As Exception
    Console.WriteLine( _
        "BeginGetHostByName failed with error: "_
        + e.Message)
End Try
```

> **Note** In the downloadable samples, a sample named ResolveName demonstrates how to synchronously perform a forward name lookup using the *Dns* class. There's also an asynchronous version of this application called AsyncResolveName.

Reverse Name Lookup

So far, we've seen how to resolve a name to an IP address, but what if you have an IP address and want to find what name is associated with the address? DNS provides reverse name lookup to perform this type of lookup. The .NET Framework *Dns* class performs DNS reverse name lookup using *GetHostByAddress(IPAddress)*. This function returns any names associated with the IP address in an *IPHostEntry* object if an IP is associated with a name. If a name can't be found, a *SocketException* will be thrown.

> **Note**   The IPv6 protocol in Windows XP and Windows Server 2003 does not register its reverse lookup information with DNS, which means that a reverse query on an IPv6 address will fail.

In DNS, more than one name can be associated with an IP address. As a result, the *IPHostEntry* object returned by *GetHostByAddress* can return multiple names. The *HostName* field of *IPHostEntry* will contain the primary host name associated with the IP address. The *Aliases* field will contain any additional names that might also be associated with an IP. The following code fragment demonstrates how to perform a reverse name lookup:

C#

```csharp
try
{
    IPHostEntry IPHost =
        Dns.GetHostByAddress("10.1.2.3");

    Console.WriteLine(
        "The Primary Host name is: " +
        IPHost.HostName.ToString());

    // Print out any Aliases that are found
    if (IPHost.Aliases.Length > 0)
    {
        Console.WriteLine("Additional names are:");
        foreach(string Alias in IPHost.Aliases)
        {
            Console.WriteLine(Alias);
        }
    }
}
```

```
catch (Exception e)
{
    Console.WriteLine(
        "GetHostByAddress failed with error: "
        + e.Message);
}
```

Visual Basic .NET

```
Try
    Dim IPHost As IPHostEntry = _
        Dns.GetHostByAddress("10.1.2.3")

    Console.WriteLine( _
        "The Primary Host name is: " + _
        IPHost.HostName.ToString())

    ' Print out any Aliases that are found
    If (IPHost.Aliases.Length > 0) Then
        Console.WriteLine( _
            "Additional names found are:")
        Dim CurAlias As String

        For Each CurAlias In IPHost.Aliases
            Console.WriteLine(CurAlias)
        Next

    End If
Catch e As Exception
    Console.WriteLine( _
        "GetHostByAddress failed with error: " + _
        e.Message)
End Try
```

Performing DNS reverse name lookup using *GetHostByAddress* can take some time, so it might cause your application to block on the call. Blocking on this call can make your application appear unresponsive, as described with forward name lookup. Therefore, two asynchronous counterpart methods, *Begin-HostByAddress* and *EndHostByAddress*, are available for reverse name lookup that use the .NET Framework asynchronous pattern. In the downloadable samples is a sample named ResolveIP that demonstrates how to synchronously perform reverse name lookup using the *Dns* class.

Summary

This chapter introduced how to identify computers and devices connected to IP networks. We described how to address computers using the IPv4 and the IPv6 addressing schemes. We also showed how to identify computers by name using the DNS service. Understanding IP addressing and DNS is essential to working with sockets in the .NET Framework to communicate over IP networks. The next two chapters introduce socket programming techniques and will use the principles learned in this chapter throughout.

8

Client Sockets

Many developers have avoided network programming using the Windows Sockets (Winsock) API because they think it's too difficult to learn and implement. Often, these developers relied on simplified interfaces such as Microsoft ActiveX network controls, which provide simplicity but often offer poor performance. At some point, the developer usually needs fine control over the communication, which isn't typically exposed through the simple interface. The Winsock API *is* large and complicated, which is why developers have looked elsewhere. However, the Microsoft Windows .NET Framework offers several classes, such as *Socket*, *TcpListener*, *TcpClient*, and *UdpClient*, that offer a simplified interface to get up and running with network programming while also exposing more complicated and powerful functionality.

The bulk of this chapter introduces the *System.Net.Sockets* class, which provides the ability for applications to communicate with one another over different protocols installed on the system. A number of transport protocols are available for Windows, such as IPv4, IPv6, IPX/SPX, and AppleTalk. However, this chapter and the next will focus only on IPv4 and IPv6, and more specifically, the TCP and UDP protocols over IPv4 and IPv6.

We introduce the *Socket* class first to introduce the concepts and underlying behavior of network programming that are sometimes hidden in the simplified *TcpListener*, *TcpClient*, and *UdpClient* classes. Also, for classes derived from these simplified classes, you can always obtain the underlying *Socket* object to perform the advanced functionality.

Additionally, our discussion of programming with the *Socket* class will be divided between the client and server operation. This chapter will cover the basics of the *Socket* class such as socket creation, setting socket options, establishing a connection, and sending and receiving data. Advanced topics such as IP multicasting and raw sockets will also be introduced. The next chapter will focus on the server-side aspects of socket programming, such as setting up a listening socket, accepting connections, and managing multiple clients. As such, the focus of the discussion in this chapter will be from the client's perspective, but many of the concepts covered apply to server-side programming as well.

Many socket operations can be invoked either synchronously or asynchronously. This chapter will focus mainly on the synchronous method calls to keep the chapter simple. Each section will mention if a particular method also has an asynchronous counterpart using the .NET Framework asynchronous pattern as described in Chapter 3, but code samples will not be given. However, Chapter 9 will fully discuss asynchronous operations because servers typically require asynchronous calls for performance and scalability reasons, although this certainly isn't always the case.

Protocol Introduction

Before getting into the details of creating and using sockets, it's necessary to understand the protocols over which communication takes place. As mentioned earlier, the sockets interface is a generic interface that can be used to communicate over a variety of transport protocols. A transport protocol is a protocol that provides a standard mechanism for addressing each computer on the network. Chapter 7 discussed the IPv4 and IPv6 transport protocols and detailed how computers address one another using these protocols.

A transport protocol might encapsulate higher-level protocols that provide a certain set of characteristics to the application using that protocol. The TCP and UDP protocols can be encapsulated within either the IPv4 or IPv6 transport protocols. Figure 8-1 illustrates IPv4 protocol encapsulation. When an application sends data over a given transport protocol, the packet sent on the network will have a transport header, followed by any number of upper-layer protocols, and finally the data sent. In this example, we see an IPv4 header and a TCP header followed by the application's data.

Figure 8-1   Protocol encapsulation

TCP

TCP is a connection-oriented, reliable, stream-oriented protocol and is used for such things as Web traffic. When a TCP connection is established, a virtual circuit is formed. The computer initiating the connection sends a request to the destination. If the message is accepted, the destination computer will acknowledge it and respond with its own connection request back to the source. This way, each side can send traffic independently of one another. In effect, there are two separate data channels for sending and receiving data.

Traffic sent on a TCP connection is stream-oriented (not to be confused with the *Stream* class), which means that the protocol controls how and when data is sent and received on the connection. So, if the sender issues two send commands of 100 bytes each, the network stack on the receiver can return any number of bytes with a receive call. Applications that use streaming protocols should never make any assumptions on how many bytes are to be received in a single receive call, which is important if fixed-size messages are being sent. The receiving application must have logic to call receive enough times to retrieve an entire message. There's no maximum send size when sending data on a TCP connection, aside from resource limitations. For example, attempting to send a 100 megabyte (MB) buffer is likely to fail because of resource limits.

The advantage of TCP is that the communication is reliable. When data is sent, the underlying network stack ensures that the data is delivered reliably. If the data is lost or corrupted, the protocol will retransmit as necessary. If the data is lost and can't be recovered, an error will be returned to the application. The drawback to TCP is the overhead involved in setting up the virtual circuit and handling reliable data transmission, which is expensive, especially if the application needs to communicate with multiple end points or if the amount of data to send to each end point is fairly small.

UDP

UDP is a connectionless, unreliable, message-oriented protocol. UDP does not require any connection to be established. The sender simply calls the send method with a destination address where the packet should be sent. Delivery of the packet is not guaranteed by the protocol. If it's absolutely imperative that the recipient receives the packet, it's up to the application's logic to ensure that it's retransmitted until the receiver receives the data.

UDP is message oriented, which means that it preserves the message boundaries. For example, if the sender sends three 100-byte packets, the receiver will call receive three times, each returning 100 bytes. Preserving the message boundaries is extremely useful when the data being sent is of a fixed size and the receiver does not require any logic to assemble a single discrete message—the message is preserved by the protocol. Note the maximum size of a UDP packet is 65,535 bytes; however, it's advisable to send small packets because large packets usually require fragmentation, which increases the probability that one fragment will be lost, causing the whole packet to be discarded at the receiver. Another benefit of UDP is that it's connectionless—there's no overhead associated with establishing a connection. The sender simply indicates the destination of each packet.

Of course, the disadvantage of UDP is that it's unreliable. If the network is congested or other problems occur, it's possible that a UDP message will get lost, and both the sender and receiver will have no idea that it occurred unless the application builds loss detection as a part of the data being sent.

Socket Basics

Now that you have a basic understanding of the common IP-based networking protocols, it's time to get into the specifics of creating sockets as well as what steps are involved in using sockets to send and receive data. Your first question is probably "What exactly is a socket?" A socket is an object that describes a network resource that's the underlying network protocol that the application is using for communication. The following sections will describe how an application creates a socket and puts it into a state so that it can be used to send and receive data. The *Socket* class resides in the *System.Net* namespace.

Socket basics are illustrated in the SimpleSocket sample located under the Chap08\SimpleSocket directory. The sample illustrates using the *Socket* class for simple TCP and UDP cases.

Creating

The first step in the process is creating the socket by instantiating an instance of the *Socket* class, which is shown here:

C#

```
public socket(
    AddressFamily addressFamily,
    SocketType socketType,
    ProtocolType protocolType
    );
```

Visual Basic .NET

```
Public Sub New( _
    ByVal addressFamily As AddressFamily, _
    ByVal socketType As SocketType, _
    ByVal protocolType As ProtocolType _
    )
```

The three parameters to the constructor define exactly which network protocol is to be created. The first parameter is an enumerated type that defines the addressing protocol to be used. The two values of this enumeration that are of interest to us are *InterNetwork* for the IPv4 protocol and *InterNetworkV6* for the IPv6 protocol.

The second and third parameters are closely related to one another and determine which upper-level protocol the socket being created is. The *Socket-Type* enumeration indicates the protocol's semantics in terms of how data is sent and received. For example, the *SocketType.Dgram* value indicates that the protocol is message- (or datagram-) oriented such that message boundaries are preserved on receive. For example, if a datagram socket sends 100 bytes, a single-100 byte packet is put on the network wire and the receiving datagram socket will receive exactly 100 bytes in a single receive call. Table 8-1 lists the values of the *SocketType* enumeration and describes their meanings.

Table 8-1   Common *SocketType* Values

SocketType Member	Description
Dgram	Datagram-oriented, where each send on a datagram socket represents a packet on the network such that message boundaries are preserved at the receiver
Raw	Raw protocol socket where the sender intends to build its own next protocol header as a part of the data payload
Rdm	Reliable datagram socket where the socket is datagram-oriented but is also reliable
Seqpacket	Sequential packet or *pseudostream* socket where each send on the socket represents a packet on the network but message boundaries are not preserved on the receiver side
Stream	Stream-oriented socket where both the sender and receiver can lump data in any size during sending or receiving of data
Unknown	Unspecified socket type where the network stack will attempt to find a protocol that matches the given *Address-Family* and *ProtocolType* parameters

The last parameter indicates the exact protocol to be used for the indicated *AddressFamily* and *SocketType*. The protocols we're interested in are *ProtocolType.Tcp* and *ProtocolType.Udp*. Note that for the TCP protocol, *Socket-Type.Stream* must be specified for the socket type, and for the UDP protocol, *SocketType.Dgram* is required. The TCP and UDP protocol have exact semantics; however, there are a few protocols, such as SPX, that allow for differing behavior (*Stream* and *Seqpacket*). If an invalid combination of socket type and protocol type are given, the *SocketException* error is thrown.

Binding

Once you have created a socket, it can't be used for data transfer until it's bound to a network interface. All data sent must originate from an address that's associated with a physical network interface, and likewise, all data received must be read from a physical interface. The process of binding a socket to a local interface is simple. First an address object must be created that describes the local address that the socket is to be bound to. In the case of IPv4 and IPv6, this address object is the *IPAddress* class. Either an *IPAddress* object is initialized with a property of the *IPAddress* class itself, or the *Parse* method is used to parse the string representation of an address into the object. Table 8-2 lists the commonly used properties and methods for binding to an interface.

Table 8-2 *IPAddress* Members

Member	Property/Method	Description
Any	Property	IPv4 wildcard address: 0.0.0.0
Broadcast	Property	IPv4 broadcast address: 255.255.255.255
Loopback	Property	IPv4 loopback address: 127.0.0.1
Ipv6Any	Property	IPv6 wildcard address: ::
Ipv6Loopback	Property	IPv6 loopback address: ::1
Parse	Method	Parses a string into the appropriate protocol

The following code illustrates how to initialize several different *IPAddress* objects with properties by using the *Parse* method:

C#

```
IPAddress  bindAddress, parsedAddress;

bindAddress = IPAddress.Any;     // Holds the IPv4 wildcard address
bindAddress = IPAddress.IPv6Any; // Now holds the IPv6 wildcard address

try
{
    parsedAddress = IPAddress.Parse("169.254.0.1");
    parsedAddress = IPAddress.Parse("fe80::2ff:abcd:1234%3");
}
catch ( FormatException err )
{
    Console.WriteLine("Invalid IP address: {0}", err.Message);
}
```

Visual Basic .NET

```
Dim bindAddress As IPAddress, parsedAddress As IPAddress

bindAddress = IPAddress.Any        ' Holds the IP4 wildcard address
bindAddress = IPAddress.IPv6Any  ' Now holds the IPv6 wildcard address

Try
    parsedAddress = IPAddress.Parse("169.254.0.1")
    ParsedAddress = IPAddress.Parse("fe80::2ff:abcd:1234%3")
Catch err As FormatException
    Console.WriteLine("Invalid IP Address: {0}", err.Message)
End Try
```

Notice that the *IPAddress* class can contain either an IPv4 or IPv6 address. If an invalid IP address is passed to the *Parse* method, a *FormatException* is thrown.

> **Note**   Support for the IPv6 protocol in the *IPAddress* class was introduced in version 1.1 of the .NET Framework. Earlier versions of the *IPAddress* class can't be used to parse and describe IPv6 addresses.

Next create an *EndPoint* object corresponding the address object. An endpoint is a combination of the local address and a local port number. A port number is a 16-bit integer used by both the TCP and UDP protocols for multiplexing multiple sockets on a single interface. This way, if a UDP packet arrives on interface 10.10.10.1 and port 5150, the stack will deliver the data to the socket bound to the same interface and port. To create an endpoint for either the IPv4 or IPv6 protocol, an *IPEndPoint* object needs to be created. The following code creates an end point describing the IPv4 wildcard address on port 5150:

C#

```
IPAddress  bindAddress = IPAddress.Any;
IPEndPoint  bindEndPoint = new IPEndPoint( bindAddress, 5150 );
```

Visual Basic .NET

```
Dim bindAddress As IPAddress = IPAddress.Any
Dim bindEndPoint As IPEndPoint = New IPEndPoint(bindAddress, 5150)
```

Once the socket is created and an *IPEndPoint* is built, the *Bind* method needs to be called with *IPEndPoint*, as shown in the following code. Notice that the *IPAddress* is created from a user-input string that can be either an IPv4 or IPv6 string because the *Parse* method will parse either. Therefore, we make sure to parse the string first and then create the *Socket* with the proper address family by passing the *AddressFamily* property of the *IPAddress* to the socket creation call. If the address families of *IPEndPoint* and the created socket do not match, a *SocketException* occurs.

C#

```
IPAddress  bindAddress = IPAddress.Parse( userInputString );
IPEndPoint bindEndPoint = new IPEndPoint( bindAddress, 5150 );
Socket     mySocket = null;

try
{
    mySocket = new Socket(
        bindAddress.AddressFamily,
        SocketType.Stream,
        ProtocolType.Tcp);
    mySocket.Bind( bindEndPoint );
}
catch ( SocketException err )
{
    if ( mySocket != null )
        mySocket.Close();
}
```

Visual Basic .NET

```
Dim bindAddress As IPAddress = IPAddress.Parse(userInputString)
Dim bindEndPoint As IPEndPoint = New IPEndPoint(bindAddress, 5150)
Dim mySocket As Socket

mySocket = Nothing
Try
    mySocket = New Socket( _
        bindAddress.AddressFamily, _
        SocketType.Stream, _
        ProtocolType.Tcp)
    mySocket.Bind( bindEndPoint )
Catch err As SocketException
    If (Not mySocket Is Nothing) Then
        mySocket.Close()
    End If
End Try
```

Note that binding a socket is not always required. The following operations will implicitly bind a socket to a local interface:

■ *Connect*

■ *SendTo* (for a datagram socket)

When one of these methods is called on an unbound socket, the network stack will bind the socket to an appropriate interface on a randomly chosen port in the range of 1024 to 5000. The advantage to explicitly binding the socket yourself is the ability to choose a specific port from the entire range of available ports, which will be discussed in more detail in the next chapter.

The most common cause of exceptions when calling the *Bind* method is when a socket of the same protocol is already bound to the requested port. For example, if UDP socket A is bound to address and port 10.10.10.1:5150, UDP socket B will get an exception if it attempts to bind to the same address and port. Note that if socket B is a TCP socket, no error will occur because the port reservations are on a per-protocol basis. In the "Socket Options" section later in this chapter, we'll cover several options that can allow several sockets of the same protocol to be bound to the same address and port. We'll also discuss this problem in detail in Chapter 9 because servers typically run into this problem more often than client sockets.

Connecting

Once a socket is created and optionally bound, it can be used as a client socket connected to a remote server. When a TCP socket is connected, the underlying protocol establishes a virtual circuit where the server actively accepts the connection if it chooses. If a connect is performed on a UDP socket, a destination address is associated with the socket so that if data is sent, the destination does not have to be supplied on each and every send call. Note that connecting a UDP socket by no means implies that a socket is waiting to receive the data on the destination—it's simply a time-saving measure.

Connecting a socket is similar to binding except that instead of a local address in the end point, a remote address is specified. The port number used to create the *IPEndPoint* must be a valid port number on which the remote server is listening. In the case of TCP, if there's no active listening socket on the given port, a *SocketException* occurs because the remote computer will forcefully reject the connection. Again, for UDP, there will be no indication as to whether a socket is listening on the destination computer.

Most client applications typically resolve the server's host name using the *Dns* class to retrieve the list of addresses registered to the server computer. For more information about the *Dns* class, see Chapter 7. A robust client application should perform the following steps:

1. Call *Dns.Resolve* with the server's host name.

2. Iterate through the *IPHostEntry.AddressList*.

3. Create a *Socket* based on the address family of the current *IPAddress* returned.

4. Call *Connect* on the created socket to the current *IPAddress*.

5. If the connection request fails, go to step 2.

6. If the connection request succeeds, break out of the loop.

Performing these steps will ensure a positive user experience because an application should attempt to connect to the requested server on every address returned, not just the first address returned from DNS. The following code illustrates a simple TCP client that follows the above steps:

C#

```
Socket       tcpSocket = null;
IPHostEntry  resolvedServer;
IPEndPoint   serverEndPoint;

try
{
    resolvedServer = Dns.Resolve( "server-name" );
    foreach( IPAddress addr in resolvedServer.AddressList )
    {
        serverEndPoint = new IPEndPoint( addr, 5150 );
        tcpSocket = new Socket(
            addr.AddressFamily,
            SocketType.Stream,
            ProtocolType.Tcp
            );
        try
        {
            tcpSocket.Connect( serverEndPoint );
        }
        catch
        {
            // Connect failed so try the next one
            //    Make sure to close the socket we opened
            if ( tcpSocket != null )
                tcpSocket.Close();
```

```
            continue;
        }
        break;
    }
}
catch ( SocketException err )
{
    Console.WriteLine("Client connection failed: {0}", err.Message);
}
// Now use tcpSocket to communicate to the server
```

Visual Basic .NET

```
Dim tcpSocket As Socket
Dim resolvedServer As IPHostEntry
Dim serverEndPoint As IPEndPoint
Dim addr As IPAddress

tcpSocket = Nothing
Try
    resolvedServer = Dns.Resolve("server-name")
    For Each addr In resolvedServer.AddressList
        serverEndPoint = New IPEndPoint(addr, 5150)
        tcpSocket = New Socket( _
            addr.AddressFamily, _
            SocketType.Stream, _
            ProtocolType.Tcp _
            )
        Try
            tcpSocket.Connect(serverEndPoint)
        Catch
            ' Connect failed so try the next one
            '    Make sure to close the socket we opened
            If (Not tcpSocket Is Nothing) Then
                tcpSocket.Close()
            End If
            GoTo ContinueLoop
        End Try
ContinueLoop:
    Next
Catch err As SocketException
    Console.WriteLine("Client connection failed: {0}", err.Message)
End Try
' Now use tcpSocket to communicate to the server
```

This code uses the synchronous connect method, but there's also an asynchronous method, *BeginConnect*. The asynchronous method is useful if the client needs to perform other tasks while the connection is taking place or if it needs to establish multiple concurrent connections.

Transferring Data

We've now covered how to create a socket and establish a connection for TCP or associate a destination for a UDP socket. Now it's time to get down to the nitty-gritty of transferring data on the socket. The next two sections will cover sending and receiving data on a socket for both the TCP and UDP protocol.

Sending Data

There are two basic methods for sending data: *Send* and *SendTo*. The former is used for connection-oriented sockets, which includes UDP sockets that have been associated with a destination via a connect method, as described earlier. The latter method is used only for connectionless protocols such as UDP. The only difference between the two methods is that *SendTo* includes a destination address parameter in addition to the parameters used with *Send*. The following code shows sending data with the *Send* method:

C#

```
Socket    clientSocket = null;
byte []   dataBuffer = new byte [ 1024 ];

// Create a TCP socket and connect to a server
try
{
    clientSocket.Send( dataBuffer );
}
catch ( SocketException err )
{
    Console.WriteLine("Send failed: {0}", err.Message);
}
```

Visual Basic .NET

```
Dim clientSocket As Socket
Dim dataBuffer(1024) As Byte

' Create a TCP socket and connect to a server
Try
    clientSocket.Send(dataBuffer)
Catch err As SocketException
    Console.WriteLine("Send failed: {0}", err.Message)
End Try
```

This code shows the simplest use of the *Send* method: simply sending a byte array of data. Several other instances of the *Send* method exist that take additional parameters such as number of bytes from the array to send, offset in the array to start sending data, and a socket flag that controls how the data is sent. The socket flag is the *SocketFlags* enumerated type, which is described in Table 8-3.

Table 8-3   Socket Flags

SocketFlag	Description
DontRoute	This flag indicates that data should be sent from the interface the socket is bound to. Most transport protocols ignore this request. It's valid for sending only.
MaxIOVectorLength	This flag is not valid for any current protocols.
None	This flag indicates no flag values.
OutOfBand	When sending, this flag indicates that data should be sent as urgent data. When receiving, it indicates that the next byte read should be urgent data. This flag is supported by TCP.
Partial	When sending, this flag indicates that this send is part of a larger block of data to send. When receiving, it indicates that the data returned is part of a larger message.
Peek	When specified, this flag indicates that data is returned to the application but is not removed from the network stack buffers. This flag is valid only for receiving.

Most of the flags are rarely used or don't apply to the TCP or UDP protocol (such as the *Partial* or the *MaxIOVectorLength* flag). The *OutOfBand* flag is used on connected TCP sockets when the sender needs to send data that's of higher importance than the data already sent on the stream, hence the name *urgent* or *out-of-band* (OOB) data. The receiver can then process this data separate from the normal data already buffered by the local network stack. Use of OOB data is discouraged because two different RFCs (793 and 1122) describe how OOB should be implemented in TCP, and they're not always compatible across different operating systems. Therefore, depending on which operating systems the client and server are running on, sending and receiving OOB data might not work if the OOB implementations differ.

The next sending method is *SendTo*, which is used for unconnected datagram sockets such as with the UDP protocol. As mentioned earlier, the only difference between *Send* and *SendTo* is that *SendTo* also takes the destination *IPEndPoint*. The following code illustrates sending a UDP datagram:

C#

```
IPAddress   destAddress = IPAddress.Parse( "10.10.10.1" );
IPEndPoint  destEndPoint = new IPEndPoint( destAddress, 5150 );
Socket      udpSocket;
```

```
byte []      message = System.Text.Encoding.ASCII.GetBytes(
                "hello world" );

udpSocket = new Socket(
    destAddress.AddressFamily,
    SocketType.Dgram,
    ProtocolType.Udp
    );
try
{
    udpSocket.SendTo( message, destEndPoint );
}
catch ( SocketException err )
{
    Console.WriteLine("SendTo failed: {0}", err.Message);
}
```

Visual Basic .NET

```
Dim destAddress As IPAddress = IPAddress.Parse("10.10.10.1")
Dim destEndPoint As IPEndPoint = new IPEndPoint(destAddress, 5150)
Dim udpSocket As Socket
Dim message() As Byte = System.Text.Encoding.ASCII.GetBytes( _
    "hello world" )

udpSocket = new Socket( _
    destAddress.AddressFamily, _
    SocketType.Dgram, _
    ProtocolType.Udp _
    )
Try
    udpSocket.SendTo( message, destEndPoint )
Catch err As SocketException
    Console.WriteLine("SendTo failed: {0}", err.Message )
End Try
```

The value returned from both the *Send* and *SendTo* methods is the number of bytes transferred on the socket. Note that the send methods will send all the data requested unless an error occurs or the socket has been put into non-blocking mode. By default, all sockets created are blocking. A socket is put into non-blocking mode by calling the *IOControl* method, in which case, there's no guarantee that the number of bytes actually sent will be the number of bytes requested. In this case, it's the application's responsibility to ensure that all data has been sent. Non-blocking mode will be discussed in more detail in the "Socket Options" and "Socket Ioctls" sections later in this chapter.

> **Tip**   One common problem encountered when sending data on the socket is that the *Send* and *SendTo* methods require byte arrays, which is not always the type of data being sent. In this case, the *BitConverter* class is useful for converting common types into byte arrays via the *GetBytes* method.

As you can see, sending data on a socket is simple and straightforward. If an error occurs while sending data, such as if the TCP connection is broken or if there's no route to the destination, a *SocketException* will be generated. Finally, the asynchronous versions of the *Send* and *SendTo* methods are *BeginSend* and *BeginSendTo*, respectively.

Receiving Data

The methods for receiving data are *Receive* and *ReceiveFrom*. To receive data on a socket, it must either be connected as with a TCP socket or a connected UDP socket, or it must be bound to a local interface as with unconnected UDP sockets. The parameters to the receive methods are very similar to the send methods. A byte buffer is specified to receive the data into, an optional number of bytes to receive is set, *SocketFlags* are set for controlling the receive operation, and the *IPEndPoint* describing who sent the data (used with the *ReceiveFrom* method) is set. If the number of bytes to receive is not set, the size of the byte array is used. The following code creates a receiving UDP socket that calls *ReceiveFrom*:

C#

```
IPAddress   bindAddress = IPAddress.Any;
IPEndPoint  bindEndPoint = new IPEndPoint( bindAddress, 5150 );
Socket      udpSocket;
byte []     receiveBuffer = new byte [ 1024 ];
IPEndPoint  senderEndPoint = new IPEndPoint(
    bindAddress.AddressFamily, 0
);
EndPoint  castSenderEndPoint = (EndPoint) senderEndPoint;
int       rc;

udpSocket = new Socket(
    bindAddress.AddressFamily,
    SocketType.Dgram,
    ProtocolType.Udp
    );
try
```

```
{
    udpSocket.Bind( bindEndPoint );
    rc = udpSocket.ReceiveFrom( receiveBuffer, ref castSenderEndPoint );
    senderEndPoint = (IPEndPoint) castSenderEndPoint;
    Console.WriteLine("Received {0} bytes from {1}", rc,
        senderEndPoint.ToString());
}
catch ( SocketException err )
{
    Console.WriteLine("Error occurred: {0}", err.Message);
}
finally
{
    udpSocket.Close();
}
```

Visual Basic .NET

```
Dim bindAddress As IPAddress = IPAddress.Any
Dim bindEndPoint As IPEndPoint = new IPEndPoint(bindAddress, 5150)
Dim udpSocket As Socket
Dim receiveBuffer(1024) As Byte
Dim senderEndPoint As IPEndPoint = New IPEndPoint( _
    bindAddress.AddressFamily, 0)
Dim castSenderEndPoint As EndPoint = CType(senderEndPoint, EndPoint)
Dim rc As Integer

udpSocket = New Socket( _
    bindAddress.AddressFamily, _
    SocketType.Dgram, _
    ProtocolType.Udp _
    )
Try
    udpSocket.Bind(bindEndPoint)
    rc = udpSocket.ReceiveFrom(receiveBuffer, castSenderEndPoint)
    senderEndPoint = CType(castSenderEndPoint, IPEndPoint)
    Console.WriteLine("Received {0} bytes from {1}", rc, _
        senderEndPoint.ToString())
Catch err As SocketException
    Console.WriteLine("Error occurred: {0}", err.Message)
Finally
    udpSocket.Close()
End Try
```

The receiver code isn't all that different from the sender code, except for the extra work involved in casting the *IPEndPoint*, which contains the address of whomever sent the datagram packet. Also, the value returned from the receive methods is the number of bytes actually received into the data buffer. For blocking sockets, this value will be at least one byte.

If an error occurs during receive, a *SocketException* is thrown. For a TCP connection, an error can occur if the connection is broken for whatever reason (for example, the remote process dies, network connectivity is lost, and so on). A UDP socket can receive this exception if the same socket has sent data to an end point where there is no socket to receive the data. This error occurs because the remote machine will send an Internet Control Message Protocol (ICMP) port unreachable message indicating that no socket is listening for the data. The sending computer's network stack will receive this error and propagate it back to the sending socket, which can cause the exception to be thrown if the socket is now attempting to receive data. Finally, a UDP socket will receive an exception if the buffer passed to the *Receive* or *ReceiveFrom* method is too small to hold the received data. In this case, the exception is thrown and the remaining portion of the message is truncated and discarded. The asynchronous versions of *Receive* and *ReceiveFrom* are *BeginReceive* and *BeginReceiveFrom*, respectively.

Closing

When an application has completed communications on a socket, it needs to close the connection to free the resource. In the case of sockets, closing the connection involves freeing both the handle and memory resources associated with the *Socket* class object as well as network resources such as the local interface and port on which the socket is bound.

When closing a TCP connection, the connection itself needs to be closed in a graceful manner—that is, the TCP peer should be notified that the connection is closing so that both sides can ensure that all data has been received on the connection. This type of closing is known as a *graceful shutdown*. To initiate a graceful shutdown, each side in the TCP connection should call the *Shutdown* method with the *SocketShutdown.Send* flag. Once this call is done, the protocol stack sends a transport-level disconnect to the peer to indicate that the local participant will no longer be sending any additional data. A socket detects a graceful close when a call to the *Receive* method returns zero bytes. The following code sample shows a simple client that sends a request to the server and waits for the response:

C#

```
Socket    tcpSocket;
Byte []   receiveBuffer = new byte [ 1024 ],
          requestBuffer = new byte [ 1024 ];
int       rc;
```

```
// Establish a TCP connection, such that tcpSocket is valid
try
{
    // Initialize the requestBuffer and send request to server
    tcpSocket.Send( requestBuffer );
    // Since this socket will not be sending anything shut it down
    tcpSocket.Shutdown( SocketShutdown.Send );
    while (1)
    {
        rc = tcpSocket.Receive( receiveBuffer );
        if ( rc > 0 )
        {
            // Process data
        }
        else if ( rc == 0 )
        {
            tcpSocket.Close();
            break;
        }
    }
}
catch ( SocketException err )
{
    Console.WriteLine("An error occurred: {0}", err.Message);
}
```

Visual Basic .NET

```
Dim tcpSocket As Socket
Dim receiveBuffer(1024) As Byte
Dim requestBuffer(1024) As Byte
Dim rc As Integer

' Establish a TCP connection, such that tcpSocket is valid
Try
    ' Initialize the requestBuffer and send request to server
    tcpSocket.Send(requestBuffer)
    ' Since this socket will not be sending anything shut it down
    tcpSocket.Shutdown(SocketShutdown.Send)
    Do While True
        rc = tcpSocket.Receive(requestBuffer)
        If (rc > 1) Then
            ' Process the data
        ElseIf (rc = 1) Then
            Exit Do
        End If
    Loop
```

```
Catch err As SocketException
    Console.WriteLine("An error occurred: {0}", err.Message)
End Try
```

Notice that because this client sends a single request, it calls *Shutdown* to indicate to the server that no more data will be sent. A TCP connection is full duplex, which means that the two send channels are independent of each other. One socket can indicate shutdown while the peer can send data as long as it wants. If the socket attempts to send additional data after shutdown, a *SocketException* will occur.

The *SocketShutdown* enumerated type also includes *Receive* and *Both* values, but these values are not of interest to TCP because the underlying transport protocol has no equivalent semantic for indicating to the peer that it will stop receiving data. Indicating *Both* shuts down both the sending and receiving channels. However, if you do use either of these values, there will be no indication to the peer, but if any receive method is called, a *SocketException* will occur. Once the socket has performed a shutdown and has received indication that the peer has also shut down the connection (by a receive method returning zero), the local resources associated with the socket are freed by calling the *Close* method.

For UDP sockets, there's no connection to gracefully shutdown because UDP is a connectionless protocol. Therefore, when an application is finished communicating with a UDP socket, it simply needs to call the *Close* method.

Socket Options

A number of properties can be set or modified on the socket, which affects the socket's behavior. An example of a property is how much data the underlying network stack buffers for the socket, which can be important if a socket is receiving very large UDP datagrams and wants the local stack to be able to buffer multiple packets.

Two methods can change certain characteristics of a socket: *GetSocketOption* and *SetSocketOption*. *GetSocketOption* retrieves the current property value, and *SetSocketOption* sets the property's value. The parameter list for these two methods is the same. The first parameter is a *SocketOptionLevel* enumerated type, and the second is the *SocketOptionName* enumerated type. The value of the options can be one of three types, depending on the option level and name: integer, byte array, or object.

SocketOptionLevel indicates on what network level the option name is being applied. Socket options can be applied at the socket level (*Socket*) or at the protocol level (IPv4, IPv6, UDP, or TCP). *SocketOptionName* is an enumerated type that indicates the property being queried or set. Note that a particular

SocketOptionName typically applies to a single *SocketOptionLevel*, although this is not always the case. Table 8-4 describes some of the common *SocketOption-Name* properties. The multicast-related options will be covered in the "IP Multicasting" section later in this chapter.

Table 8-4 Common *SocketOptionName* Options

Option Name	Option Level	Description
Broadcast	*Socket*	Boolean value that enables the sending of broadcast packets on a socket. Only valid for protocols that support broadcast data.
DontLinger	*Socket*	Boolean value that disables any linger value set with the *Linger* option.
ExclusiveAddressUse	*Socket*	Boolean value that disallows any subsequent socket from binding to the same port regardless of whether the socket sets the *Reuse-Address* option.
HeaderIncluded	*IP* or *IPv6*	Boolean value that's used with raw sockets and indicates that the protocol header is included as part of data to send.
IpTimeToLive	*IP* or *IPv6*	Sets the integer time to live (TTL) value in the IP header.
KeepAlive	*Tcp*	Boolean value that enables TCP keepalives. Note that by default keepalives are sent on the order of hours.
Linger	*Socket*	Sets a time limit on unacknowledged data after the *Close* method has been called on a connection-oriented socket. A *LingerOption* object is passed to the call.
NoDelay	*Tcp*	Boolean value that disables the Nagle algorithm.
ReceiveBuffer	*Socket*	Sets the integer size in bytes (default of 8 KB) of the per-socket buffer maintained by the stack for receiving data.
ReceiveTimeout	*Socket*	Sets the timeout value for receive operations in milliseconds. An exception is thrown if timeout occurs.
ReuseAddress	*Socket*	When enabled, indicates a socket can be bound to an address even if another socket is bound to the same address and port.

Table 8-4 **Common *SocketOptionName* Options**   *(continued)*

Option Name	Option Level	Description
SendBuffer	*Socket*	Sets the integer size in bytes (default of 8 KB) of the per-socket buffer maintained by the stack for sending data.
SendTimeout	*Socket*	Sets the timeout value for send operations in milliseconds. If the send can't complete in the specified time, an exception is thrown.

> **Warning**   The *ReceiveTimeout* and *SendTimeout* socket options should never be used on TCP sockets because data might be lost when a timeout occurs.

A few notes about socket options. First, the majority of the options are Boolean values. When setting an option's value, simply pass an integer where zero is *false* and non-zero is *true*. Retrieving the option's value is a little more complex because a byte array must be used. The following code illustrates setting the *ReceiveBuffer* option and then retrieving the value just set:

C#

```
Socket    mySocket;
byte []   optionBuffer = new byte [ 4 ];
int       sendBufferSize = 16384;

// First create a valid Socket - mySocket
mySocket.SetSocketOption(
    SocketOptionLevel.Socket,
    SocketOptionName.SendBuffer,
    sendBufferSize
    );
mySocket.GetSocketOption(
    SocketOptionLevel.Socket,
    SocketOptionName.SendBuffer,
    optionBuffer
);
sendBufferSize = BitConverter.ToInt32( optionBuffer, 0 );
Console.WriteLine("Retrieved SendBuffer size = {0}", sendBufferSize);
```

Visual Basic .NET

```
Dim mySocket As Socket
Dim optionBuffer(4) As Byte
Dim sendBufferSize As Integer = 16384

' First create a valid socket - mySocket
mySocket.SetSocketOption( _
    SocketOptionLevel.Socket, _
    SocketOptionName.SendBuffer, _
    sendBufferSize _
    )
mySocket.GetSocketOption( _
    SocketOptionLevel.Socket, _
    SocketOptionName, _
    optionBuffer _
    )
sendBufferSize = BitConverter.ToInt32(optionBuffer, 0)
Console.WriteLine("Retrieved SendBuffer size = {0}", sendBufferSize)
```

Second, some of the socket options can be set or retrieved, but not both. For example, the multicast-related options can be used only with *SetSocket-Option*, and the *AcceptConnection* option can only be retrieved. The *Accept-Connection* option is not in Table 8-4 because it isn't very useful; it simply indicates whether *Listen* has been called on the socket.

The options *ReuseAddress*, *ExclusiveAddressUse*, and *Linger* will be covered in greater detail in Chapter 9, and *HeaderIncluded* and multicast-related options are covered later in this chapter.

Socket Ioctls

Socket I/O control codes (ioctls) are somewhat related to socket options. Socket ioctls typically return information about the socket or some network characteristic, such as enumerating all the local IP addresses. The *Socket* method for calling an ioctl is *IOControl*. Unfortunately, the .NET Framework does not offer any predefined ioctls and their corresponding structures, so to call an ioctl, you might need to use the *StructLayout* class to define the data returned. For a complete listing of the Winsock ioctls, consult *Network Programming for Microsoft Windows, Second Edition* by Anthony Jones and Jim Ohlund (Microsoft Press, 2002), which devotes a chapter to Winsock ioctls. The Microsoft Platform SDK contains information about the most common ioctls under the *WSAIoctl* entry. The following code shows the prototype for the *IOControl* method:

C#

```
public int IOControl(
    int ioControlCode,
    byte [] optionInValue,
    byte [] optionOutValue
    );
```

Visual Basic .NET

```
Public Function IOControl( _
    ByVal ioControlCode As Integer, _
    ByVal optionInvValue() As Byte, _
    ByVal optionOutValue() As Byte _
    )
```

The *ioControlCode* value is the ioctl being called. These values can be found in the C header files winsock2.h and ws2tcpip.h. Note that the ioctls in the C header file are unsigned, which can lead to some annoying compilation errors in C# and Microsoft Visual Basic .NET because the *ioControlCode* is defined as a signed integer. In this case, the values simply have to be converted to the equivalent negative number, or the *Unchecked* operator may be used in C# to prevent integer overflow validation. The input value is the byte array of the expected value, and because few ioctl objects are defined in the .NET Framework, applications will have to build these byte arrays by hand to match the required ioctl object's layout. Likewise, the output is a byte array specific to each ioctl that applications will have to decode appropriately.

The RawSocket sample located at Chap08\rawsocket\cs illustrates calling the *IOControl* with the Winsock ioctl *SIO_ROUTING_INTERFACE_QUERY*. This ioctl takes the equivalent of a *SocketAddress* structure (the equivalent of the Winsock *sockaddr* structure for a particular address family) that indicates the address of a remote destination. On output, a *SocketAddress* structure is returned that describes the local interface on which the destination is reachable; the *SIO_ROUTING_INTERFACE_QUERY* ioctl performs a route lookup.

Setting a Socket to Non-Blocking Mode

If you are familiar with the Winsock API, you know that the most common ioctl is the Winsock define *FIONBIO*, which is used to change a socket from blocking to non-blocking mode. All code samples in this chapter so far have shown blocking sockets. When a socket is put into the non-blocking mode, the operation will throw an exception if it can't be completed immediately. In the .NET Framework, however, the *FIONBIO* ioctl is not exposed through the *IOControl* method but as a property of the *Socket* class called *Blocking*.

Non-blocking sockets should be avoided if possible because they're inefficient and prone to logic errors. The non-blocking mode is a carryover from BSD Sockets and Winsock 1.1, where it was the only alternative to blocking sockets; there were no asynchronous operations. Setting a socket to non-blocking mode allowed the application to service multiple sockets at once with the drawback of requiring the application to poll for events (such as read and write) on the socket. The *Socket* class exposes a *Poll* method that does this. However, polling for events leads to inefficient network usage because the application must spend time querying each socket for certain events. It's much simpler and more efficient to use asynchronous pattern method operations instead, as described in Chapter 3.

IP Multicasting

Earlier in the chapter, we introduced the concept of multicasting data, a method of delivering data from one source to many receivers that's accomplished by each receiver "joining" a particular multicast address. All receivers that are interested in the same traffic join the same multicast group. Both the IPv4 and IPv6 address spaces reserve a portion for multicast addresses.

A multicast socket is simply a UDP socket that uses the *SocketOptionName.AddMembership* and *SocketOptionName.DropMembership* socket options to join one or more groups. Both IPv4 and IPv6 support multicasting, so the option levels specified are *SocketOptionLevel.IP* and *SocketOptionLevel.IPv6*, respectively.

An IPv4 and IPv6 multicast *Socket* sample exists under the Chap08\Multicast folder.

Joining a Group

To join a multicast group, the UDP socket must be bound to a local address and port. When joining a group, the multicast address and the local interface on which to join the group are parameters to the *SetSocketOption* call, which means that it's possible to join one or more multicast groups on one or more local interfaces all on the same socket. Therefore, the UDP socket should be bound to the wildcard address.

When joining an IPv4 multicast group, a *MulticastOption* object must be created that identifies the multicast group *IPAddress* and the local interface *IPAddress* to be joined. The following code illustrates IPv4 and multicasting:

C#

```csharp
Socket          mcastSocket;
IPEndPoint      localAddress = new IPEndPoint( IPAddress.Any, 5150 );
MulticastOption mcastOption;

try
{
    mcastOption = new MulticastOption(
        IPAddress.Parse( "234.6.7.8"),
        IPAddress.Parse( "10.10.10.1" )
        );
    mcastSocket = new Socket(
        localAddress.AddressFamily,
        SocketType.Dgram,
        ProtocolType.Udp
        );
    mcastSocket.Bind( localAddress );
    mcastSocket.SetSocketOption(
        SocketOptionLevel.IP,
        SocketOptionName.AddMembership,
        mcastOption
        );
}
catch( SocketException err )
{
    Console.WriteLine("Error: {0}", err.Message);
}
```

Visual Basic .NET

```vbnet
Dim mcastSocket As Socket
Dim localAddress As IPEndPoint = New IPEndPoint(IPAddress.Any, 5150)
Dim mcastOption As MulticastOption

Try
    mcastOption = New MulticastOption( _
        IPAddress.Parse("234.6.7.8"), _
        IPAddress.Parse("10.10.10.1") _
        )
    mcastSocket = New Socket( _
        localAddress.AddressFamily, _
        SocketType.Dgram, _
        ProtocolType.Udp _
        )
    mcastSocket.Bind( localAddress )
    mcastSocket.SetSocketOption( _
        SocketOptionLevel.IP, _
```

```
        SocketOptionName.AddMembership, _
        mcastOption _
        )
Catch err As SocketException
    Console.WriteLine("Error: {0}", err.Message)
End Try
```

This code creates an IPv4/UDP socket, binds it to the wildcard address and port 5150, and joins the group 234.6.7.8 on the local interface 10.10.10.1. If no such local interface exists, a *SocketException* is thrown. Once joined, the socket can receive data via the *ReceiveFrom* method for multicast data sent to the group 234.5.6.8 and port 5150.

Joining multicast groups on an IPv6 socket is slightly different in that it takes a different structure to join the group on an interface. Instead of a *MulticastOption* object, an *IPv6MulticastOption* is required, which is constructed with the IPv6 multicast group's *IPAddress* and the *ScopeId* of the local interface's *IPAddress* object. Because IP addresses tend to be transient, IPv6 multicasting allows only joining groups given the interface's index, which never changes (unless the interface is disabled or removed or the machine is rebooted). The following code shows how to create an IPv6 socket and join a multicast group:

C#

```
Socket       mcastSocket;
IPEndPoint   localAddress = new IPEndPoint( IPAddress.IPv6Any, 5150 );
IPv6MulticastOption  mcastOption;

try
{
    mcastOption = new IPv6MulticastOption(
        IPAddress.Parse( "ff12::1" ),
        IPAddress.Parse( "::%5" ).ScopeId
        );
    mcastSocket = new Socket(
        localAddress.AddressFamily,
        SocketType.Dgram,
        ProtocolType.Udp
        );
    mcastSocket.Bind( localAddress );
    mcastSocket.SetSocketOption(
        SocketOptionLevel.IPv6,
        SocketOptionName.AddMembership,
        mcastOption
        );
}
```

```
catch ( SocketException err )
{
    Console.WriteLine("Error: {0}", err.ToString());
}
```

Visual Basic .NET

```
Dim mcastSocket As Socket
Dim localAddress As IPEndPoint = New IPEndPoint(IPAddress.IPv6Any, 5150)
Dim mcastOption As IPv6MulticastOption

Try
    mcastOption = New IPv6MulticastOption( _
        IPAddress.Parse("ff12::1"), _
        IPAddress.Parse("::%5").ScopeId _
        )
    mcastSocket = New Socket( _
        localAddress.AddressFamily, _
        SocketType.Dgram, _
        ProtocolType.Udp _
        )
    mcastSocket.Bind(localAddress)
    mcastSocket.SetSocketOption( _
        SocketOptionLevel.IPv6, _
        SocketOptionName.AddMembership, _
        mcastOption _
        )
Catch err As SocketException
    Console.WriteLine("Error: {0}", err.ToString() )
End Try
```

Notice that when the *IPv6MulticastOption* is created, the string "::%5" is parsed into an *IPAddress* and the *ScopeId* is passed to the object's constructor, but we could have simply specified the *long* value *5*. Attempting to parse the string "%5" results in a *FormatException* because the string is not a valid IPv6 address.

Because multicasting is a one-to-many communication, it's possible that multiple sockets on the same computer will want to receive data from the same multicast group and port. To do so, each socket will have to bind to the same port, which is not allowed by default. In this case, each socket calls *SetSocket-Option* with *SocketOptionName.ReuseAddress*, as described in Table 8-4. This call will allow multiple sockets to bind to the same address and port, and any multicast data received on that address and port will be delivered to each multicast socket bound to it. For more information on the *ReuseAddress* option and possible security implications, see Chapter 9.

Sending Data to a Multicast Group

Receiving data sent to a multicast group is the same as with non-multicast sockets, but sending data to a multicast group has a catch. Because any computer can join a group on any interface, the network stack has no clue as to which local interface multicast data should be sent from. With non-multicast traffic, the local interface to originate traffic from is determined by the routing table. With multicast traffic, this does not work because multicast recipients might be present on any or all of the local computer's networks if the local computer has multiple network interfaces. (A computer with multiple network interfaces is *multihomed*.) By default, the network stack will send the multicast traffic on the first interface in the routing table unless specified otherwise.

An application can specify the local interface that multicast traffic should be sent from on a socket by using *SetSocketOption* and the *SocketOption-Name.MulticastInterface*. The option level is IP or IPv6, depending on which protocol is being used. The option value is the IPv4 *IPAddress* object or the *ScopeId* field of the IPv6 *IPAddress* that identifies the local interface that multicast data should be sent from.

Note that to send data to a multicast group, it's not required for the socket to join the group it's sending to or for it to join any group at all. Also note that the default time-to-live (TTL) value for sent multicast traffic is one, which means that any data sent will not travel beyond the first router on the network. However, the *SocketOptionName.MulticastTimeToLive* socket option can change the default TTL.

Leaving a Group

Membership to a multicast group can be dropped by following the same steps for joining except specifying *SocketOptionName.DropMembership* instead of *SocketOptionName.AddMembership*. This ability to drop membership is useful if the multicast groups that the socket is interested in change over time, such as an application that receives various channels of streaming media and each media channel is sent to a separate multicast group. Otherwise, if the socket is closed with the *Close* method, all multicast groups joined will be dropped implicitly.

Raw Sockets

Another very useful socket type is *SocketType.Raw*, which is used by applications that need to build custom protocol headers encapsulated in the given transport protocol header, which in our case can either be an IPv4 or IPv6 header. A raw socket is created by creating a *Socket* object and specifying either

IPv4 or IPv6, *SocketType.Raw*, and the *ProtocolType* of the protocol being built by the application. For example, if *ProtocolType.Icmp* is specified, any data sent on that socket is expected to have a valid ICMP protocol header followed by the data payload. Both the IPv4 and IPv6 headers contain an 8-bit value that identifies the next upper-layer protocol header that's set by the *ProtocolType* parameter to the *Socket* constructor. The ICMP and ICMPv6 protocols are defined in RFCs 792 and 2463, respectively.

After the raw socket is created, it must be bound to an explicit local interface before any operation can be performed on it. Once bound, it can be used to send and receive protocol-specific data, which we'll cover in the following sections.

A raw socket sample is provided under the Chap08\RawSocket folder that implements IPv4 and IPv6 ping as well as an IPv4 and IPv6 raw UDP sender.

Sending with Raw Sockets

To send data, the protocol header must be built correctly. A protocol header is defined by a series of bit fields that have distinct values with specific meanings. Figure 8-2 shows the ICMP header for the IPv4 protocol. Each field must be set to valid values for the remote host to respond. For example, to issue an ICMP echo request (otherwise known as a *ping*), the *Type* field is set to 8 while the *Code* field is set to 0. Also, the *Checksum* field must be correctly calculated. Protocol headers typically require the 16-bit one's complement checksum of the protocol header and any payload. (See the Chap08\RawSocket code sample for implementation details.) When a remote machine receives this packet, it sends back an ICMP echo response packet (*Type* and *Code* both 0).

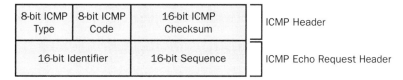

Figure 8-2   ICMP protocol header

When building the protocol header, it's important to remember that all data must be converted to network byte order. Additionally, most values used by the *Socket* class that are related to the protocol (such as the IP address and port) are also subject to this rule. However, this conversion is hidden from the application because the constructors for these various object (such as *IPAddress* and *IPEndPoint*) implicitly perform the necessary byte order conversion when getting and setting the values—that is, when a value is assigned into the object, it's converted to network byte order, and when the value is retrieved, it's converted into host byte order.

An application can perform byte order conversion by using the static methods *IPAddress.NetworkToHostOrder* and *IPAddress.HostToNetworkOrder*. Each of these methods is overloaded to perform conversion on different basic types. The inputs supported are *short*, *int*, and *long* (or *Short*, *Integer*, and *Long* in Visual Basic .NET).

Note   Unsigned variables passed into a byte order conversion function should be cast as the signed equivalent and cast back to the original unsigned type. Otherwise, the method mangles the resulting value. Additionally, the *Unchecked* operator may be used in C#.

Receiving with Raw Sockets

When receiving data on a raw socket, there are a few behavioral differences between IPv4 and IPv6 raw sockets. With IPv4, data received on the socket will include the IPv4 header, all subsequent headers, and the packet payload. With IPv6, data received on the raw socket will start with the protocol header following the IPv6 header; that is, a raw IPv6 socket will *never* receive the IPv6 header. Also, don't forget that the protocol headers returned from the receive call will be in network byte order and will require manual translation to host byte order when decoding the header.

A complete raw socket sample is located at Chap08\rawsocket\cs. The various protocol headers are defined in protocol.cs, while the process of sending and receiving a ping request is implemented in ping.cs.

Sample: IPv4 Raw Socket and ICMP

Let's look at how to create a raw socket and build the protocol header. In this example, we'll create an IPv4/ICMP echo request packet, which is the same thing ping.exe does to determine if a remote computer is alive and on the network. The associated code sample also performs IPv6/ICMPv6 echo requests.

1.   Create a raw IPv4 socket and specify the ICMP protocol, as shown here:

C#

```
Socket  rawSocket = new Socket(
    AddressFamily.InterNetwork,
```

```
SocketType.Raw,
ProtocolType.Icmp
);
```

Visual Basic .NET

```
Dim rawSocket As Socket = New Socket( _
    AddressFamily.InterNetwork, _
    SocketType.Raw, _
    ProtocolType.Icmp _
    )
```

2.   Bind the raw socket to an explicit local interface. In this example, the interface is 10.10.10.1. Because the ICMP protocol does not contain port fields, the *IPEndPoint* is created by specifying zero for the port.

C#

```
IPEndPoint  bindEndPoint = new IPEndPoint(
    IPAddress.Parse("10.10.10.1"),
    0
    );
rawSocket.Bind( bindEndPoint );
```

Visual Basic .NET

```
Dim bindEndPoint As IPEndPoint = New IPEndPoint( _
    IPAddress.Parse("10.10.10.1"), _
    0 _
    )
rawSocket.Bind(bindEndPoint)
```

3.   Build the ICMP and echo request header. A byte array is allocated to contain the 4-byte ICMP base header plus another 4 bytes for the echo request header followed by a 32-byte payload. The *Checksum* field is initially set to 0. For the *Identifier* field, we use the process ID, which is used to verify that any responses received are responses to our requests (because the echo reply will use the same identifier).

C#

```
byte []  icmpData = new byte [ 40 ],
         byteArray;
int      offset = 0;
short    icmpIdentifier = 0,
icmpSequence = IPAddress.HostToNetworkOrder( (short) 1 );
System.Diagnostics.Process proc =
    System.Diagnostics.Process.GetCurrentProcess();
```

```
icmpIdentifier = IPAddress.HostToNetworkOrder( (short) proc.Id );
icmpData[ offset++ ] = (byte) 8; // ICMP echo request type
icmpData[ offset++ ] = (byte) 0; // ICMP echo request code
icmpData[ offset++ ] = 0;        // Checksum set to zero
icmpData[ offset++ ] = 0;
byteArray = BitConverter.GetBytes(
    IPAddress.HostToNetworkOrder( icmpIdentifier ) );
Array.Copy(byteArray, 0, icmpData, offset, byteArray.Length);
offset += byteArray.Length;
byteArray = BitConverter.GetBytes(
    IPAddress.HostToNetworkOrder( icmpSequence ) );
Array.Copy(byteArray, 0, icmpData, offset, byteArray.Length);

for( ; offset < icmpData.Length; offset++)
    icmpData[ offset ] = (byte) 'e';
```

Visual Basic .NET

```
Dim icmpData(40) As Byte
Dim byteArray() As Byte
Dim offset As Integer = 0
Dim icmpIdentifier As Short = 0
Dim icmpSequence As Short = IPAddress.HostToNetworkOrder(CShort(1))
Dim proc As System.Diagnostics.Process = _
    System.Diagnostics.Process.GetCurrentPRocess()

icmpIdentifier = IPAddress.HostToNetworkOrder(CShort(proc.Id))
icmpData(offset) = 8      ' ICMP echo request type
offset = offset + 1
icmpData(offset) = 0      ' ICMP echo request code
offset = offset + 1
icmpData(offset) = 0      ' Checksum set to zero
offset = offset + 1
icmpData(offset) = 0
offset = offset + 1
byteArray = BitConverter.GetBytes( _
    IPAddress.HostToNetworkOrder(icmpIdentifier))
Array.Copy(byteArray, 0, icmpData, offset, byteArray.Length)
offset = offset + byteArray.Length
byteArray = BitConverter.GetBytes( _
    IPAddress.HostToNetworkOrder(icmpSequence))
Array.Copy(byteArray, 0, icmpData, offset, byteArray.Length)
offset = offset + byteArray.Length
```

4.   Compute the checksum. The following method computes the 16-bit one's complement checksum on a byte array. Assume that this static method is a member of the class *ProtocolHeader*.

C#

```csharp
static public ushort ComputeChecksum( byte [] payLoad )
{
    uint    xsum = 0;
    ushort  shortval = 0,
            hiword = 0,
            loword = 0;

    // Sum up the 16-bits
    for(int i=0; i < payLoad.Length / 2; i++)
    {
        hiword = (ushort) (((ushort) payLoad[i*2]) << 8);
        loword = (ushort) payLoad[ ( i*2 ) + 1 ];
        shortval = (ushort) (hiword | loword);
        xsum = xsum + (uint)shortval;
    }
    // Pad the last byte if necessary
    if ( ( payLoad.Length % 2 ) != 0 )
    {
        xsum += (uint) payLoad[ payLoad.Length-1 ];
    }

    xsum =  ( ( xsum >> 16 ) + ( xsum & 0xFFFF ) );
    xsum =  ( xsum + ( xsum >> 16 ) );
    shortval = (ushort) (~xsum);

    return shortval;
}
```

5. Call the checksum routine, and assign the value into the ICMP packet.

C#

```csharp
ushort  checksumValue;
// Compute the checksum
checksumValue = ProtocolHeader.ComputeChecksum( icmpData );
// Assign value back into ICMP packet
byteArray = BitConverter.GetBytes(
    IPAddress.HostToNetworkOrder( checksumValue ) );
Array.Copy( byteArray, 0, icmpData, 3, byteArray.Length );
```

Visual Basic .NET

```vbnet
Dim checksumValue As UInt16
' Compute the checksum
checksumValue = ProtocolHeader.ComputeChecksum(icmpData)
```

```
' Assign value back into the ICMP packet
byteArray = BitConverter.GetBytes( _
    IPAddress.HostToNetworkOrder(checksumValue))
Array.Copy(byteArray, 0, icmpData, 0, byteArray.Length)
```

6. Send the packet with a simple call to *SendTo* with the *icmpData* buffer built earlier that contains the ICMP header and payload.

C#

```
IPEndPoint  pingDestination = new IPEndPoint(
    IPAddress.Parse("10.10.10.1"), 0);
rawSocket.SendTo( icmpData, pingDestination );
```

Visual Basic .NET

```
Dim pingDestination As IPEndPoint = New IPEndPoint( _
    IPAddress.Parse("10.10.10.1"), 0)
rawSocket.SendTo(icmpData, pingDestination)
```

7. Wait for a response. After the ICMP echo request is sent, the response needs to be received, which is a simple call to *Receive-From*. See the Chap08\RawSocket code sample for the full details of implementing ping.

Using the *HeaderIncluded* Option

Raw sockets are ideal in cases where the custom protocol being created is encapsulated in IPv4 or IPv6, but what if an application needs to modify the fields of the IPv4 or IPv6 header itself? In this situation, the *SocketOption-Name.HeaderIncluded* option is useful. When this option is set on a raw socket, the application must build the IPv4 or IPv6 header itself and pass it along with all encapsulated headers and data payload to a send method (*Send* or *SendTo*). The *HeaderIncluded* option is a simple Boolean value that must be set on the socket before binding.

In the ping example, if the option was set, an IPv4 header would need to have been built. The byte array passed to *SendTo* would be 28 bytes plus any payload, and would be composed of the following entries:

- 20-byte IPv4 header

- 8-byte ICMP echo request header

- n bytes for the ICMP echo payload

Setting the *HeaderIncluded* option does not affect how data is received on the raw socket. For IPv4 raw sockets, the IPv4 header will still be part of any data received on the socket, and for IPv6, the IPv6 header will not be returned with received data (as is the case for raw sockets when *HeaderIncluded* isn't set).

Computing Protocol Checksums

The ping sample earlier illustrated the method that computes a checksum over an arbitrary byte array, which is a fairly simple algorithm. However, depending on the protocol, the checksum might need to be calculated over different parts of the protocol packet. Many protocols, such as IPv4 and ICMP, require the checksum to be calculated over its own header and any payload.

On the other hand, protocols such as UDP and ICMPv6 require what is known as a *pseudoheader checksum*. This is a checksum that's calculated over parts of multiple headers. Figure 8-3 shows the pseudoheader checksum for IPv4/UDP.

32-bit IPv4 source address		
32-bit IPv4 destination address		
8-bit zero	8-bit protocol	16-bit UDP length
16-bit UDP source port		16-bit UDP destination port
16-bit UDP length		16-bit UDP checksum
Data (and possible pad byte)		

Figure 8-3   IPv4/UDP pseudoheader checksum fields

You'll notice that checksum is calculated over parts of the encompassing IPv4 header as well as parts of the UDP header followed by whatever UDP payload is present. If an application was using raw sockets with the *HeaderIncluded* option set to build IPv4/UDP packets, the UDP header would be built and the checksum would be calculated according to the pseudoheader in Figure 8-3. Once it is calculated, the IPv4 checksum is calculated over the IPv4 header, the UDP header (with its checksum field already calculated), and the payload.

The IPv6 protocol is a bit different from IPv4. The IPv6 protocol header does not contain a checksum field. It relies on the upper-level protocols such as UDP or ICMPv6 to perform any checksum calculations. Therefore, IPv6 also states that these encapsulated protocols must calculate checksums over a pseudoheader that includes portions of the IPv6 protocol. Figure 8-4 shows the IPv6/UDP pseudoheader checksum.

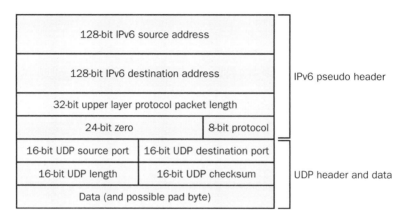

Figure 8-4   IPv6/UDP pseudoheader checksum fields

Simplified Socket Classes

The .NET Framework offers several simplified socket-oriented classes for the TCP and UDP protocols: *TcpClient*, *TcpListener*, and *UdpClient*. Typically, these classes offer multiple constructors that take most of the common parameters used to set up the socket and thereby remove a few steps from the creation process when compared to using the *Socket* class. Each class exposes the underlying *Socket* object as a protected property that can be used to perform the more powerful actions that the *Socket* class offers, which is only useful for derived classes. Note that each of these simplified classes offers constructors that have become obsolete because they were designed with IPv4 in mind. However, they have been extended and brought up-to-date in version 1.1 of the .NET Framework to support IPv6 as well. The next sections will look at each of these three classes in more detail.

See the SimplifiedSocketClasses sample located in Chap08\Simplified-SocketClasses for examples on how to use these three classes.

TcpClient

The *TcpClient* class is a simplified interface for a TCP socket that connects to a server. This connection is typically accomplished by calling the *TcpClient* constructor that takes the string server name and port to establish a connection to. If a host name is specified in the constructor, only the first DNS resolved name is attempted. If that connection fails, an exception is thrown. This behavior is not desirable because, for example, the DNS server might return an IPv4 address but the server might be listening on IPv6. The *TcpClient* class also offers a *Connect* method if a connection is not established as part of the constructor. This method allows a client to be more robust by performing DNS resolution itself and attempting to connect to each address returned. Because the underlying socket object is not public, *TcpClient* exposes a number of properties (listed in Table 8-5) that map directly to socket options but remove the necessity of the application making the call to *SetSocketOption*.

Table 8-5   *TcpClient* Properties and Equivalent Socket Options

Property	Socket Option Equivalent
LingerState	*SocketOptionName.Linger*
NoDelay	*SocketOptionName.NoDelay*
ReceiveBufferSize	*SocketOptionName.ReceiveBuffer*
ReceiveTimeout	*SocketOptionName.ReceiveTimeout*
SendBufferSize	*SocketOptionName.SendBuffer*
SendTimeout	*SocketOptionName.SendTimeout*

Once a connection is established, the *TcpClient* class does not expose a send or receive method. Instead, it offers a *NetworkStream* object that's obtained via the *GetStream* method. The *NetworkStream* class was introduced in Chapter 2. To send and receive data, the *NetworkStream* object exposes *Read* and *Write* methods as well as asynchronous versions.

Finally, *TcpClient* does not offer a method to shut down the connection, but the *Close* method should be called when the connection is done to release the underlying network resources. It's questionable that the *TcpClient* by itself greatly simplifies a TCP client because an application running on an IPv4- or IPv6-enabled network will most likely have to implement DNS resolution to connect to a server.

TcpListener

The *TcpListener* class is very simple, but then again, setting up a TCP listening socket isn't too difficult to begin with. An instance of *TcpListener* is created by specifying an *IPEndPoint* or an *IPAddress* and a port on which to listen for incoming TCP connection requests. Once created, the TCP server must be started by invoking the *Start* method, which actually puts the server into the listening mode.

Once *TcpListener* is listening for client connections, there are two methods for accepting connections: *AcceptSocket* and *AcceptTcpClient*. The former accepts a connection and returns it as a *Socket* object, and the latter accepts the connection and returns it as a *TcpClient* object. When finished with the

TcpListener, the *Stop* method will close the underlying listening socket and network resources.

The *TcpListener* class is ideal for simple applications that don't expect a high volume of client connections because there's no control over the listen backlog as well as no asynchronous method for accepting a connection. Chapter 9 will cover more details of accepting client connections.

UdpClient

The *UdpClient* class is a simplified interface for sending and receiving UDP data over IPv4 or IPv6. It differs from the *Socket* class in that the binding step is removed. The *UdpClient* object can be constructed two different ways: by specifying the local address and port to bind to or by specifying the remote destination to connect the UDP socket to. If *UdpClient* is to be used as a receiver, it should not be connected.

In addition to simplifying the socket creation step, *UdpClient* has a simplified interface for joining multicast groups. The *JoinMulticastGroup* method is overloaded to allow joining both IPv4 and IPv6 multicast groups. However, when joining IPv4 groups, the method does not allow you to specify the local interface to join, unlike the IPv6 version, which also takes the interface index on which the group is joined. This functionality makes the *UdpClient* class unsuitable for IPv4 multicasting because on a multihomed machine, the interface on which the group is actually joined can't be determined unless the routing table is consulted.

Once the socket is set up, the *Send* and *Receive* methods can be used for sending and receiving data. If *UdpClient* is not connected to an endpoint, the *Send* method is overloaded and offers an instance that specifies the destination host name and port. Of course, this class suffers the same problem as the *TcpClient* class in that the first DNS resolved name is used as the destination. This name might not correspond to the address family the receiver is on.

In truth, the *UdpClient* doesn't save too many steps over a direct *Socket* implementation, but it's useful when a quick-and-dirty UDP sender or receiver is required (but multicasting is not).

Code Access Security

The *Socket* class requires the *SocketPermission.Accept* permission to create a listening socket, and the *SocketPermission.Connect* privilege is required to connect a remote socket. These permissions apply to all instances of the *Socket* class, including TCP and UDP.

Code access security defines a security policy that grants different privileges based on the zone in which the application is running. There are three zones: My Computer, Local Intranet, and Internet. The My Computer zone defines any application run from the local computer, and Local Intranet consists of applications run from network shares residing on the Local Area Network (LAN). The Internet zone is the network beyond the LAN, such as a Web server on the Internet.

In version 1.1 of the .NET Framework, both the *SocketPermission.Accept* and *SocketPermission.Connect* permissions are granted only to applications run in the My Computer zone. Code executed from either of the other two zones will result in a *System.Security.SecurityException* being thrown. As an experiment, create a network share on your local computer with the SimpleServer.exe sample (in the Chap08\SimpleSocket folder) in it. Map a driver letter to that share, and execute the sample from the mapped drive. An exception will be thrown. Of course, the default policy might be changed to allow this connection.

Summary

This chapter introduced the basics of programming with the UDP and TCP protocol over IPv4 and IPv6. We began by introducing the protocols themselves and continued with an introduction to the *Socket* class, followed by advanced topics such as socket options, IP multicasting, and raw sockets. The last few sections covered the *TcpClient*, *TcpListener*, and *UdpClient* classes, which are very basic classes for TCP and UDP networking. The topics in this chapter mostly covered the client-side aspect of network programming. The next chapter will cover in detail the server side of socket programming, and it will go into detail about asynchronous socket operations.

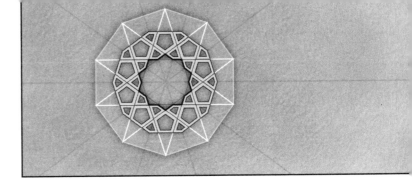

9

Server Sockets

In the previous chapter, the *Socket* class was introduced, as well as the basic concepts of setting up a socket and establishing client connections when using a connection-oriented protocol such as TCP. This chapter details how to create a server, or *listening* socket, with the *Socket* class that accepts one or more client connections. The previous chapter covered the *TcpListener* class and illustrated how this process basically works.

This chapter is divided into three sections: creating server sockets, socket security, and asynchronous socket operations. The first part discusses how to create a server socket using the *Socket* class and how to accept a client connection. The second part covers socket security, including how to prevent malicious processes from creating sockets that are bound to the same interface and port as an existing server socket as well as controlling what clients can connect to the server socket. The final section discusses how to use asynchronous operations on the *Socket* class, which is the building block for high-performance network applications.

Server Creation

As mentioned earlier, this chapter uses the term *server socket* to refer to an instance of the *Socket* class for a connection-oriented protocol used to accept incoming client connections. Once a server is created and set to listen for incoming connections, it can accept only connections—it can't be used as a client socket. Server sockets have two parts: creating a listening socket and accepting client connections. The next two sections discuss these concepts in detail.

Listening Sockets

The steps for creating a server socket are similar to client sockets: the socket is created and *must* be bound followed by calling the *Listen* method. A server socket must call the *Bind* method to indicate which interface the server will listen on. In general, the server can listen on one specific interface or on all interfaces. For example, if a TCP/IPv4 server is being created on a machine with two network interfaces with the addresses 10.10.10.1 and 192.168.1.1, the server can be bound specifically to one of these addresses, such as the 10.10.10.1 address and port 5150. If a client TCP connection request is received on the 192.168.1.1 interface and port 5150, it will be rejected because no server is listening on that address and port. If the server wants to receive connections across all interfaces, it should bind to the wildcard address for the address family being used, which for IPv4 is *IPAddress.Any* (equal to 0.0.0.0).

Once the socket is bound, the call to *Listen* indicates that the socket will be a server socket that accepts client connections received on the interface and port the socket was bound to. Note that *Listen* can be called only on sockets for protocols that are connection-oriented (such as TCP). If *Listen* is called on a non-connection-oriented protocol, a *SocketException* is generated. Also, if *Listen* is called on a *Socket* object that's not bound, a *SocketException* is thrown.

The netstat.exe command-line utility can be used to display TCP and UDP sockets and what addresses and ports they are bound to, as well as indicate the state of the socket (connected, listening, and so on). The following code is the output of *netstat.exe -aon*. On Microsoft Windows XP and later, the *-o* switch will include the process ID of the process owning the given socket entry.

```
Active Connections

  Proto  Local Address          Foreign Address        State          PID
  TCP    0.0.0.0:135            0.0.0.0:0              LISTENING      940
  TCP    0.0.0.0:445            0.0.0.0:0              LISTENING      4
  TCP    4.65.4.128:3295       207.46.196.119:80      ESTABLISHED    620
  TCP    4.65.4.128:3302       131.107.39.8:1723      ESTABLISHED    4
  TCP    4.65.4.128:11424      0.0.0.0:0              LISTENING      3328
  TCP    172.30.45.183:3312    157.54.7.23:80         ESTABLISHED    620
  TCP    [::]:135              [::]:0                 LISTENING      940
  TCP    [::]:1025             [::]:0                 LISTENING      988
  TCP    [::]:42510            [::]:0                 LISTENING      1572
  UDP    0.0.0.0:445           *:*                                   4
  UDP    0.0.0.0:500           *:*                                   748
```

The following code illustrates creating a TCP/IPv4 server socket listening on the wildcard address:

C#

```
IPEndPoint listenEndPoint = new IPEndPoint( IPAddress.Any, 5150 );
Socket tcpServer = new Socket(
    listenEndPoint.AddressFamily,
    SocketType.Stream,
    ProtocolType.Tcp
    );
tcpServer.Bind( listenEndPoint );
tcpServer.Listen( int.MaxValue );
```

Visual Basic .NET

```
Dim listenEndPoint As IPEndPoint = New IPEndPoint(IPAddress.Any, 5150)
Dim tcpServer As Socket = New Socket( _
    listenEndPoint.AddressFamily, _
    SocketType.Stream, _
    ProtocolType.Tcp _
    )
tcpServer.Bind(listenEndPoint)
tcpServer.Listen(Integer.MaxValue)
```

The only parameter to *Listen* is known as the *backlog*, which indicates how many client TCP connections can be queued on the listening socket at any given time. A server socket can dequeue a client connection by calling the *Accept* method or by using the asynchronous *BeginAccept*. If the backlog is set to 1, it means that if the server does not accept the client connection, only a single TCP client connection will be accepted. Any subsequent connection requests will be refused by the networking stack. Once the server accepts the connection, the pending connection is removed from the queue and another connection can be queued. The client that's refused will receive a *SocketException* on its connection request.

In the previous code sample, the backlog is set to the maximum integer value, but note that the underlying network stack will reset this value to its internal maximum value. Currently, on Windows Server, the maximum is 200. On professional and home versions of Windows, the maximum backlog is 5. If a server is expected to handle a large number of incoming connections, the backlog should be set to the maximum.

> **Note** On Windows Server 2003 SP1 and later, the home and client versions will have the same backlog limit as server versions.

Accepting Client Connections

After the server socket has been established, the server can make a blocking call to *Accept* to accept a client connection. If a client connection is pending, it's dequeued from the listen backlog, and if no connection is pending, the *Accept* call blocks until a client connection request is received. The asynchronous call to accept a connection is *BeginAccept* and will be covered in detail in the "Asynchronous Accept" section later in this chapter.

The *Accept* method takes no arguments and simply returns a *Socket* object that references the client connection. All data transfers then occur on the *Socket* object returned. The *RemoteEndPoint* property of the returned *Socket* object contains the address information of the connecting client.

The following code continues the previous example. In this code, once the listening socket is established, the server sits in an infinite loop waiting for a client connection. Once a client connection is accepted, data is received from the client until the connection is closed, at which point the server will handle the next client connection.

C#

```
Socket  tcpClient;
byte [] receiveBuffer = new byte [ 4096 ];

while ( true )
{
    try
    {
        tcpClient = tcpServer.Accept();
        Console.WriteLine("Accepted connection from: {0}",
            tcpClient.RemoteEndPoint.ToString());
        try
        {
            while ( true )
            {
                int rc = tcpClient.Receive( receiveBuffer );
                if ( rc == 0 )
                    break;
            }
        }
        catch ( SocketException err )
        {
            Console.WriteLine("Error occurred on accepted socket: {0}",
                err.Message);
        }
        finally
        {
            tcpClient.Close();
        }
```

```
    }
    catch ( SocketException err )
    {
        Console.WriteLine("Accept failed: {0}", err.Message);
    }
}
```

Visual Basic .NET

```
Dim tcpClient As Socket
Dim receiveBuffer(4096) As Byte
Dim rc As Integer

While (True)
    Try
        tcpClient = tcpServer.Accept()
        Console.WriteLine("Accepted connection from: {0}", _
        tcpClient.RemoteEndPoint.ToString())
        Try
            While (True)
                rc = tcpClient.Receive(receiveBuffer)
                If (rc = 0) Then
                    Exit While
                End If
            End While
        Catch err As SocketException
            Console.WriteLine("Error occurred on accepted socket: {0}", _
                err.Message)
        Finally
            tcpClient.Close()
        End Try
    Catch err As SocketException
        Console.WriteLine("Accept failed: {0}", err.Message)
    End Try
End While
```

Take a look at the SimpleSocket sample in Chapter 8 for an example on setting up a blocking TCP server.

Closing the Server

When a server no longer wants to accept client connections, it simply needs to call the *Close* method on the listening socket. Any queued client connection requests that have not been accepted with a blocking or an asynchronous accept will be reset. All client connections already accepted will not be affected when the server socket closes because each client is its own network connection that will not be closed until the *Close* method is called on its *Socket* object.

Socket Security

There are many aspects to adding security to sockets, ranging from preventing malicious local processes from stealing ports to authenticating client connections to detecting a denial of service attack. In this chapter, we focus mainly on the socket sharing issue, but we'll also discuss the *SocketPermission* class, which can be used to override the default socket security policy enforced by the Microsoft Windows .NET Framework. Chapter 14 will discuss how to detect malicious clients by managing server resources and limiting how long a client can be idle.

Sharing Ports

Under certain circumstances, it's possible to have several sockets bound to the same address and port. However, depending on the protocol, the effects can be undesirable. For TCP and UDP, it's undetermined which socket will receive traffic. The only case where it's truly useful to have several sockets bound to the same address and port is for IP multicasting, where each socket bound to the same local interface and port and joined to the same multicast group will each receive a copy of the data. Normally, if an attempt is made to bind a socket to an interface and port already in use, a *SocketException* occurs.

For all versions of Windows prior to Windows Server 2003, sockets were shareable by default. On a pre–Windows Server 2003 machine, if a second socket is created and *SocketOptionName.ReuseAddress* is set via *SetSocketOption*, the socket can be bound to an interface and a port already being used by another socket. To prevent another socket from doing this, a new socket option, *SocketOptionName.ExclusiveAddressUse*, was introduced on Windows NT 4 Service Pack 4 and later (but not on Windows 9x). If a socket sets this option before binding, then after the socket is bound, no other sockets can reuse the same address and port regardless of whether the *ReuseAddress* option is set.

On Windows Server 2003 and later, the default security model for sockets was changed so that sockets are not shareable. As a result of this change, the uses of the two socket options, *ReuseAddress* and *ExclusiveAddressUse*, have changed somewhat. Now if a socket wants to allow others to bind to the same address and port, the first socket must set the *ReuseAddress* option, which is in effect setting the permission to allow others to steal the address and port. Then the second socket must also set the *ReuseAddress* option to bind to the same address and port.

There is one catch, however, when binding a socket to the wildcard address under the new security scheme. Even though the socket is not shareable, it's not exclusive when it comes to the wildcard address. Therefore, the first socket can bind to the wildcard address and specific port, but a second socket can come along and bind to an explicit address on the same port. For example, on a computer with two interfaces, 10.10.10.1 and 10.10.10.2, the first socket can bind to 0.0.0.0:5150, and a second socket can bind to 10.10.10.1:5150. In this case, all traffic received on 10.10.10.1:5150 will be handled by the second socket, and all traffic received on port 5150 for interfaces other than 10.10.10.1 will be handled by the first socket.

As you can see, in the case where the socket is bound to the wildcard address on Windows Server 2003 and later, another socket can't bind to the wildcard address and same port (or a *SocketException* will be thrown), but it can bind to an explicit interface and port. However, if the server socket sets *ExclusiveAddressUse*, even binding to the explicit interface will fail. In general, a server should *always* set the *ExclusiveAddressUse* option regardless of which operating system it's running on. The only exception is for multicast UDP sockets.

Socket Permissions

As we saw in Chapter 8, different levels of code access security are available for socket applications depending on the zone in which the application is run. Under certain circumstances, an application can invoke untrusted assemblies or another application that resides in a more restrictive zone. In this case, the executed code is subjected to the code access permissions, which can result in socket operations failing. However, the *SocketPermission* class can be used to grant access to socket resources for subsequently invoked socket code.

The *SocketPermission* class enables applications to specify the resources to which subsequent socket calls have access to. For example, the permissions set could limit code to creating TCP sockets that connect to a single destination. Any attempt to connect to a different destination will fail. The permission properties that are used to grant or deny access are listed in Table 9-1.

Table 9-1   Socket Permission Properties

Property	Description
Transport type	Defines the transport on which to control. The transport value can be all, connection-oriented, connectionless, or the specific transports (TCP or UDP).
Host name/ address	Indicates the host name or string address being granted access to.
Port number	Indicates the port number being granted access to, which can either be a specific port or all ports.

Set socket permissions

1.   Create an instance of the *SocketPermission* class. There are two con-
     structors: one which sets the initial permission state (to either unre-
     stricted or none) and one that allows a specific transport, host name,
     and port to allow access to. The following code shows how to create
     a *SocketPermission* instance with no permissions:

C#

```
SocketPermission sockPerm1;

sockPerm1 = new SocketPermission(
    System.Security.Permissions.PermissionState.None);
```

Visual Basic .NET

```
Dim sockPerm1 As SocketPermission

sockPerm1 = New SocketPermission( _
    System.Security.Permissions.PermissionState.None)
```

2.   Once the initial *SocketPermission* object is created, individual per-
     missions can be added to the object. The following code allows
     sockets to connect to any port on the host "AllowedHost" using the
     TCP transport:

C#

```
sockPerm1.AddPermission(
    NetworkAccess.Connect,
    TransportType.Tcp,
    "AllowedHost",
    SocketPermission.AllPorts
    );
```

Visual Basic .NET

```
sockPerm1.AddPermission( _
    NetworkAccess.Connect, _
    TransportType.Tcp, _
    "AllowedHost", _
    SocketPermission.AllPorts _
    )
```

Note that the *SocketPermission* constructor can be used to specify a single allowed host from step 2.

C#

```
sockPerm1 = new SocketPermission(
    NetworkAccess.Connect,
    TransportType.Tcp,
    "AllowedHost",
    SocketPermission.AllPorts
    );
```

Visual Basic .NET

```
sockPerm1 = New SocketPermission( _
    NetworkAccess.Connect, _
    TransportType.Tcp, _
    "AllowedHost", _
    SocketPermission.AllPorts _
    )
```

3. Enforce the socket permission for all subsequent socket calls by calling the *Demand* method.

C#

```
sockPerm1.Demand();
```

Visual Basic .NET

```
sockPerm1.Demand()
```

4. The *Deny* method will prevent any function higher in the call stack from modifying the socket permissions granted. Once the desired permissions are established and demanded, the *Deny* method should be invoked before calling the untrusted code.

C#

```
sockPerm1.Deny();
InvokeUntrustedSocketCode();
```

Visual Basic .NET

```
sockPerm1.Deny()
InvokeUntrustedSocketCode()
```

If multiple *SocketPermission* classes are created, the *Union* and *Intersect* methods can be used to perform logical operations on sets of permissions. These methods return a new *SocketPermission* instance containing the results of the operation.

Finally, note that the permissions granted by the *SocketPermission* class are applied only when the executed code does not have socket permissions. For example, creating and demanding a *SocketPermission* that allows a connection to a single host will not be enforced when run in the local computer zone because socket operations are unrestricted in that zone. In other words, the *SocketPermission* class can't deny access to socket resources if the executed code has permission to access them.

Asynchronous Socket Operations

The key to writing server applications that scale to many thousands of concurrent connections is using asynchronous socket calls. Chapter 3 introduced the concept of threading as well as asynchronous operations. Using a separate thread to handle each client connection along with blocking I/O calls is acceptable if the server is not expected to handle many connections. However, threads are an expensive resource, and depending on the physical resources available, the maximum number of threads that can be created could be small. If the server is expected to handle thousands of connections, asynchronous socket calls must be used to ensure efficient use of the local resources.

The *Socket* class implements asynchronous socket operations using completion ports on Windows NT, Windows 2000, Windows XP, and Windows Server 2003. On Windows 9*x* and Windows Me, overlapped I/O is used. Table 9-2 lists the asynchronous *Socket* class methods. Note that the maximum number of outstanding asynchronous calls is limited only by local resources.

Table 9-2   Asynchronous Socket Methods

Start Method	End Method	Description
BeginAccept	*EndAccept*	Accepts a client connection on a connection-oriented server socket and returns a *Socket* object for the client connection
BeginConnect	*EndConnect*	Initiates a client connection to the indicated server

Table 9-2   Asynchronous Socket Methods   *(continued)*

Start Method	End Method	Description
BeginReceive	*EndReceive*	Receives data into the specified buffer on the connected socket
BeginReceiveFrom	*EndReceiveFrom*	Receives data into the specified buffer and returns the *EndPoint* from which the data originated
BeginSend	*EndSend*	Sends the given data buffer on the connected socket
BeginSendTo	*EndSendTo*	Sends the given data buffer to the specified destination

Posting Asynchronous Operations

As we saw in Chapter 3, all asynchronous socket operations take a delegate and a context object. The delegate is a method that's invoked when the asynchronous operation completes either successfully or with an error. The following code shows the prototype for the delegate:

C#

```
public delegate void AsyncCallback( IAsyncResult ar );
```

Visual Basic .NET

```
Public Delegate Sub AsyncCallback(ByVal ar As IAsyncResult)
```

Perhaps the most important part of posting and managing multiple asynchronous operations is the context information associated with each *Begin* operation. This context blob can be any object to identify the operation—typically, it's a class that contains at a minimum the *Socket* object on which the asynchronous operation was posted as well as an indicator of the type of operation completed. This context information is especially relevant if multiple asynchronous operations are posted simultaneously, such as sends and receives.

The following *IoPacket* class is an example of the state information associated with an operation:

C#

```csharp
public enum IoPacketType
{
    Accept,
    Connect,
    Send,
    SendTo,
    Receive,
    ReceiveFrom
}

public class IoPacket
{
    public IoPacketType ioType;
    public Socket        ioSocket;

    public IoPacket( ioPacketType type, Socket asyncSocket )
    {
        ioType = type;
        ioSocket = asyncSocket;
    }
}
```

Visual Basic .NET

```vbnet
Public Enum IoPacketType
    Accept
    Connect
    Send
    SendTo
    Receive
    ReceiveFrom
End Enum

Public Class IoPacket
    Public ioType As IoPacketType
    Public ioSocket As Socket

    Public Sub New(ByVal type As IoPacketType, ByVal asyncSocket As Socket)
        ioType = type
        ioSocket = asyncSocket
    End Sub
End Class
```

For each operation posted on the socket object, an instance of the *IoPacket* class is created that indicates the *Socket* object and operation type for the asynchronous operation posted. This way, when the delegate is executed, the

IoPacket context information can be retrieved to determine the *Socket* and operation just completed. The following few sections discuss posting and processing specific asynchronous *Socket* operations.

This chapter's AsyncSocket sample provides examples of asynchronous TCP client and server applications.

Asynchronous Accept

The *BeginAccept* method posts an asynchronous connection accept request on a listening socket. When the delegate registered with *BeginAccept* is fired, the *EndAccept* method on the listening *Socket* should be called, which returns a *Socket* object for the client connection request just accepted. The following code snippet shows how to post a *BeginAccept* on an already created TCP listening socket:

C#

```
try
{
    IoPacket ioContext = new IoPacket(
        IoPacketType.Accept, tcpListenSocket
    );
    tcpListenSocket.BeginAccept( new AsyncCallback( AcceptCallback ),
        ioContext );
}
catch ( SocketException err )
{
    Console.WriteLine("Socket error: {0}", err.Message );
}
```

Visual Basic .NET

```
Try
    Dim ioContext As IoPacket

    ioContext = New IoPacket(IoPacketType.Accept, tcpListenSocket)
    tcpListenSocket.BeginAccept(New AsyncCallback(AddressOf _
        AcceptCallback), ioContext)
Catch err As SocketException
    Console.WriteLine("Socket error: {0}", err.Message)
End Try
```

Once the operation is posted, the delegate will be invoked on completion. The delegate is required to call the corresponding method to terminate the asynchronous operation, which in this case is the *EndAccept* method. Each terminating operation will return the result of the asynchronous operation that includes the result of the operation as well as the context information.

C#

```
public static void AcceptCallback( IAsyncResult ar )
{
    IoPacket ioContext = (IoPacket) ar.AsyncState;
    Socket   tcpClient = null;

    switch ( ioContext->ioType )
    {
        case IoPacketType.Accept:
            try
            {
                tcpClient = ioContext.ioSocket.EndAccept( ar );
            }
            catch ( SocketException err )
            {
                Console.WriteLine("Socket error: {0}", err.Message);
            }
            catch ( System.NullReferenceException err )
            {
                Console.WriteLine("Socket closed: {0}", err.Message);
            }
            break;
        default:
            Console.WriteLine("Error: Invalid IO type! ");
            break;
    }
}
```

Visual Basic .NET

```
Public Sub AcceptCallback(ByVal ar As IAsyncResult)
    Dim ioContext As IoPacket = ar.AsyncState
    Dim tcpClient As Socket = Nothing

    If ioContext.ioType = IoPacketType.Accept Then
        Try
            tcpClient = ioContext.ioSocket.EndAccept(ar)
        Catch err As SocketException
            Console.WriteLine("Socket error: {0}", err.Message)
        Catch err As System.NullReferenceException
            Console.WriteLine("Socket closed")
        End Try
    Else
        Console.WriteLine("Error: Invalid IO type! ")
    End If
End Sub
```

The delegate retrieves the *IoPacket* context object from the *IAsyncResult* passed. It then calls the *EndAccept* method for the *IoPacketType.Accept* operation that completed. Note that the terminating asynchronous method should always be called in a *try...except* block. If an error occurs on the asynchronous operation, an exception will be thrown when the termination method is called. In the case of an asynchronous accept, if the connecting client resets the connection, an exception will occur.

Additionally, the only way to cancel an asynchronous socket operation is to close the *Socket* object itself via the *Close* method. If there are any pending asynchronous operations, the delegate associated with the operation will be invoked and the *System.NullReferenceException* error is thrown when the corresponding termination method is called.

It's possible and often desirable to post multiple *BeginAccept* operations on a TCP listening socket to ensure that a high volume of client connections can be handled simultaneously. Remember that a listening socket can queue a limited number of client connections; by posting multiple asynchronous accept operations, the backlog value is effectively increased. This ability to increase the backlog is true for *Socket*-based applications running on Windows NT–based operating systems such as Windows 2000, Windows XP, and Windows Server 2003 because the underlying Winsock API call is *AcceptEx*. If a listening socket sets the backlog value to the maximum allowed and also posts 100 asynchronous accept operations, the effective backlog is now 300. Chapter 14 will discuss high-performance servers in more detail.

Asynchronous Connect

The asynchronous connect method is useful for applications that need to have multiple sockets simultaneously connecting to servers, possibly with already connected sockets performing asynchronous data transfers. Because a single socket can be connected to only one destination, there can be only one outstanding asynchronous connect call on a given socket.

Posting an asynchronous operation is similar to using *BeginAccept* except that the *BeginConnect* method also takes the *EndPoint* describing the server to connect to. Aside from this difference, posting and completing asynchronous connect operations follow the same guidelines as the *BeginAccept* example shown earlier in this chapter.

Asynchronous Data Transfer

Because sockets generally spend most of their time sending and receiving data, the asynchronous data transfer methods are the most useful of all the asynchronous *Socket* methods. The asynchronous data transfer methods are somewhat simpler than their corresponding synchronous methods because they're not overloaded—that is, each asynchronous function has only one instance of the method. The asynchronous send method, *BeginSend*, is prototyped as shown in the following code:

C#

```
public IAsyncResult BeginSend(
    byte[] buffer,
    int offset,
    int size,
    SocketFlags socketFlags,
    AsyncCallback callback,
    object state
);
```

Visual Basic .NET

```
Public Function BeginSend( _
    ByVal buffer() As Byte, _
    ByVal offset As Integer, _
    ByVal size As Integer, _
    ByVal socketFlags As SocketFlags, _
    ByVal callback As AsyncCallback, _
    ByVal state As Object _
) As IAsyncResult
```

The asynchronous *BeginSendTo* method is the same as *BeginSend* except that the *EndPoint* parameter describing the datagram destination is specified after the *SocketFlags* parameter. The asynchronous receive methods are *BeginReceive* and *BeginReceiveFrom*, for connection-oriented and connectionless receive operations, respectively. The *BeginReceive* method is prototyped as shown here:

C#

```
public IAsyncResult BeginReceive(
    byte[] buffer,
    int offset,
    int size,
    SocketFlags socketFlags,
    AsyncCallback callback,
    object state
);
```

Visual Basic .NET

```
Public Function BeginReceive( _
    ByVal buffer() As Byte, _
    ByVal offset As Integer, _
    ByVal size As Integer, _
    ByVal socketFlags As SocketFlags, _
    ByVal callback As AsyncCallback, _
    ByVal state As Object _
) As IAsyncResult
```

The *BeginReceiveFrom* method takes the same parameters as *BeginReceive* except for an *EndPoint* parameter passed by reference after *SocketFlags*.

We've seen all the parameters to these functions before because they're the same as the synchronous versions except for the callback and state information. However, note that each data transfer operation takes a byte array for sending or receiving data. This array should not be touched or modified between the time the operation is posted and the time the operation completes.

Preserving the array is especially important when sending data on a connection-oriented streaming protocol such as TCP. Because the TCP protocol performs flow control, the receiver can indicate to the sender to stop sending data when the receiver is not handling the incoming data fast enough. At this point, if a *BeginSend* is posted, it will not complete until the TCP receiver indicates to resume sending, at which point the local network stack will transmit the byte array and call the associated callback routine. If the buffer is modified, it's undetermined what the actual data sent will be.

Another consideration when calling the asynchronous data methods is posting multiple operations on the same socket. The order in which asynchronous callbacks are invoked is not guaranteed. If two *BeginReceive* operations, *R1* and *R2*, are queued on a connected socket, it's possible that the callbacks for the completion of these events could be *R2* followed by *R1*, which can cause headaches when processing the results of these operations. This problem can be solved by encapsulating the code that posts the *BeginReceive* operation with a *Monitor.Enter* call on the *Socket* object, as follows:

C#

```csharp
Monitor.Enter( tcpSocket );
ioPacket.ReceiveCount = gGlobalReceiveCount++;
tcpSocket.BeginReceive(
    byteArray,
    0,
    byteArray.Length,
    SocketFlags.None,
    new AsyncCallback( recvCallback ),
    ioPacket
    );
Monitor.Exit( tcpSocket );
```

Visual Basic .NET

```vbnet
Monitor.Enter(tcpSocket)
ioPacket.ReceiveCount = gGlobalReceiveCount + 1
tcpSocket.BeginReceive( _
    byteArray, _
    0, _
    byteArray.Length, _
    SocketFlags.None, _
    New AsyncCallback(AddressOf recvCallback), _
    ioPacket _
    )
Monitor.Exit(tcpSocket)
```

In this code, execution is synchronized on the *tcpSocket* object, which is an instance of a connected TCP *Socket* class. A global counter is maintained, *gGlobalReceiveCount*, for marking the order in which the *BeginReceive* operations are posted. *BeginReceive* is invoked in the synchronized code to ensure that another thread using the same socket doesn't get swapped in between the assignment of the count and the execution of the operation. Of course, the synchronization is required only if asynchronous socket operations are being posted from multiple threads. When the asynchronous operation completes, the delegate can look at the *ReceiveCount* property to determine the order in which the operations were posted.

Because the send and receive data channels are independent, there's generally no problem with having a single asynchronous send along with a single asynchronous receive operation posted simultaneously.

Canceling Pending Asynchronous Operations

Once one or more asynchronous operations are posted on a *Socket* object, it might be necessary to cancel all outstanding asynchronous operations on that socket. The only way to cancel these operations is to close the *Socket* object via the *Close* method. Once the *Socket* object is closed, all pending asynchronous operations will complete. When the corresponding termination method is called (for example, *EndReceive* or *EndSend*), a *System.NullReferenceException-Error* exception will occur.

In general, it's always recommended to keep track of the number of pending asynchronous operations on each socket, for several reasons. First, limit the total number of outstanding asynchronous I/O operations. Consider a TCP server with 25,000 client connections on a 100 megabit (Mb) Ethernet connection. It's not feasible to post a 4 kilobyte (KB) send on each connection because that would amount to over 102 megabytes (MB) of data. It's likely an out-of-memory exception would occur because the sheer number of outstanding asynchronous operations as well as the number of send buffers submitted.

Second, the number of pending operations needs to be tracked in the event that the socket closes while socket operations are outstanding. This commonly occurs when the process terminates or the connection abortively closes because of a network attack or an excessively idle connection. In this case, where the process is being terminated, the process should close all active *Socket* objects and then wait for all outstanding asynchronous calls to complete with an exception before exiting the process. This way, you ensure that all events are handled gracefully and prevent timing issues that can cause exceptions (such as when a delegate fires while the process is cleaning up).

Summary

This chapter introduced the basics of creating a connection-oriented server socket that handles client requests. It also discussed the importance of socket security for servers and gave an introduction to the asynchronous *Socket* methods. Server sockets should always set the *ExclusiveAddressUse* option to ensure that no other socket can bind to the same interface. Also, robust servers should use asynchronous I/O to efficiently use resources. We also saw that asynchronous socket I/O is not much more difficult than blocking I/O. The next chapter will introduce the .NET Framework classes that deal with the HTTP protocol, and in Chapter 14, we'll discuss what can be done to ensure high performance with .NET Framework–based networking.

10

HTTP with .NET

In the previous two chapters we examined how to access the network protocols directly through the *Socket* class, which allows for precise control over what is sent and received on a socket. While the *Socket* class is powerful, it is also cumbersome to implement higher-level protocols, such as Hypertext Transfer Protocol (HTTP), because the application has to handle the network transactions as well as build and parse the HTTP commands, which can be quite complex. This chapter introduces the HTTP-related classes, an application-level protocol built on top of TCP for accessing Web resources. The .NET Framework Web classes encapsulate the TCP details for retrieving Web resources into simple and easy-to-use classes.

This chapter is divided into several parts. First, we'll introduce the basics of accessing HTTP-based Web resources via the *HttpWebRequest* and *HttpWebResponse* classes. This will be followed by the *WebRequest* and *WebResponse* classes that expose a uniform method of accessing any network resource based on request-response, such as files and HTML that can be extended to support other application-level protocols, including FTP and file sharing.

Following that, we'll cover more advanced topics such as the asynchronous model for accessing Web resources, as well as connection management, establishing secure connections over a Secure Sockets Layer (SSL), and application models that use Web-based classes from different areas (ASP.NET, console applications, etc.). We'll finish the discussion with code-access security considerations when using the Web classes.

Web Class Basics

There are four classes of interest for accessing Web resources: *HttpWebRequest*, *HttpWebResponse*, *WebRequest*, and *WebResponse*. The first two are used specifically for HTTP communication, while the second two offer an extensible interface to a variety of application protocols, including HTTP.

The Web classes in this chapter are all request-response transactions. The client makes a request to a server to perform some action. The server receives the request and generates a response that is returned to the client. Following the response, the requested entity or content is transmitted.

The HTTP protocol defines several actions a client can request of the server. These actions are listed in Table 10-1. The most common method, *GET*, requests to retrieve a URI resource. For example if a *GET* request is made for *http://www.microsoft.com/* an HTTP request is generated and sent to *www.microsoft.com*. The server then examines the request, generates a response indicating success, and sends the entity, which is the default HTML page for the Web site. The second column of the table indicates which version of the HTTP protocol introduced the method.

Table 10-1   HTTP Request Methods

Method	Minimum Version	Description
GET	0.9	Retrieves a URI resource
HEAD	1	Retrieves only the metadata of a URI resource
POST	1	Submits a form or other data (such as a SOAP message)
PUT	1.1	Uploads a file
DELETE	1.1	Deletes a URI resource
TRACE	1.1	Traces proxy chains
OPTIONS	1.1	Queries HTTP server options

Additionally, the HTTP protocol defines a series of header options that affect the behavior of the response. These options are simple string name/value pairs. The HTTP protocol defines numerous header options. The majority of these HTTP headers are exposed as properties of the *HttpWebRequest*, *HttpWebResponse*, *WebRequest*, and *WebResponse* classes. The *ContentLength* property that maps to the "Content-Length:" header is an example. Notice that some headers are valid only for requests, others for response, some for both request and response, and others for entities only. Table 10-2 lists the HTTP headers exposed as properties.

In addition to many of the headers being exposed as properties, the property *Headers* returns a *WebHeaderCollection* object that contains the entire set of headers associated with the request or response. The *Add* method of the *WebHeaderCollection* class can be used to set additional HTTP headers in the collection. Notice that the headers exposed directly as properties cannot be set using the *WebHeaderCollection*. Instead, they should be accessed through their strongly typed properties.

Table 10-2   HTTP Header Properties

Property	HTTP Header	Valid Method	Description
Accept	"Accept:"	Request	Specifies acceptable media types (e.g., text/html, image/jpeg, etc.)
Connection	"Connection:"	Request, Response	Controls how connections are handled (e.g., disable persistent connections)
ContentLength	"Content-length:"	Entity	Specifies the length of the returned entity in bytes
ContentType	"Content-type:"	Entity	Specifies the media type of the returned entity (e.g., text\html, image\jpeg, etc.)
Expect	"Expect:"	Request	Indicates expected behavior of client by the server
IfModifiedSince	"If-Modified-Since:"	Request	Used to verify cache is up-to-date
Referer	"Referer:"	Request	Specifies the URL of the document containing the reference to the requested URL
TransferEncoding	"Transfer-encoding:"	Request, Response	Specifies any transformations applied to content (e.g., chunked)
UserAgent	"User-Agent:"	Request	Specifies the client software issuing the request

Only the most relevant headers are covered here; for a full listing of the HTTP headers and their corresponding properties, consult the .NET Framework SDK and RFC 2616.

HttpWebRequest and *HttpWebResponse*

The *HttpWebRequest* and *HttpWebResponse* provide HTTP-specific implementations of the *WebRequest* and *WebResponse* classes (which are discussed later) and allow access to URI-based HTTP resources. These classes offer a complete implementation of the HTTP 1 and 1.1 protocols.

As we mentioned earlier, HTTP traffic is based on request-response, and the first step of accessing HTTP-based Web resources is to create an instance of an *HttpWebRequest* object that indicates a Web resource. This is done by calling the *Create* method of the *WebRequest* class as in the following sample:

C#

```
HttpWebRequest  httpRequest;

httpRequest = (HttpWebRequest) WebRequest.Create(
    "http://www.winisp.net/goodrich/default.htm"
    );
```

Visual Basic .NET

```
Dim httpRequest as HttpWebRequest

httpRequest = WebRequest.Create( _
    "http://www.winisp.net/goodrich/default.htm" _
    )
```

The example creates an *HttpWebRequest* object that points to the URI *http://www.winisp.net/goodrich/default.htm*. Notice that the constructor for the *HttpWebRequest* class should not be called—only the *WebRequest.Create* method. See the *WebRequest* and *WebResponse* section of this chapter for more details on the requirements of calling the *WebRequest.Create* method. Once an instance of the Web object is created, the HTTP headers and properties can be modified. Also, by default the *HttpWebRequest* method is *GET*. At this point, nothing has hit the network because an object needs to be created in order to set properties before the request is initiated.

The next step is to issue the request and receive the response from the destination. This is done by calling the *GetResponse* method, which returns a *WebResponse* object that can be cast to an *HttpWebResponse* object if you need to access the HTTP-specific properties:

C#

```
HttpWebResponse  httpResponse;

httpResponse = (HttpWebResponse) httpRequest.GetResponse();
```

Visual Basic .NET

```
Dim httpResponse As HttpWebResponse

httpResponse = httpRequest.GetResponse()
```

The returned *HttpWebResponse* object will indicate the response code of the request via the *StatusCode* property, as well as a text description of the result in *StatusDescription*. If an entity is to be sent following the request, the next step is to call *GetResponseStream*, which returns a *Stream* object that is then used to receive the entity data. Refer to Chapter 2 for information on manipulating *Stream* objects. If no response stream is associated with the *HttpWebResponse*, a *ProtocolViolationException* is thrown when *GetResponseStream* is called.

Finally, once all data is received from the response stream, the stream should be closed either by calling the *Stream.Close* method or by calling *HttpWebResponse.Close*. Note that both methods can be called, but at least one must be invoked to free the connection. The *HttpResponse.Close* method essentially calls the *Close* method of the stream and is provided as a convenience. If neither is called, the application will leak resources and run out of allowed connections. Notice that since HTTP 1.1 is implemented, keepalives are enabled by default.

Web Exceptions

As shown, setting up an HTTP Web request and receiving the response is easy and straightforward; however, the previous example didn't handle any exceptions. Exceptions are most commonly encountered when retrieving the response for a Web request and these exceptions take the form of an instance of a *WebException* class. Once a *WebException* occurs, the *Status* property indicates the type of failure. Common failures include underlying protocol failure, request timeout, etc. The *Status* property is *WebExceptionStatus*-enumerated type. Table 10-3 lists typical failures and their description, but consult the .NET Framework SDK for a complete description of each of the enumerated error types.

Table 10-3   *WebExceptionStatus* **Members**

Error	Description
ConnectFailure	An error occurred at the transport (e.g., TCP) level.
ConnectionClosed	The connection was unexpectedly closed.
Pending	The asynchronous request is pending.
ProtocolError	A response was received but a protocol-level error occurred (see Table 10-4 for HTTP protocol-level errors).
ReceiveFailure	An error occurred receiving the response.
RequestCanceled	The request was canceled by the *Abort* method. This error is used for any error not classified by the *WebExceptionStatus* enumeration.
SendFailure	An error occurred sending the request to the server.
Success	The operation completed successfully.
Timeout	No response was received during the specified timeout period.
TrustFailure	The server certificate could not be validated.

If the indicated exception status is *WebExceptionStatus.ProtocolError*—which means a response from the server was retrieved but a protocol error was detected—then an *HttpWebResponse* object has been created and can be accessed to obtain more information about the failure. In the case of the HTTP protocol, the HTTP-specific error code can be retrieved from the *HttpWebResponse* class as the *HttpStatusCode* property. Table 10-4 lists the common HTTP return codes and their descriptions. Again, consult the .NET Framework SDK for a complete list of the errors and meanings.

Table 10-4   *HttpStatusCode* **Members**

Status Code	HTTP Error Code	Description
Accepted	202	The request has been accepted for further processing.
BadRequest	400	The server could not understand the request. This error is also used for any errors not classified by the *HttpStatusCode* enumeration.
Continue	100	The client can continue with the request.

Table 10-4 *HttpStatusCode* **Members**   *(continued)*

Status Code	HTTP Error Code	Description
Forbidden	403	The server has refused to respond to the request.
GatewayTimeout	504	An intermediate proxy server timed out while waiting for a response.
InternalServerError	500	A generic error occurred on the server while responding to the request.
NotFound	404	The requested resource does not exist on the server.
OK	200	The request was successful and the requested information was sent.
ProxyAuthenticationRequired	407	The proxy server requires an authentication header.
RequestTimeout	408	The client did not send the request in the time expected by the server.
ServiceUnavailable	503	The server cannot handle the request due to high load or because it is down.
Unauthorized	401	The requested resource requires authentication to access.

The following example verifies in the catch block whether a response was returned and, if so, prints the HTTP status code information:

C#

```csharp
HttpWebRequest    httpRequest;
HttpWebResponse   httpResponse;

try
{
    httpRequest = (HttpWebRequest) WebRequest.Create(
        "http://www.winisp.net/goodrich"
    );
    httpResponse = (HttpWebResponse) httpRequest.GetResponse();
}
catch ( WebException wex )
{
    if ( wex.Status == WebExceptionStatus.ProtocolError )
    {
        httpResponse = (HttpWebResponse) wex.Response;
        Console.WriteLine("HTTP Response Code: {0}",
```

```
                        httpResponse.StatusCode.ToString());
                httpResponse.Close();
        }
}
```

Visual Basic .NET

```
Dim httpRequest As HttpWebRequest
Dim httpResponse As HttpWebResponse

Try
    httpRequest = WebRequest.Create("http://www.winisp.net/goodrich" )
    httpResponse = httpRequest.GetResponse()
Catch wex As WebException
    If wex.Status = WebExceptionStatus.ProtocolError Then
        httpResponse = wex.Response
        Console.WriteLine("HTTP Response Code: {0}", _
            httpResponse.StatusCode.ToString())
        httpResponse.Close()
    End If
End Try
```

Common Scenarios

Now that we've covered the basics for HTTP Web requests and responses, we'll move on to discuss some common scenarios in more detail. In this section, we present detailed samples for making HTTP requests with the *GET* and *POST* methods.

GET   *GET* retrieves content from Web servers and is the default method for most Web transactions. In the previous examples we showed how to construct instances of the *HttpWebRequest* class and how to retrieve the response header, but not how to retrieve the entity. The basic steps for issuing a *GET* request and handling the response are:

1. Create an *HttpWebRequest* object with the URL to retrieve

2. Retrieve the *HttpWebResponse* object for the request

3. Retrieve the stream to receive the entity data

4. Receive the data until the end of the stream is reached

The following code sample illustrates these steps. Once it obtains the *HttpWebResponse* object, it retrieves the stream handle and reads the returned data until the end. If the retrieved entity is text, a *StreamReader* is created to retrieve the data; otherwise, if the entity is an image, a *BinaryReader* is used.

C#

```csharp
HttpWebRequest  httpRequest = null;
HttpWebResponse httpResponse = null;
BinaryReader    binReader = null;
StreamReader    streamReader = null;

try
{
    // Create the HTTP request object
    httpRequest = (HttpWebRequest) WebRequest.Create(
        "http://www.winisp.net/goodrich");

    // Set some HTTP specific headers
    httpRequest.UserAgent = "My User Agent/1.0";

    // Get the response object
    httpResponse = (HttpWebResponse) httpRequest.GetResponse();

    if ( httpResponse.ContentType.StartsWith( @"image" ) )
    {
        // For image entities, use the binary reader
        binReader = new BinaryReader(
            httpResponse.GetResponseStream() );

        byte [] responseBytes;

        // Read the response in 4KB chunks
        while ( true )
        {
            responseBytes = binReader.ReadBytes( 4096 );

            if ( responseBytes.Length == 0 )
                break;

            // Do something with the data
        }
    }
    else if ( httpResponse.ContentType.StartsWith( @"text" ) )
    {
        // For text entities, use the text reader.
        streamReader = new StreamReader(
            httpResponse.GetResponseStream(), Encoding.UTF8 );

        string httpContent = streamReader.ReadToEnd();

        // Do something with the data
    }
}
```

```csharp
catch ( WebException wex )
{
    Console.WriteLine("Exception occurred on request: {0}",
        wex.Message );
    if ( wex.Status == WebExceptionStatus.ProtocolError )
        httpResponse = wex.Response;
}
finally
{
    if ( httpResponse != null )
        httpResponse.Close();
    if ( binReader != null )
        binReader.Close();
    if ( streamReader != null )
        streamReader.Close();
}
```

Visual Basic .NET

```vbnet
Dim httpRequest As HttpWebRequest = Nothing
Dim httpResponse As HttpWebResponse = Nothing
Dim binReader As BinaryReader = Nothing
Dim streamReader As StreamReader = Nothing

Try
    ' Create the HTTP request object
    httpRequest = WebRequest.Create( _
        "http://www.winisp.net/goodrich")

    ' Set some HTTP specific headers
    httpRequest.UserAgent = "My User Agent/1.0"

    ' Get the response object
    httpResponse = httpRequest.GetResponse()

    If httpResponse.ContentType.StartsWith("image") Then
        ' For image entities, use the binary reader
        binReader = New BinaryReader( _
                httpResponse.GetResponseStream())

        Dim responseBytes() As Byte

        ' Read the response in 4KB chunks
        While (True)
            responseBytes = binReader.ReadBytes(4096)

            If responseBytes.Length = 0 Then
                GoTo AfterLoop
            End If
```

```vb
            ' Do something with the data
        End While
AfterLoop:
    ElseIf httpResponse.ContentType.StartsWith("text") Then
        ' For text entities, use the text reader.
        streamReader = New StreamReader( _
            httpResponse.GetResponseStream(), Encoding.UTF8)

        Dim httpContent As String = streamReader.ReadToEnd()

        ' Do something with the data
    End If
Catch wex As WebException
    Console.WriteLine("Exception occurred on request: {0}", _
        wex.Message)
    If wex.Status = WebExceptionStatus.ProtocolError Then
        httpResponse = wex.Response
    End If
Finally
    If Not httpResponse Is Nothing Then
        httpResponse.Close()
    End If
    If Not binReader Is Nothing Then
        binReader.Close()
    End If
    If Not streamReader Is Nothing Then
        streamReader.Close()
    End If
End Try
```

The Chap10\HttpGetRequest code sample illustrates retrieving a URI, as well as linked documents and images in that URI to a local directory, and provides a progress indicator for each file as it downloads.

POST   Issuing a *POST* request is similar to issuing an HTTP *GET* request. One difference is that the request stream is retrieved from the *HttpWebRequest* object to send the post data. The general steps for issuing a *POST* request are:

1.   Create an *HttpWebRequest* object with the URL to post to

2.   Change the *Method* property to "POST" and the *ContentType* property to "application/x-www-form-urlencoded"

3.   Retrieve the request stream from the *HttpWebRequest* object

4.   Send the post data on the stream

5.   Retrieve the *HttpWebResponse* object

6.   Retrieve the response stream from *HttpWebResponse* and read the response

The following code sample illustrates issuing a *POST* request and receiving the response:

C#

```csharp
HttpWebRequest httpRequest;
HttpWebResponse httpResponse;
BinaryReader httpResponseStream;

try
{
    // Create HTTP Web request
    httpRequest = (HttpWebRequest) WebRequest.Create(
        "http://www.microsoft.com" );

    // Change method from the default "GET" to "POST"
    httpRequest.Method = "POST";

    // Posted forms need to be encoded so change the content type
    httpRequest.ContentType = "application/x-www-form-urlencoded";

    // Data to POST
    string postData = "s1=foo&s2=bar";

    // Retrieve a byte array representation of the data
    byte [] postBytes = Encoding.UTF8.GetBytes(
        postData.ToString() );

    // Set the content length
    httpRequest.ContentLength = postBytes.Length;

    // Retrieve the request stream so we can write the POST data
    Stream httpPostStream = httpRequest.GetRequestStream();

    // Write the POST request
    httpPostStream.Write( postBytes, 0, postBytes.Length );

    httpPostStream.Close();

    // Retrieve the response
    httpResponse = (HttpWebResponse) httpRequest.GetResponse();

    // Retrieve the response stream
    httpResponseStream = new BinaryReader(
        httpResponse.GetResponseStream(),
        Encoding.UTF8
        );

    byte [] readData;
```

```
    while ( true )
    {
        readData = httpResponseStream.ReadBytes( 4096 );
        if ( readData.Length == 0 )
            break;
        // Process response
    }
    httpResponseStream.Close();
    httpResponse.Close();
}
catch ( WebException wex )
{
    Console.WriteLine("Exception occurred: {0}", wex.ToString());
    httpResponse = (HttpWebResponse) wex.Response;
    httpResponse.Close();
}
```

Visual Basic .NET

```
Dim httpRequest As HttpWebRequest
Dim httpResponse As HttpWebResponse
Dim httpResponseStream As BinaryReader

Try
    ' Create HTTP Web request
    httpRequest = WebRequest.Create("http://www.microsoft.com/")

    ' Change method from the default "GET" to "POST"
    httpRequest.Method = "POST"
    ' Posted forms need to be encoded so change the content type
    httpRequest.ContentType = "application/x-www-form-urlencoded"

    ' Data to POST
    Dim postData As String = "sl=foo&s2=bar"

    ' Retrieve a byte array representation of the data
    Dim postBytes() As Byte = Encoding.UTF8.GetBytes( _
        postData.ToString())

    ' Set the content length
    httpRequest.ContentLength = postBytes.Length

    ' Retrieve the request stream so we can write the POST data
    Dim httpPostStream As Stream = httpRequest.GetRequestStream()

    ' Write the POST request
    httpPostStream.Write(postBytes, 0, postBytes.Length)

    httpPostStream.Close()
```

```
' Retrieve the response
httpResponse = httpRequest.GetResponse()

' Retrieve the response stream
httpResponseStream = New BinaryReader( _
    httpResponse.GetResponseStream(), Encoding.UTF8())

Dim readData() As Byte

While (True)
    readData = httpResponseStream.ReadBytes(4096)
    If readData.Length = 0 Then
        GoTo afterwhile
    End If
    ' Process response
End While
afterwhile:

httpResponseStream.Close()
httpResponse.Close()
Catch wex As WebException
Console.WriteLine("Exception occurred: {0}", wex.ToString())
httpResponse = wex.Response
httpResponse.Close()
End Try
```

The Chap10\HttpPostRequest code sample illustrates posting a form to a URI and receiving the response.

Web Proxies

Corporate environments often incorporate a firewall that requires a proxy server to be specified for Web traffic to travel beyond the corporate network. If a request is made for a resource outside the local proxied network, the request will fail and a *WebException* is thrown. For Web requests to traverse the proxy, the *Proxy* property of the *HttpWebRequest* class must be set. To set the proxy, an instance of the *WebProxy* class is created with the string name of the proxy server. The following code illustrates creating a *HttpWebRequest* and setting the *Proxy* property. Notice that the property needs to be set before invoking the request with the *GetResponse* method.

C#

```
WebProxy proxyServer = new WebProxy("http://corpproxy/");
HttpWebRequest httpRequest = (HttpWebRequest) WebRequest.Create(
    "http://www.winisp.net/goodrich");
httpRequest.Proxy = proxyServer;
HttpWebResponse httpResponse = (HttpWebResponse) httpRequest.GetResponse();
```

Visual Basic .NET

```
Dim proxyServer As WebProxy = New WebProxy("http://corpproxy:80")
Dim httpRequest As HttpWebRequest = WebRequest.Create( _
    "http://www.winisp.net/goodrich")
httpRequest.Proxy = proxyServer
HttpWebResponse httpResponse = httpRequest.GetResponse()
```

In the preceding example, a specific proxy server is set for the request by specifying the proxy server name in the *WebProxy* constructor. If Microsoft Internet Explorer is configured with a static proxy server, the static *WebProxy* method *GetDefaultProxy* will return the currently configured proxy server as a *WebProxy* object, as shown by the following statement:

```
WebProxy proxyServer = WebProxy.GetDefaultProxy();
```

If the proxy server requires authentication, the necessary credentials to access the server must be specified in the *Credentials* property of the *WebProxy* class. Creating and assigning network credentials is covered in detail later on in this chapter.

> **Note**   The next version of the .NET Framework is likely to add automatic proxy discovery—that is, support Web Proxy Auto Discovery (WPAD).

In addition to the ability to set the proxy server information on each request, the .NET Framework maintains a global proxy setting for use as the default proxy for all Web requests if a proxy setting is not explicitly provided. This is done through the *GlobalProxySelection* class. The property of interest is *Select*, which is assigned a *WebProxy* object that will be the default proxy server for subsequent requests when a proxy server is not explicitly assigned. The *GlobalProxySelection.GetEmptyWebProxy* method is of interest because it can be assigned to *GlobalProxySelection.Select* to turn off all use of a proxy server across the entire application.

Finally, a default proxy setting for System.Net can be specified in the machine.config file located in the .NET Framework runtime installation directory usually found under <drive>:\<windir>\Microsoft.Net\Framework\<version>\ config. The default setting should appear as follows:

```
<system.net>
    <defaultProxy>
        <proxy usesystemdefault="true"/>
    </defaultProxy>
</system.net>
```

This setting indicates that System.Net will use the computer's proxy settings, as specified in the Internet Options control panel applet. The system default settings for proxy servers will generally suffice and applications do not have to set a specific proxy on the request.

WebRequest and *WebResponse*

The *WebRequest* and *WebResponse* classes offer protocol agnostic abstract interfaces to request-response communication. Currently, the .NET Framework offers handlers for file and HTTP transfers, and it is possible for other protocols to be plugged into the same harness by inheriting from the *WebRequest* and *WebResponse* classes.

We've seen how the *WebRequest* class plays a role in issuing an HTTP request. Earlier, when we created an HTTP request, we called the *WebRequest.Create* method with the URI of the resource being requested. Because the URI begins with the protocol *http*, the *WebRequest* class is able to determine that the HTTP handler should be called to service this request. Likewise, if the URI passed to *Create* was *file://c:\files\myfile.txt*, then the file handler *FileWebRequest* is called to service the request.

The advantage of using the *WebRequest* and *WebResponse* classes, rather than casting the returned object to its specific type, such as *HttpWebRequest*, is that all operations for issuing the request and handling the response are available in these base classes. That is, a Web page can be retrieved solely by creating a *WebRequest* object and retrieving the *WebResponse* or by using *WebClient*, which builds on *WebRequest* and *WebResponse*. Notice that for C#, it is necessary to cast the Web object to its specific type to access properties specific to that protocol (for example, the *Connection* property of the *HttpWebRequest* class).

As mentioned earlier, the sequence of calls for handling a request-response operation with *WebRequest* is the same as it is for the *HttpWebRequest* class. The following code illustrates this point:

C#

```
// Create the request object
WebRequest  request = WebRequest.Create(address);

// Issue the request
WebResponse  response  = request.GetResponse();
```

```
// Read the content
StreamReader reader = new StreamReader(response.GetResponseStream(),
    Encoding.ASCII);

string content = reader.ReadToEnd();

// Display the content to the console
Console.WriteLine(content);

// Close the response
response.Close()
```

Visual Basic .NET

```
' Create the request object
Dim request As WebRequest = WebRequest.Create(address)

' Issue the request
Dim response As WebResponse = request.GetResponse()

' Read the content
Dim reader As New StreamReader(response.GetResponseStream(), _
    Encoding.ASCII)

Dim content As String = reader.ReadToEnd()

' Display the content to the console
Console.WriteLine(content)

' Close the response
response.Close();
```

Cookies

Cookies are used by Web servers to associate information with a particular user so that context information can be maintained for a given user across multiple Web requests. When a Web request is received by the server, the server might include a cookie (via the *Set-Cookie* header) for the client to include in each subsequent request to that server. This way, each subsequent request to the server will include the cookie information in the *Cookie* header.

A cookie itself is simply a collection of name/value strings. Cookies are defined in RFC 2109 and RFC 2965. A single name/value pair is exposed in the .NET Framework through the *Cookie* class while the *CookieCollection* class stores multiple *Cookie* objects as a single store. A *Cookie* has several properties besides the name and value (expiration date, for example). The following code creates two simple cookies and adds them to a *CookieCollection* object.

C#

```
Cookie  cookieObj;
CookieCollection cookieJar = new CookieCollection();

cookieObj = new Cookie("user", "Joe");
cookieJar.Add( cookieObj );

cookieObj = new Cookie("item", "ISBN0123456789");
cookieJar.Add( cookieObj )
```

Visual Basic .NET

```
Dim cookieObj As Cookie
Dim cookieJar As CookieCollection = New CookieCollection

cookieObj = New Cookie("user", "Joe")
cookieJar.Add(cookieObj)

cookieObj = New Cookie("item", "ISBN0123456789")
cookieJar.Add(cookieObj)
```

The cookies associated with a Web request are exposed through the *CookieContainer* property of the *HttpWebRequest* class, which is of the type *CookieContainer*. Before issuing the request, the *CookieContainer* can be set by instantiating a new instance of a *CookieContainer* with either a single *Cookie* object or a *CookieCollection*. The cookie values in the container will then be a part of the Web request as the cookie header. Notice that the *CookieContainer* object is a collection and can be accessed through array index notation.

After the client issues a Web request, the server sends a response received by the client as an *HttpWebResponse* object. The cookies set by the server are available through the *Cookies* property, which is a *CookieContainer* object.

Asynchronous HTTP Model

As we've seen with most other classes, the Web request-response classes (both the HTTP-specific classes as well as the generic Web classes) offer an asynchronous I/O pattern for retrieving the request stream and the response. The asynchronous Web pattern is useful when issuing multiple Web requests concurrently from a single application as well as for maximizing performance.

The first asynchronous method is *BeginGetRequestStream*, which is used for HTTP methods other than *GET* and *HEAD*. When this asynchronous request is issued, the callback is invoked and the request stream can be retrieved from the request object to send data associated with the Web request. If *BeginGet-RequestStream* is invoked on a Web request whose method is *GET* or *HEAD*, a *ProtocolViolationException* exception is thrown. The *BeginGetRequestStream* is most commonly used with the *POST* method, as shown in the following example:

C#

```
// Common state information
public class HttpState
{
    public HttpWebRequest     httpRequest;
    public HttpWebResponse    httpResponse;
}
public class AsyncPost
{
    public void DoAsyncPost()
    {
        try
        {
            HttpState    httpRequestState = new HttpState();

            // Setup the request
            httpRequestState.httpRequest =
                (HttpWebRequest)WebRequest.Create(
                    "http://www.microsoft.com/");
            httpRequestState.httpRequest.Method = "POST";
            httpRequestState.httpRequest.ContentType =
                "application/x-www-form-urlencoded";

            // Post the async operation
            IAsyncResult ar =
                httpRequestState.httpRequest.BeginGetRequestStream(
                    new AsyncCallback( HttpRequestStreamCallback ),
                    httpRequestState
                );

            // Process the response stream
            httpRequestState.httpResponse =
                (HttpWebResponse)
                httpRequestState.httpRequest.GetResponse();
```

```csharp
                // Retrieve the response stream
                StreamReader responseStream = new StreamReader(
                    httpRequestState.httpResponse.GetResponseStream());

                // Receive the response

                httpRequestState.httpResponse.Close();
            }
            catch( Exception ex )
            {
                Console.WriteLine("Exception occurred: {0}", ex.Message);
            }
        }
        private static void HttpRequestStreamCallback(IAsyncResult ar)
        {
            try
            {
                // State of request is set to asynchronous.
                HttpState httpRequestState = (HttpState) ar.AsyncState;

                // End of the Asynchronous request.
                Stream streamResponse =
                    httpRequestState.httpRequest.EndGetRequestStream(ar);

                byte [] postData = new byte [ 1024 ];

                // Setup data to write on the request stream
                streamResponse.Write( postData, 0, postData.Length );
                streamResponse.Close();
            }
            catch( Exception ex )
            {
                Console.WriteLine(ex.ToString());
            }
        }
    }
}
```

Visual Basic .NET

```vbnet
' Common state information
Public Class HttpState
    Public httpRequest As HttpWebRequest
    Public httpResponse As HttpWebResponse
End Class

Public Class AsyncPost
    Public Sub DoAsyncPost()
```

```
    Try
        Dim httpRequestState As HttpState = New HttpState

        ' Setup the request
        httpRequestState.httpRequest = WebRequest.Create( _
            "http://www.microsoft.com/")
        httpRequestState.httpRequest.Method = "POST"
        httpRequestState.httpRequest.ContentType = _
            "application/x-www-form-urlencoded"

        ' Post the async operation
        Dim ar As IAsyncResult = _
            httpRequestState.httpRequest.BeginGetRequestStream(_
                AddressOf HttpRequestStreamCallback, _
                httpRequestState _
                )

        ' Process the response stream
        httpRequestState.httpResponse = _
            httpRequestState.httpRequest.GetResponse()

        ' Retrieve the response stream
        Dim responseStream As StreamReader = New StreamReader( _
            httpRequestState.httpResponse.GetResponseStream())

        ' Receive the response

        httpRequestState.httpResponse.Close()
    Catch ex As Exception
        Console.WriteLine("Exception occurred: {0}", ex.Message)
    End Try
End Sub

Private Sub HttpRequestStreamCallback(ByVal ar As IAsyncResult)
    Try
        ' State of request is set to asynchronous.
        Dim httpRequestState As HttpState = ar.AsyncState

        ' End of the Asynchronous request.
        Dim streamResponse As Stream = _
            httpRequestState.httpRequest.EndGetRequestStream(ar)

        Dim postData(1024) As Byte
```

```
                ' Setup data to write on the request stream
                streamResponse.Write(postData, 0, postData.Length)
                streamResponse.Close()
            Catch ex As Exception
                Console.WriteLine(ex.ToString())
            End Try
        End Sub
    End Class;
```

The second asynchronous method is *BeginGetResponse*, which invokes the callback once the request has been sent to the server and the response headers received. Within the callback, the application can retrieve the entity by first retrieving the Web response via the *GetResponseStream* method followed by retrieving the response stream. The following code shows how to issue an asynchronous *BeginGetResponse*, as well as the asynchronous delegate method.

C#

```csharp
public class AsyncGet
{
    public void DoAsyncGet( )
    {
        try
        {
            HttpState    httpStateRequest = new HttpState();

            httpStateRequest.httpRequest = (HttpWebRequest)
                WebRequest.Create(
                    "http://www.microsoft.com/");

            // Get the response object
            IAsyncResult ar =
                httpStateRequest.httpRequest.BeginGetResponse(
                    new AsyncCallback( HttpResponseCallback ),
                    httpStateRequest
                    );
        }
        catch ( WebException wex )
        {
            Console.WriteLine("Exception occurred on request: {0}",
                wex.Message );
        }

    }
    private static void HttpResponseCallback(IAsyncResult ar)
    {
        try
        {
```

```csharp
            HttpState      httpRequestState = (HttpState)
                ar.AsyncState;

            // Complete the asynchronous request
            httpRequestState.httpResponse = (HttpWebResponse)
                httpRequestState.httpRequest.EndGetResponse( ar );

            // Read the response into a Stream object.
            Stream httpResponseStream =
                httpRequestState.httpResponse.GetResponseStream();

            // Post asynchronous Read operations on stream

            return;
        }
        catch(WebException ex)
        {
            Console.WriteLine("Exception: {0}", ex.Message);
        }
    }
}
```

Visual Basic .NET

```vbnet
Public Class AsyncGet
    Public Sub DoAsyncGet()
        Try
            Dim httpStateRequest As HttpState = New HttpState

            httpStateRequest.httpRequest = WebRequest.Create( _
                "http://www.microsoft.com/")

            ' Get the response object
            Dim ar As IAsyncResult

            ar = httpStateRequest.httpRequest.BeginGetResponse( _
                AddressOf HttpResponseCallback, _
                httpStateRequest _
                )
        Catch wex As WebException
            Console.WriteLine("Exception occurred on request: {0}", _
                wex.Message)
        End Try
    End Sub

    Private Sub HttpResponseCallback(ByVal ar As IAsyncResult)
        Try
            Dim httpRequestState As HttpState = ar.AsyncState
```

```
        ' Complete the asynchronous request
        httpRequestState.httpResponse = _
            httpRequestState.httpRequest.EndGetResponse(ar)

        ' Read the response into a Stream object.
        Dim httpResponseStream As Stream = _
            httpRequestState.httpResponse.GetResponseStream()

        ' Post asynchronous Read operations on stream

        Return
    Catch ex As WebException
        Console.WriteLine("Exception: {0}", ex.Message)
    End Try
End Sub
End Class;
```

It is possible to cancel an asynchronous Web request after it is issued. This can be desirable if the operation is taking too long, such as with a heavily burdened Web server. Cancellation is done by calling the *Abort* method on the Web request object. There are a number of ways to structure an application to handle timing out a Web request and aborting the connection. A simple method is to use the thread pool to schedule a timer event using the *WaitOrTimer-Callback* and specifying the context information for the request along with the timeout length, as the following code illustrates:

C#

```
public void DoAsyncWithTimeout()
{
    HttpState  httpRequestState = new HttpState();

    // Create the request
    httpRequestState.httpRequest = (HttpWebRequest)
        WebRequest.Create("http://www.microsoft.com/");

    // Post the async get response
    IAsyncResult ar = httpRequestState.httpRequest.BeginGetResponse(
        new AsyncCallback( HttpResponseCallback ),
        httpRequestState
        );

    // Register for a timeout
    ThreadPool.RegisterWaitForSingleObject(
        ar.AsyncWaitHandle,
        new WaitOrTimerCallback( RequestTimeoutCallback ),
        httpRequestState,
```

```csharp
            10 * 1000,  // 10 second timeout
            true
            );
}

static void RequestTimeoutCallback( object state, bool timedout )
{
    if ( timedout == true )
    {
        HttpState   requestState = state as HttpState;

        if ((requestState != null) &&
            (requestState.httpRequest != null))
        {
            requestState.httpRequest.Abort();
        }
    }
}
```

Visual Basic .NET

```vbnet
Public Sub DoAsyncWithTimeout()
    Dim httpRequestState As HttpState = New HttpState

    ' Create the request
    httpRequestState.httpRequest = WebRequest.Create( _
        "http://www.microsoft.com/")

    ' Post the async get response
    Dim ar As IAsyncResult = _
        httpRequestState.httpRequest.BeginGetResponse( _
            AddressOf HttpResponseCallback, _
            httpRequestState _
            )

    ' Register for a timeout
    ThreadPool.RegisterWaitForSingleObject( _
        ar.AsyncWaitHandle, _
        AddressOf RequestTimeoutCallback, _
        httpRequestState, _
        10 * 1000, _
        True)
End Sub

Private Sub RequestTimeoutCallback(ByVal state As Object, _
    ByVal timedout As Boolean)
```

```
    If timedout = True Then
        Dim requestState As HttpState = state

        If (Not requestState Is Nothing) And _
               (Not requestState.httpRequest Is Nothing) Then
            requestState.httpRequest.Abort()
        End If
    End If
End Sub
```

In the preceding code sample, if the asynchronous delegate registered with the *BeginGetResponse* call does not fire within 10 seconds, the *Request-TimeoutCallback* delegate will be invoked. Notice that the state information associated with the asynchronous *GET* request is also passed to the timeout function. This context block should contain the *HttpWebRequest* object so that the *Abort* method can be called on it. Note that due to the way asynchronous methods use a thread pool, it is not recommended that you mix synchronous and asynchronous method calls. This is because calling from within an asynchronous delegate will block the thread, which leaves fewer threads to service other asynchronous delegates—leading to potential starvation. For example, if your application calls *HttpWebResponse.BeginGetResponseStream* to retrieve the stream, it should then use the *Stream.BeginRead* method on the stream rather than *Stream.Read*.

Connection Management

When retrieving multiple URIs, it is often the case that many of the resources reside on the same host. If an application needs to retrieve hundreds or thousands of URIs, the application should limit the number of concurrent HTTP requests. This allows efficient use of network bandwidth and lessens the load on the Web server. To accomplish this, the .NET Framework offers the *Service-PointManager* and *ServicePoint* classes for managing HTTP requests.

The *ServicePointManager* class defines limits for a destination, such as the maximum number of concurrent connections allowed at any given time. The first step for managing Web connections is to establish the limits on the *Service-PointManager* that will be applied to subsequent connection requests. Table 10-5 lists the important properties of the *ServicePointManager* class.

Table 10-5 *ServicePointManager* **Properties**

Property	Description
DefaultConnectionLimit	Maximum number of concurrent connections to a single *ServicePoint*
MaxServicePointIdleTime	Maximum time in milliseconds a *ServicePoint* can be idle before being garbage collected
MaxServicePoints	Maximum number of concurrent *ServicePoint* objects

Once the restrictions are set on the *ServicePointManager*, a *ServicePoint* object is retrieved for a given server before any Web requests are issued to that server. A *ServicePoint* is retrieved by calling *FindServicePoint*. If a *ServicePoint* already exists from a previous request, the same object is returned; otherwise, a new *ServicePoint* is created so long as the *MaxServicePoints* limit is not exceeded. The following code illustrates this:

C#

```
ServicePoint    sp;

GlobalProxySelection.Select = new WebProxy("http://myproxy:80/");

ServicePointManager.MaxServicePoints        = 2;
ServicePointManager.DefaultConnectionLimit  = 2;
ServicePointManager.MaxServicePointIdleTime = 20000; // 20 seconds

sp = ServicePointManager.FindServicePoint(new Uri("http://www.one.com"));
// GetUriResource retrieves a URI
GetUriResource("http://www.one.com/one.html");

sp = ServicePointManager.FindServicePoint(new Uri("http://www.two.com"));
GetUriResource("http://www.two.com/two.html")
```

Visual Basic .NET

```
Dim sp As ServicePoint

GlobalProxySelection.Select = New WebProxy("http://myproxy:80/")

ServicePointManager.MaxServicePoints = 2
ServicePointManager.DefaultConnectionLimit = 2
ServicePointManager.MaxServicePointIdleTime = 20000 ' 20 seconds
```

```
sp = ServicePointManager.FindServicePoint(New Uri("http://www.one.com"))
' GetUriResource retrieves a URI
GetUriResource("http://www.one.com/one.html")

sp = ServicePointManager.FindServicePoint(New Uri("http://www.two.com"))
GetUriResource("http://www.two.com/two.html");
```

In this example, the application establishes a limit of two concurrent servers (*MaxServicePoints*) with two concurrent requests to each sever (*DefaultConnectionLimit*). It then sets *www.one.com* as the first *ServicePoint* to be managed and *www.two.com* as the second managed site. The *GetUri-Resource* function issues an asynchronous *HttpWebRequest* for the resource.

The service point limit in the example is two, and only two concurrent *ServicePoint* objects are requested; therefore, the subsequent Web requests succeed. However, if a third call to *FindServicePoint* was requested to a server (for example, *www.three.com*) that had not been requested previously, an *Invalid-OperationException* would be thrown because this third *ServicePoint* would exceed the established limit.

Only a single Web request is issued for each *ServicePoint*. If three concurrent instances of *HttpGetRequest* are issued for URIs residing on a single *Service-Point* host (such as *www.one.com*), the first two are allowed while the third is blocked until one of the initial requests completes.

Secure Connections

A Web site is often structured to restrict access to authorized users or encrypt the data stream to prevent prying eyes from viewing sensitive information. The .NET Framework Web classes support several methods of security.

First, a request can contain user information that authenticates the request. The .NET Framework supports several authentication methods such as NTLM and Kerberos, but it is also extensible so that other authentication technologies can be added. Secondly, encrypted connections can be created by sending a request using the Secure Sockets Layer (SSL) protocol. The next couple sections in this chapter discuss these concepts in more detail.

Authentication

Many Web pages restrict access to authorized users in order to protect sensitive personal information or to safeguard services for pay, for example. Providing authentication information with a request is simple: an instance of the *Network-Credential* class is created with the user and password information and is then associated with the request object via the *Credentials* property of the *Web-Request* and *HttpWebRequest* classes. An instance of a *CredentialCache* object also can be assigned to the *Credentials* property. This class is a container for multiple credentials, which we'll talk about later in this section.

The *NetworkCredential* class has several constructors that take a combination of username, password, and domain. These values are exposed as the properties *UserName*, *Password*, and *Domain*. The following code shows how to create credentials and associate them with an HTTP request:

C#

```
HttpWebRequest     httpRequest;
HttpWebResponse    httpResponse;

httpRequest = (HttpWebRequest) WebRequest.Create("http://payroll");
httpRequest.Credentials = new NetworkCredential(
    "joe", "password", "DOMAIN");
httpResponse = (HttpWebResponse) httpRequest.GetResponse();
```

Visual Basic .NET

```
Dim httpRequest As HttpWebRequest
Dim httpResponse As HttpWebResponse

httpRequest = WebRequest.Create("http://payroll")
httpRequest.Credentials = New NetworkCredential( _
    "joe", "password", "DOMAIN")
httpResponse = httpRequest.GetResponse()
```

When a request is made with security credentials, multiple security providers might be installed, such as NTLM, Kerberos, etc. When the Web request is issued and a challenge is returned from the server, each installed security provider is queried until one accepts the challenge and returns a valid *Authorization* class object. These providers are queried in the order they are registered with the .NET Framework and the *AuthenticationManager* class.

The *AuthenticationManager* is a static class that can be used to enumerate the registered security providers or to register a custom security provider. The *AuthenticationManager* maintains an ordered collection of providers that can be queried by accessing the *RegisteredModules* property. The following code illustrates this scenario:

C#

```
IEnumerator           registeredModules;
IAuthenticationModule currentModule;

registeredModules = AuthenticationManager.RegisteredModules;
Console.WriteLine("Authentication Modules:");

while( registeredModules.MoveNext() )
{
    currentModule = (IAuthenticationModule)registeredModules.Current;

    Console.WriteLine("  Module : {0}",
        registeredModules.Current);
    Console.WriteLine("    Supports Pre-Authentication : {0}",
        currentModule.CanPreAuthenticate );
}
```

Visual Basic .NET

```
Dim registeredModules As IEnumerator
Dim currentModule As IAuthenticationModule

registeredModules = AuthenticationManager.RegisteredModules
Console.WriteLine("Authentication Modules:")

While (registeredModules.MoveNext())
    currentModule = registeredModules.Current
    Console.WriteLine("  Module : {0}", registeredModules.Current)
    Console.WriteLine("    Supports Pre-Authentication : {0}", _
        currentModule.CanPreAuthenticate)
End While
```

It is possible to plug in custom authentication schemes. This is accomplished by creating a class that implements the *IAuthenticationModule* interface. The interface requires two methods and two read-only properties to be implemented. The two read-only properties are:

- *AuthenticationType* This string is a read-only property that returns the authentication scheme name

- *CanPreAuthenticate* This Boolean read-only property indicates whether the authentication module supports pre-authentication

The two methods are:

```
public Authorization PreAuthenticate(WebRequest request,
    ICredentials credentials)
public Authorization Authenticate(String challenge, WebRequest request,
    ICredentials credentials)
```

The *PreAuthenticate* method is used when the authentication scheme allows a user to be pre-authenticated. Pre-authentication is enabled when the *PreAuthenticate* property of a *WebRequest* or *HttpWebRequest* is set to true. For those security schemes that support pre-authentication, this causes the "WWW-authenticate" header to be sent with the request that supplies the credential information so that subsequent requests do not have to specify the same information again.

If the given security scheme doesn't support pre-authentication, the *Pre-Authenticate* method still must be implemented but should return *null* (or *Nothing* in Visual Basic .NET). Both the *PreAuthenticate* and *Authenticate* methods return an *Authorization* object containing the encrypted message that is expected by the server and sent with the request. An *Authorization* object is constructed by passing the generated authentication string to the constructor.

For the *Authenticate* method, the input parameter challenge contains the string indicating the type of authentication required. The *Authenticate* method should verify whether to handle the authorization request based on the challenge string. If so, it returns a valid *Authorization* object, and if not, it returns *null* or *Nothing*. The credentials parameter is the *NetworkCredential* object associated with the Web request used in the authentication process.

The *PreAuthenticate* method is called for providers that support pre-authentication after the *Authenticate* method has been called in response to a challenge. This method takes the *WebRequest* object on which the pre-authentication is taking place along with the credentials associated with the request.

As mentioned earlier in this section, a *CredentialCache* object can be used to track different user credentials for different URIs. This relieves the burden on the application of having to set up a *NetworkCredential* object for each request. After a *CredentialCache* object is created, a *NetworkCredential* instance is added via the *Add* method along with the URI on which the credentials are to be used and the authentication scheme for the credentials, such as "Basic," "Digest," or "NTLM." Remember, the *AuthenticationManager* can enumerate the available authentication schemes.

The Chap10\Authentication sample illustrates NTLM authentication and enumerating the available authentication packages.

Note that while this section shows you how to associate credentials with each request, it is recommended that *CredentialCache.DefaultCredentials* be used instead as it supplies the current user's credentials (including whether the application is impersonating someone else). This use of *DefaultCredentials* prevents the application from having to prompt for a user's password, which can lead to security vulnerabilities. Also, note that *DefaultCredentials* only applies to NTLM- and Kerberos-based authentication.

Unsafe Authentication

Under normal circumstances, NTLM authentication occurs on the connection level—not for each individual request. This means that if the client application impersonates a different user after the initial authentication, subsequent requests that should be from different users will be made in the context of the original authenticated user. Because of this potential security hole, the .NET Framework Web classes authenticate on every request—not just the first.

Of course, this behavior can degrade performance, especially if no impersonation is taking place. Because of this, the *HttpWebRequest* Boolean property *UnsafeAuthenticatedConnectionSharing* is exposed to disable the behavior. If this property is set to true, it is important to ensure that the application doesn't blindly use impersonation. If impersonation is required, the *ConnectionGroup-Name* string property provides a way to partition different request into groups. All the requests associated with a single user should contain the same *ConnectionGroupName*, as this allows the correct authentication credentials to be sent for each group.

SSL

One of the great advantages to using the .NET Framework Web classes is that SSL support is nearly transparent. The only difference between a normal request and an SSL-encrypted request is that *https* is the URI scheme instead of *http*. The SSL negotiation that occurs to establish the underlying connection, send the request, and retrieve the response is transparent and requires no intervention by the application.

> **Note** In NET Framework version 1 only SSL 3 and not TLS 1 is used for requests. This is a confirmed bug. See Knowledge Base article 330965 at *http://msdn.microsoft.com* for more information.

Any of the HTTP request samples in this chapter can be used to retrieve a URI with the *https* scheme.

Certificates

Certificates are a part of the authentication process when using public and private key security technologies, such as SSL. The .NET Framework supports the use of X.509 version 3 certificates, which are a mechanism for validating that the private and public keys used to access a resource are correct. In this section we'll discuss methods for associating a specific certificate with a request in addition to programming considerations when using X.509 certificates. However, a discussion of how certificate validation occurs is beyond the scope of this book. For more information on X.509 certificates consult RFC2459 or a cryptography book such as *Applied Cryptography* by Bruce Schneier (John Wiley & Sons, 2nd edition, 1995).

The *HttpWebRequest* class allows specific certificates to be associated with the request by the *ClientCertificates* property, which is an *X509Certificate-Collection* object. Individual *X509Certificate* objects can be added to or removed from the *X509CertificateCollection* via the *Add* and *Remove* methods. An *X509Certificate* object is created one of several ways. Using the constructor, an *X509Certificate* can be created from a byte array representing the actual X.509 certificate, from a handle to an existing certificate, or from an already created *X509Certificate* class.

Alternately, the static methods *CreateCertFromFile* and *CreateCertFrom-SignedFile* return *X509Certificate* objects when given the path and filename to a valid certificate file. Notice that only the ASN.1 DER format for X.509 certificates is supported regardless of which method is used to create a certificate object.

There are several considerations when using certificate objects. First, the *X509Certificate* created is only a reference to the certificate within the certificate store—not the actual certificate. This is important if impersonation is used, as accessing the *X509Certificate* might fail if the current user does not have the correct rights. Of course, the Access Control Lists (ACLs) can be set on the certificate store, as well as on the certificate itself, to allow a different user to access the certificate.

Secondly, when a certificate is referenced, the certificate store for the current user, the "My" store, is accessed followed by the machine store. However, the My store is often unavailable in middle-tier scenarios, such as ASP.NET. Because of this, if a certificate is accessed from a process that does not have access to the My store, the operation will fail, an exception will be generated, and the machine store will not be queried. A fix to this problem is available for version 1 of the .NET Framework as a QFE (Quick Fix Engineering). This is described in Knowledge Base article 817854 at *http://support.microsoft.com*.

As mentioned earlier, a primary reason for using certificates is to validate the public and private keys match. It is also important to validate the X.509 certificate because a certificate can expire, be revoked, or have other problems. Certificate verification is handled differently depending on the .NET Framework version. For example, version 1 of the .NET Framework did not check for certificate revocation or certificate name (CN) mismatches. Additionally, in the .NET Framework versions that support checking for certificate revocation, the feature is disabled by default. To enable this feature, the *ServicePoint-Manager.CheckCertificateRevocationList* property must be set to true. Certificate revocation checking and CN mismatch checking also can be enabled globally through the machine.config file or for a specific application by the configuration file.

Finally, an application can define its own certificate policy by implementing the *ICertificatePolicy* interface and assigning it to the *ServicePoint-Manager.CertificatePolicy* property. It is not recommended to override the default policy, however, as this could lead to potentially dangerous security problems. There is a single method for the *ICertificatePolicy* interface, which is *CheckValidationResult*, as shown in the following sample:

C#

```
bool CheckValidationResult(
    ServicePoint srvPoint,
    X509Certificate certificate,
    WebRequest request,
    int certificateProblem
);
```

Visual Basic .NET

```
Function CheckValidationResult( _
    ByVal srvPoint As ServicePoint, _
    ByVal certificate As X509Certificate, _
    ByVal request As WebRequest, _
    ByVal certificateProblem As Integer _
) As Boolean
```

The *CheckValidationResult* simply returns a Boolean value indicating whether to accept or reject the certificate. The parameters to the function are *X509Certificate* and *ServicePoint*, which will use the certificate along with the *WebRequest* that received the request. The *certificateProblem* parameter is the error code encountered while using the certificate. *CheckValidationResult* must determine whether the error code truly is a failure according to the custom policy. The actual error codes are dependent on the underlying security packages defined by the Security Support Provider Interface (SSPI). Consult the platform SDK for detailed information on SSPI, its security providers, and their error codes. The *CheckValidationResult* method determines whether the returned error is truly an error or should be ignored. Returning true indicates the certificate should be honored, whereas returning false causes the request to fail.

> **Note**   ASP.NET applications cannot set a client certificate when calling a secure Web service. This is a confirmed bug in the .NET Framework. See Knowledge Base article 817854 at *http:// msdn.microsoft.com* for more information.

Application Models

The .NET Framework Web classes can be accessed from a variety of application types, including console applications, ASP.NET, XML-based Web Services, Windows Forms, and Windows Services. However, it is important to realize that these application models can run under different environments. For example, a Windows Service or ASP.Net application can run under a different user account or impersonate different users, meaning it might not have the ability to change proxy settings or access to certain resources such as certificates.

The threading models also can vary from one application to another. For example, the ASP.NET environment uses a thread pool to satisfy incoming HTTP requests. This thread pool is also used by the *HttpWebRequest* class. This means that, if you are building a middle-tier application, you should be aware that both the Web server (ASP.NET) and any back-end Web requests issued will share the same limited set of threads and you should adjust the limits accordingly. This is a significant contrast to using *HttpWebRequest* from within a console-based application where all work is started from a "main" execution thread.

Code Access Security

As seen with other .NET network classes, use of the Web classes is restricted depending on where the executable is running from. Table 10-6 lists resources the Web classes can access from the various application zones. For example, an application accessed from an intranet share can only connect back to the same machine on which it is running (the localhost). Notice that version 1.1 of the .NET Framework allows applications run from the Internet zone to access the localhost, whereas this was not allowed in version 1.

Table 10-6 Code Access Permissions for Web Classes

.NET Framework Version	Internet	Intranet	Local Machine
1	None	Localhost	Anywhere
1.1	Localhost	Localhost	Anywhere

Summary

The .NET Framework offers extensive support for the HTTP protocol. In addition, the *WebRequest* classes offer an abstract interface to protocols oriented as request-reply, including HTTP. This makes accessing these protocols extremely easy. We also demonstrated how to configure Web requests for common network scenarios such as proxy servers. Finally, we discussed how to secure Web requests by using SSL and supplying credentials and security certificates. The next chapter is the first chapter in the advanced topics section of this book. It covers programming with XML Web services.

Part III
Advanced Concepts

11

XML Web Services and the Network

This chapter won't dwell on what Web services are in the .NET Framework. Instead, we'll look at how Web services interact with the lower-level network aspects of the stack. If you are unfamiliar with the basics of Web services, you might want to check out *Building XML Web Services for the Microsoft .NET Platform*, by Scott Short (Microsoft Press, 2002).

We'll start this chapter by examining the components that make up a Web service in the .NET Framework. Then we'll dive into the details of controlling how Web services interact with the Hypertext Transfer Protocol (HTTP) and how to override a Web service request to change the protocol. Next we'll talk about how to get the best performance and scalability out of your Web service applications while avoiding some of the common pitfalls. Finally, we'll talk about the future of Web services and how to design your applications such that they will continue to work well as Web services evolve.

Web Services

In version 1.1 of the Microsoft Windows .NET Framework, Web services are exposed in the form of matching client and server technologies that map to the HTTP request-response model. Figure 11-1 illustrates the flow of a message as it travels from client to server and back.

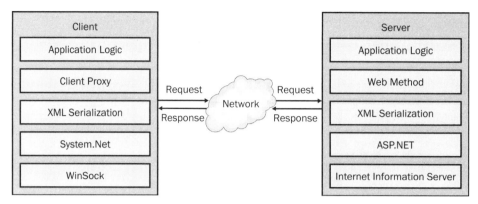

Figure 11-1 Web service message flow over HTTP in the .NET Framework

A client application issues a request by calling a method on a class that represents a client "proxy" for the server. The .NET Framework takes care of serializing that call into a SOAP message and sending it in an HTTP *POST* command to the server. On the server side, Internet Information Server (IIS) receives the request and passes it up through ASP.NET, where it gets deserialized and exposed to the server application code in the form of a method call. The method is then called. When the method completes, the server responds, and the response data gets serialized and sent back to the client application.

Interacting with the Network

There are two critical points to bear in mind as you consider how Web services interact with the network. First, it's important to understand the relationship between a Web service call and the underlying transport used to flow that call from one location to another. It's also necessary to understand the APIs available to help control the flow of a message as it originates from the client, gets transported and processed on the server, and is received back in the form of a response.

Web Services and HTTP

From a network perspective, it's important to understand that Web services in version 1.1 of the .NET Framework use the HTTP protocol. Most production Web services use HTTP, but because SOAP is transport-protocol independent, you can expect more services to use SOAP in the future. The Web services implementation in the framework allows an application to call a Web service, using either the HTTP *POST* verb or the HTTP *GET* verb. In practice, most applications use HTTP *POST* because it passes a SOAP envelope to the server within a request body, as opposed to including it as part of the query string parameters. This approach is more in line with the design of the HTTP protocol and, therefore, is better understood by the HTTP infrastructure that handles the message, which makes it more efficient and reliable.

HTTP protocol bindings for a Web service are specified in two locations: in the machine.config file stored in the config subdirectory within the .NET Framework version directory on the machine, or in a Web.config file associated with a particular application on the server. The following code sample demonstrates using the configuration settings in the *System.Web* section of the configuration system to control these bindings:

```
<configuration>
<system.Web>
  <WebServices>
    <protocols>
      <add name="HttpSoap1.2"/> <!--- reserved for future use -->
      <add name="HttpSoap"/>
      <!-- <add name="HttpPost"/> -->
      <!-- <add name="HttpGet"/> -->
      <add name="HttpPostLocalhost" />
      <add name="Documentation"/>
    </protocols>
  </WebServices>
</system.Web>
</configuration>
```

Notice that *HttpPost* and *HttpGet* are disabled by default. This is because they are intended for certain interoperability scenarios and do not offer the same level of control or efficiency as the *HttpSoap* binding. Although the *HttpSoap* binding uses an HTTP *POST* to send the data, it's different from the *HttpPost* binding because *HttpSoap* sends a SOAP message in the HTTP payload, whereas *HttpPost* simply sends form-encoded XML data in the HTTP payload. The original intent of *HttpPost* was for interoperability with XML and RPC (Remote Procedure Call) services that didn't understand SOAP. The SOAP protocol is now common, however, and *HttpPost* is rarely needed. Documentation provides the documentation page that comes up when you hit the service URL with a browser. *POST* on the local host enables you to locally test a service with basic types such as *int* or *string* by typing values into an auto-generated HTML page in the browser and hitting a button.

Understanding the dependency that exists between Web services and the HTTP infrastructure is important as it will help you to realize that Web services can be managed, monitored, debugged, and so on using the same or similar models as those used for Web sites in general. A critical difference, however, is the role that the client plays in the conversation. In the world of static or dynamically generated HTML and the browser, most of the control over network-related elements in an application is given to the developer and administrators on the server only. In the world of Web services decisions made by the application developer, both the client and the server can have a significant influence over the end-user experience in terms of performance, scalability, and security.

Extending Your Service

Web services in the .NET Framework include an extensibility model that enables an application to gain access to a message before and after it gets serialized or deserialized by the framework. This model is known as a SOAP extension. SOAP extensions make it possible for an application to modify the stream used to represent the message body to add support for features such as encryption, custom logging, and compression.

> **Note** Good examples of SOAP extensions are available online at *http://msdn.microsoft.com/Webservices* and *www.gotdotnet.com*.

Controlling the HTTP Request-Response Pair

In addition to extending a SOAP message, the framework provides a way for an application to control the actual HTTP protocol being emitted by the client request. This functionality is when you want to add custom HTTP headers. This is often done in cases in which infrastructure, or other parts of the system, rely on certain patterns or values in the HTTP message, and these values must be added to the Web service call so that it can interoperate with these systems. The following code demonstrates how you can use access to the HTTP headers to send custom HTTP information to the server:

C#

```
using System;
using System.Net;

/// <summary>
/// Sample class that demonstrates calling a Web service
/// with a custom HTTP header.
/// </summary>
```

```
class WebServicesMathClient
{
    [STAThread]
    static void Main(string[] args)
    {
        // Get x,y from the console
        Console.Write("X:");
        int x = int.Parse(Console.ReadLine());
        Console.Write("Y:");
        int y = int.Parse(Console.ReadLine());

        // Instantiate the derived math service
        MyMathService mathService = new MyMathService();

        // Call the add method and print the result
        float result = mathService.Add(x,y);
        Console.WriteLine(x + " + " + y + " = " + result);
    }
}


/// <summary>
/// MyMathService gets a WebRequest and sets the default credentials
/// and a custom header on the request.  If you need control over the
/// HTTP semantics of a Web service request it is much better to override
/// the auto generated proxy class so that you don't lose the changes when
/// the proxy gets regenerated.
/// </summary>
class MyMathService : WebServicesClient.localhost.MathService
{
    // GetWebRequest is called before the SOAP request is sent
    protected override WebRequest GetWebRequest(Uri url)
    {
        // Create a request based on the supplied URI
        WebRequest request = WebRequest.Create(url);

        // Set default credentials
        request.Credentials = CredentialCache.DefaultCredentials;

        // Set a custom header value on the request
        request.Headers["custom-header"] = "caleb";

        return request;
    }
}
```

Visual Basic .NET

```vbnet
Imports System
Imports System.Net
'Sample class that demonstrates calling a Web service
'with a custom HTTP header.
Module WebServicesMathClient

    Sub Main()
        'Get x,y from the console
        Console.Write("X:")
        Dim x As Integer = Integer.Parse(Console.ReadLine())
        Console.Write("Y:")
        Dim y As Integer = Integer.Parse(Console.ReadLine())

        'Instantiate the derived math service
        Dim mathService As MyMathService = New MyMathService

        'Call the add method and print the result
        Dim result = mathService.Add(x, y)

        Console.WriteLine(x & " + " & y & " = " & result)
    End Sub

End Module

'MyMathService gets a WebRequest and sets the default credentials
'and a custom header on the request.  If you need control over the
'HTTP semantics of a Web service request it is much better to override
'the auto generated proxy class so that you don't lose the changes when
'the proxy gets regenerated.
Class MyMathService
    Inherits localhost.MathService

    'GetWebRequest is called before the SOAP request is sent

    Protected Overrides Function GetWebRequest(ByVal url As Uri) As WebRequest
        'Create a request based on the supplied URI
        Dim request As WebRequest = WebRequest.Create(url)

        'Set default credentials
        request.Credentials = CredentialCache.DefaultCredentials

        'Set a custom header value on the request
        request.Headers("custom-header") = "caleb"

        Return request
    End Function
End Class
```

The custom header added in this example can be used to route the request or to handle other HTTP-level processing. Also notice that the override to *GetWebRequest* happens in a class that derives from the Web service, rather than in the automatically generated client proxy itself. This is because if the client proxy gets regenerated, Microsoft Visual Studio .NET will overwrite the previous proxy file and any overrides will need to be reinserted. By making the changes in a derived class, the overrides will continue to work even after the client proxy is regenerated. Furthermore, the derived class changes can be applied to other Web services that also need this functionality.

Performance

The Web services platform in the .NET Framework is built with high performance in mind on IIS and *System.Net*; therefore, it can be quite fast. A number of common "gotchas" can arise, however, as you deploy Web services in a production environment that requires high performance. The performance tips given here will be discussed in detail in Chapter 14. The purpose of this section is to call out common elements that often apply to applications using Web services, so that they can be avoided.

100 Continue and *POST*

Because Web services are usually sent via an HTTP *POST*, they are subject to the 100 Continue logic, which will be described in Chapter 14. While 100 Continue is often the ideal semantic because it can save the client from sending data that doesn't have to be sent, 100 Continue does cause an extra roundtrip between the client and the server for each Web-service call. If the data is small enough, it might be faster to simply turn off the 100 Continue feature for Web services. The 100 Continue feature is controlled via the *System.Net.ServicePoint-Manager.Expect100Continue* property.

Preauthentication

Preauthentication can save time in cases in which the application repeatedly calls the same set of services. At least one major Web services client product sends basic authentication credentials with every request if preauthentication is turned on in the client API. We know this because we occasionally get requests to do this for Web services calls. *System.Net* does not send the basic credentials on the first request when preauthentication is enabled. This is because the client doesn't know which authentication scheme is desired by the server until it has made at least one request to the server. Basic authentication alone provides little defense in terms of protection from credential theft. It would be unfortunate if the client sent basic credentials across the network when the server wanted some stronger form of authentication, such as Kerberos. In general, we recommend that basic authentication be used only if it is done in concert with some other encryption mechanism, such as HTTPS (Secure HTTP) or encryption at the network's IP layer or lower. In cases where the environment is controlled, however, and the benefits of using basic authentication are deemed to outweigh the risks, you can add your own basic header to the Web service request using the custom header logic described earlier in this chapter.

Connection Pooling

In Visual Studio .NET the *UnsafeAuthenticatedConnectionSharing* property is exposed on each of the automatically generated client proxies. *UnsafeAuthenticatedConnectionSharing* is used in conjunction with the *ConnectionGroupName* property, which is also exposed on the Web services proxy. If the service is using authentication, these two properties can have a significant impact on the performance of your Web service, as they enable connection pooling for the authenticated connections. Be sure to use them carefully according to the description in Chapter 14.

Also notice that the *System.Net* connection semantics apply to Web service requests made with the .NET Framework. For example, setting the *System.Net.ServicePointManager.DefaultConnectionLimit* to 20 when the application domain is starting will cause all Web service requests to use a connection limit of 20 rather than the default of 2.

Nagle Algorithm

The Nagle algorithm increases network efficiency by decreasing the number of packets sent across the network. It accomplishes this by instituting a delay on the client of up to 200 milliseconds when small amounts of data are written to the network. The delay is a wait period for additional data that might be written. New data is added to the same packet. The practice of compiling data is not always ideal for Web services, however, because a *POST* request often contains a small amount of data in the HTTP headers without the body (because of 100 Continue, as described earlier). The Nagle algorithm can be turned off for Web services calls via the *System.Net.ServicePointManager.UseNagleAlgorithm* property. Yet disabling the Nagle algorithm might not provide the best performance either—you'll need to experiment with disabling the algorithm to fine-tune your application. Whether you should disable the algorithm in this case depends on several factors, including the size of the Web services call, the latency of the network, and whether HTTP authentication is involved.

Scalability

Certain decisions can significantly increase system scalability when using Web services. The following tips are related to managing the use of threads and connections within the system.

Calling a Web Service from Within ASP.NET

Developers who use the .NET Framework frequently call Web services from within ASP.NET. This practice is known as a "middle-tier" scenario. Because ASP.NET and *System.Net* share the same thread pool, however, the threads must be well managed when used together. When threads are not well managed, a middle-tier ASP.NET application that calls a Web service can run in an underutilized state while the server waits for available threads. An even worse outcome is a deadlocked application caused by ASP.NET worker threads waiting for back-end requests to complete. Back-end requests require additional threads to complete, so nothing can happen until the requests start to time out. An obvious way to guard against such thread starvation is to always move the methods being called into a local dynamic link library (DLL) and call them directly from code whenever possible.

However, an off-machine, Web services call is often necessary as part of processing an ASP.NET page. In this case, there are a number of concepts to keep in mind.

- By default, *System.Net* limits the number of connections to two connections per application domain and host pair. The number of available connections can be increased either programmatically or through configuration in the *System.Net* section. In middle-tier scenarios, the connection limit should be bumped higher than two to better utilize the server.

- Back-end calls that involve redirection or authentication can exacerbate the thread problem. It is possible for *System.Net* to require two threads to complete in cases where redirection or authentication is required.

- A number of parameters in the machine.config file can help to further fine-tune application scalability in middle-tier scenarios. These values include *maxWorkerThreads*, *maxIoThreads*, *minFreeThreads*, *minLocalRequestFreeThreads*, *maxconnection*, and *executionTimeout*. The best use of these values can be found in Microsoft Knowledge Base article 821268 at *http://support.microsoft.com/?id=821268*.

Another option available to middle-tier applications that need to call a Web service as a result of an ASP.NET page request is to use the asynchronous framework provided in ASP.NET to include a module that issues the request asynchronously before the page starts to load. This way, the server will have no threads blocking while I/O completes and pages will have the necessary data when they load. This option is fairly complex, but it can enable applications to get the most out of the available resources on the server. The following sample demonstrates a page that uses an asynchronous module to call a Web service and process a request with ASP.NET support for asynchronous modules. For brevity, this sample is only for C#. See the downloadable samples for this book to obtain a copy of a Visual Basic .NET sample.

C#

```
// Contents of asyncmodule.cs
using System;
using System.Web;
using System.Threading;
using System.Text.RegularExpressions;

/// <summary>
/// Demonstrates an async module in ASP.NET
/// </summary>
public class AsyncModule : IHttpModule
{

    // static data members
    static int counter = 0;
    static int modCounter = 0;
    const string RedirectLocation = "accessdenied.aspx";

    // instance data members
    int instanceCounter;
    bool isAuthorized;
    HttpContext ctx;
    Regex locationRegex = new Regex(RedirectLocation,
        RegexOptions.IgnoreCase);

    public void Init(HttpApplication app)
    {
        // register for our async event
        app.AddOnAuthorizeRequestAsync(new BeginEventHandler(
            ref AsyncBeginHandler),
            new EndEventHandler(ref AsyncEndHandler));
```

```
        // add a sync EndRequest handler to explain what happened if
        // access is denied
        app.EndRequest += new EventHandler(ref OnEndRequest);

        int modCount = Interlocked.Increment(ref modCounter);
        TraceHelper.WriteLine("Initializing module instance", modCount);
    }

// Required on this interface
    public void Dispose()
    {
    }

    public IAsyncResult AsyncBeginHandler(object src, EventArgs e,
        AsyncCallback cb, object extraData)
    {
        HttpApplication app = (HttpApplication)src;

        // per-request init
        instanceCounter = Interlocked.Increment(ref counter);
        isAuthorized = false;
        ctx = app.Context;

        // let anyone into the access denied page
        Match m = locationRegex.Match(ctx.Request.FilePath);

        // is it something other than accessdenied.aspx?
        // Check authorization...
        if(!m.Success)
        {
            // create service proxy, async result, and callback
            AsyncAuthModule.localhost.Service1 authServ =
                new AsyncAuthModule.localhost.Service1();

            MyAsyncResult myAr = new MyAsyncResult(cb,
                authServ, instanceCounter);

            AsyncCallback myCb = new AsyncCallback(
                ref WebServiceAsyncCallback);

            // start async call
            TraceHelper.WriteLine("Begin Authorization", instanceCounter);
            authServ.BeginIsAuthorized(ctx.User.Identity.Name, myCb, myAr);
            return myAr;
        }
        else // otherwise, complete synchronously
        {
```

```
                isAuthorized = true;
                TraceHelper.WriteLine("Request for accessdenied page, " +
                    "skipping", instanceCounter);

                return new MyAsyncResult(null, null, true, true, null,
                    instanceCounter);
            }
        }


    public void AsyncEndHandler(IAsyncResult ar)
    {
        MyAsyncResult myAr = (MyAsyncResult)ar;
        TraceHelper.WriteLine("End Authorization", instanceCounter);

        // if this user isn't authorized, then bail out
        if(!isAuthorized)
        {
            ctx.Response.StatusCode = 403;
            ctx.ApplicationInstance.CompleteRequest();
            TraceHelper.WriteLine("Request Rejected", instanceCounter);
        }

        // clear variables
        ctx = null;
        instanceCounter = -1;
        isAuthorized = false;
        myAr.EndOp(); // Throw if necessary
    }

    public void WebServiceAsyncCallback(IAsyncResult ar)
    {
        MyAsyncResult myAr = (MyAsyncResult)ar.AsyncState;
        AsyncAuthModule.localhost.Service1 authServ =
            (AsyncAuthModule.localhost.Service1)myAr.AsyncState;

        // get back result
        isAuthorized = authServ.EndIsAuthorized(ar);
        TraceHelper.WriteLine("WebService call completed", instanceCounter);

        // tell ASP.NET we're done
        int cnt = instanceCounter;
        TraceHelper.WriteLine("Begin notify ASP.NET", cnt);
        myAr.Complete(false, isAuthorized, null);
        TraceHelper.WriteLine("End notify ASP.NET", cnt);
    }
```

```csharp
    public void OnEndRequest(object src, EventArgs E)
    {
        HttpApplication app = (HttpApplication)src;

        // did we block someone?
        if(app.Response.StatusCode == 403)
            app.Response.Redirect(RedirectLocation, false);
    }
}


// Contents of MyAsyncResult.cs
using System;
using System.Threading;
using System.Diagnostics;


/// <summary>
/// Implementation of IAsyncResult
/// </summary>

public class MyAsyncResult : IAsyncResult
{
    // data members
    AsyncCallback cb;
    object state;
    bool completed;
    bool completedSync;
    object result;
    Exception err;
    int counter;

    public MyAsyncResult(AsyncCallback callb, object st, int cnt)
    {
        this.cb = callb;
        this.state = st;
        this.counter = cnt;
    }

    // constructor with predefined results,
    // useful for errors that occur before async work is done
    public MyAsyncResult(AsyncCallback callb, object st, bool complete,
        object res, Exception e, int cnt)
    {
        this.cb = callb;
        this.state = st;
        this.completed = complete;
        this.counter = cnt;
```

```
        this.completedSync = this.completed;
        this.result = res;
        this.err = e;

        if(null!=cb)
            cb(this);

        if(this.completed)
            TraceHelper.WriteLine("MyAsyncResult completed sync", counter);
    }

    public object AsyncState
    {
        get
        {
            return state;
        }
    }

    public bool CompletedSynchronously
    {
        get
        {
            return completedSync;
        }
    }

    public WaitHandle AsyncWaitHandle
    {
        get
        {
            return null;
        }
    }

    public bool IsCompleted
    {
        get
        {
            return completed;
        }
    }

    // non IAsyncResult Stuff
    public Exception AsyncError
    {
        get
        {
```

```
            return err;
        }
    }

    public void Complete(bool sync, object res, Exception e)
    {
        TraceHelper.WriteLine("MyAsyncResult.Complete called", counter);
        completed = true;
        completedSync = sync;
        result = res;
        err = e;
        if(null != cb)
            cb(this);
    }

    public object EndOp()
    {
        if(err!=null)
            throw new Exception("AsyncOperation filed", err);

        return result;
    }
}
```

> **Note**   The next major release of the .NET Framework is expected to significantly simplify the model for dealing with asynchronous execution calls associated with a page and the related Web service call.

Load Balancing Back-End Web Service Calls

Let's begin by reviewing how network load balancers work. Network load balancers are used to balance the load of Web service calls between a Web server and a number of back-end machines. The load balancer represents a virtual address that Web service calls go to from the Web server to the back-end machines. The load balancer attempts to distribute the Web service calls based on a hash of the caller's IP address and the client wildcard port used to connect to the virtual address.

Now we'll look at problems with Web services that can occur in this environment. As we've said throughout this chapter, Web services in the .NET Framework use the *System.Net* HTTP implementation. To trim the significant overhead associated with creating a new connection, the HTTP stack keeps TCP connections to the server open for as long as possible through use of the

HTTP keepalive behavior. However, a problem can occur when you want the connections torn down in order to force the client to make requests over a different client port and enable load balancing to occur. But because *System.Net* doesn't want to close the connections, you might see a situation where the load between two servers behind a network load balancer is not balancing evenly. Two options can be helpful in this situation—both options involve closing the connections periodically so that the load balancer can balance the requests across the back-end machines:

■ **Close the connection from the client**   One option is to set *Http-WebRequest.KeepAlive* to false on every request or with enough frequency that load balancing can occur. This is the easiest solution, but it has a couple of drawbacks. The first drawback is that turning off keepalive can cause the authentication to fail when you are using a connection-oriented authentication scheme, such as NTLM, to authenticate to the back-end machines. The second drawback is that you have to write the logic to close the connection, rather than having it provided by the stack, if you only want the closing behavior to kick in every so often.

■ **Close the connection from the server**   A second option is to have a Web service on the back end that sets the connection close header on every request or at a predetermined interval. Like the previous option, this one requires you to implement your own logic for when to close the connection; however, there is no restriction against using NTLM because the request will never be closed in the middle of an NTLM handshake.

> **Note**   The next major release of the .NET Framework is expected to improve support for load balancing by allowing the *System.Net* HTTP stack to forcefully tear down the connections at specified intervals.

Avoiding Common Pitfalls

As with any technology, it is possible to make assumptions about how an API should work that are incorrect and potentially problematic. In this section, we'll present a list of the most common issues we've heard from developers using production Web services in the .NET Framework.

Consuming an External Web Service

Visual Studio .NET includes an Add Web Reference dialog box that makes it easy to consume a Web service from within a code project. In the dialog box, you simply type in the service URI, and the dialog box displays the contents of the Web service. You then click the Add Web Reference button, which causes Visual Studio .NET to build a client class that calls the service when you call its methods. In versions 1 and 1.1 of the .NET Framework, a feature known as "automatic proxy detection" is supported by Microsoft Internet Explorer, but not by *System.Net*. This feature is accessible through the Control Panel, Internet Options, Connections tab, LAN Settings button. If you are attempting to build a client that consumes a Web service that is external to your network, and the Automatically Detect Settings check box enabled, it is possible that you'll be able to see the service with Internet Explorer, but not be able to use Visual Studio .NET to build the client class that consumes the service. The fix for this situation is to clear the Automatically Detect Settings check box and specify your proxy settings directly. The next major release of the .NET Framework is likely to include support for automatic proxy detection.

Using Certificates from the Middle Tier

The .NET Framework supports the ability to call a Web service over the Secure Socket Layer (SSL) protocol. When SSL is used over an HTTP connection it is known as Secure HTTP or HTTPS. In some scenarios, it's desirable to send a client certificate as part of the handshake that occurs when an HTTPS session is established. In versions 1 and 1.1 of the Framework, this is done by installing a certificate in the My User account certificate store, then exporting the public key for that certificate, and then using the exported file when you construct an *X509Certificate* class, which is then set on the Web services client instance.

The problem with using this approach on the middle tier is that the My User account is associated with the current user, and there is no current user when running under a service such as ASP.NET. As a result, the certificate is not found when *System.Net* tries to use it at execution time. To improve this situation, an update is available for the version 1 platform at *http://support.microsoft.com/default.aspx?scid=kb;en-us;817854*. The update also will be included in Service Pack 3 for version 1 and Service Pack 1 for version 1.1. The fix for this issue enables *System.Net* to look in the Computer account, also known as the Machine store, in addition to the My User account. This way, if you want to use a client certificate to authenticate from the middle tier, you can install the certificate in the Machine store and *System.Net* will find it there at execution time.

Handling Network Failures

Occasionally, network failures occur in the middle of a Web service call. The cause of the failures can range from a faulty driver in a network device, to a power outage on the server, to someone simply tripping over a cable. The fact is, the network connection might fail. This problem presents Web service developers with a difficult situation. Because Web services use HTTP *POST*, the *System.Net* stack cannot simply retry the request—a client calling, say, the pizza ordering Web service might end up with two orders rather than one. This network failure problem will be solved over time as Web-service specifications for reliable messaging evolve and are implemented in the stack. Until that time, however, developers must continue to be aware of this issue and factor it into their application design. Here are some tips that can help:

- Because the network call can fail, client applications should always include Web service calls in a *try/catch* block so that failure cases are handled accordingly.

- When failures occur, client applications should be programmed to either retry the call or alert the user or system administrator of the failure. You should use caution when retrying the call to avoid the "two pizzas ordered instead of one" effect.

- Services might have retry logic built in so that duplicate detection logic is included on the server. This logic enables clients to retry in cases where a minor network glitch caused the failure as opposed to a catastrophic event such as a power outage.

Transferring Large Amounts of Data

Sending attachments or other large amounts of data within a single Web services call can have a negative effect on performance and network utilization. There are two primary reasons for this. The first reason for diminished performance is that a Web service encodes the message within a "SOAP envelope" that is included in the HTTP request or response, depending on whether the data is being sent or being received. This encoding can increase the data size, which is not desirable with an already large block of data. The second reason for suboptimal performance is that in version 1.1 of the Framework a Web services call is an all-or-nothing proposition. This means that, if a particular Web service method is designed to return a 10-MB file and it fails after sending 9 MB of the response, the application cannot simply request the remaining 1 MB. Contrast this to the HTTP *GET* verb that enables client applications to specify which portion of the response is desired.

There are a few options to consider when programming a Web services solution that needs to work with large amounts of data.

- Don't send or receive the data in a Web service, use a URI instead. If the data being sent or received is extremely large, it might be best to pass a URI within the Web services call and use a more suitable protocol for the file transfer, such as FTP or HTTP.

- You can use different forms of compression to reduce the content size and minimize the impact of large data elements. A SOAP extension enables you to compress various parts of the Web service message. The HTTP protocol also supports compression on downloads, so HTTP transport compression is an option if the large data is being downloaded.

- When designing the application, you should consider including caching logic that avoids costly calls whenever possible.

- Efforts are underway to better address this issue within the context of a Web service call. Check out *http://msdn.microsoft.com/Webservices* for more information on Direct Internet Message Encapsulation (DIME) and WS-Attachments.

Preparing for the Future

Web Services Enhancements for Microsoft .NET (WSE) releases provide a glimpse of where Microsoft is heading with Web services. WSE is an ideal way to become familiar with the evolving standards in Web services while getting solutions to some of the challenges present in Web services today.

Web services are moving from implementation that is bound to the HTTP protocol to Web services that are protocol-independent. Independence from the underlying network transport protocol will broaden the possible solutions that can be built using Web services. It will also enable programmers to move beyond HTTP-related challenges with Web services discussed in this chapter, such as the 100 Continue behavior. One of the best things you can do to help your applications evolve along with this trend toward protocol independence is to keep business logic in your service separate from transport protocol logic. For example, code that modifies HTTP headers or changes other properties described in this chapter should be separated from logic that could be applied to the message independent of the protocol being used.

Summary

In this chapter, we looked at how Web services in the .NET Framework interact with the network. We discussed the ways in which Web services bind to the HTTP protocol, and we outlined mechanisms available for extending the service and customizing the underlying protocol. Next, we went through network performance, scalability, and load balancing scenarios for Web services. Finally, we covered the most common network-related pitfalls that occur when developing Web services and recommended tips on how to best deal with them.

12

.NET Remoting

The Microsoft Windows .NET Framework offers an easy way to develop highly distributed network applications by using .NET remoting. With .NET remoting you can develop applications that seamlessly access classes on one or more computers across a network—without having to deal with the complexities of programming to the network layer itself.

This chapter will examine how .NET remoting relates to the network and how remoting and the network enable you to build applications that communicate across a network to access class types in other application domains on other computers. We will focus on how to set up remoting to communicate over a network by selecting an appropriate channel. We'll assume you are familiar with core concepts. For more comprehensive instruction in .NET remoting, we recommend *Microsoft .NET Remoting* by Scott McLean, James Naftel, and Kim Williams (Microsoft Press, 2002).

In this chapter, we'll describe application domains and how .NET remoting allows you to access class types across application domains between two processes. You'll learn that this technique requires first setting up a .NET remoting communication channel to form a link (or channel) between application domains and that setting up a communication channel requires using a built-in channel in the .NET Framework, such as the Hypertext Transfer Protocol (HTTP) channel. Developing a custom channel is also an option. We'll describe the built-in channels and their features and discuss their strengths and weaknesses. We'll also explain how to develop a custom channel that can communicate across a network. Understanding how to develop a channel will give you insight into how .NET remoting communicates between application domains. Further, developing a custom channel will help you build distributed applications that can run across almost any data transmission medium, such as a satellite link.

Application Domains

.NET remoting allows you to easily develop highly distributed applications in which an application running in one application domain can access the properties and methods of another class running in a different application domain. An application domain is an isolated operating environment where a .NET assembly can execute. You can think of an application domain as a process in a traditional operating system. The application domain provides isolation for your application and its operating system resources from other applications. However, an application domain is not a process at all, because a process in the .NET world potentially can have more than one application domain. In fact, every process has at least one application domain that is known as the default domain.

The .NET remoting infrastructure provides a mechanism that allows your application to seamlessly access class types across application domains. In Figure 12-1 you can see that one or more application domains can operate within a process. Process A has two application domains, X and Y. Figure 12-1 also shows you that class type 1 in application domain X is accessing class type 2 in application domain Z. .NET remoting provides the channel of communication needed for class type 1 to access class type 2.

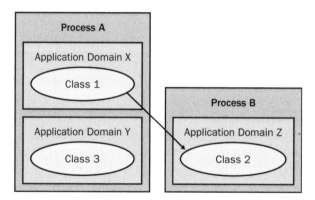

Figure 12-1   Application domain overview

The nice thing about application domains is that you can isolate the running of class types. If a class is running in another application domain in your application and crashes, it will not harm the rest of your application running in another application domain, such as the default domain.

A remote class type is a class library running in another application domain. The ability to communicate over a network to access remote class types in another application domain without having to deal with the semantics of the network layer is one of the greatest strengths of .NET remoting. When an application accesses properties and methods of a class in another application domain, the process is known as crossing application domain boundaries. Crossing application domain boundaries can be accomplished only by using .NET remoting channels.

Accessing Remote Class Types

To access a remote class type in another application domain, you have to make a class *remotable*. Making a class remotable requires telling the .NET remoting infrastructure to marshal the class type in order to access it across application domain boundaries. Marshaling is a process of packaging up a class in one application domain, sending it to another application domain, and unpackaging the class for use in the other application domain. The two styles of marshaling are *marshal by value* and *marshal by reference*.

Marshal by Value

Marshal by value occurs when a class type is copied from one application domain to another. When a calling application domain references a class in another application domain, the caller receives a copy of the class from the remoting infrastructure and the caller can access only the methods and properties of the copied class in the calling application domain. Marshal by value is useful when you need to pass a data structure, such as an array of strings, from one application domain to another.

To marshal a class by value requires adding the *Serializable* attribute to a class definition as shown in the following code:

C#

```
[Serializable]
public class MyData
{
    public int     Field1;
    public string  Field2
}
```

Visual Basic .NET

```
<Serializable()> _
Public Class MyData
    Public Field1 As Integer
    Public Field2 As String
End Class
```

When a class type is passed from one application domain to another, adding the *Serializable* attribute informs the .NET remoting infrastructure to package up and copy the class type to another application domain. For more information on how class types are serialized, see Chapter 4.

Marshal by Reference

Marshal by reference occurs when you remotely access the properties and methods of a class in another application domain. To marshal a class by reference requires that a class inherit the *MarshalByRefObject* class. The following code demonstrates a class named *DemoClass* that can be marshaled by reference across application domains.

C#

```
namespace Demo
{
    public class DemoClass : MarshalByRefObject
    {
        public int m_TheValue = 0;

        public void PrintMessage(string Message)
        {
            Console.WriteLine(Message);
        }
    }
}
```

Visual Basic .NET

```
Namespace Demo
    Public Class DemoClass : Inherits MarshalByRefObject
        Public m_TheValue As Integer = 0
        Public Sub PrintMessage(ByVal Message As String)
            Console.WriteLine(Message)
        End Sub
    End Class
End Namespace
```

Marshal by reference allows an application on computer A to invoke class methods and access class properties on computer B. For example, if there is an application on computer A that references *DemoClass* on computer B, then computer A can call *PrintMessage* and make the method run on computer B.

The .NET remoting architecture performs marshal by reference by setting up a transparent proxy in the calling application domain that handles making method calls and accessing properties. The proxy makes the remote class look as if it is available in the client's application domain when in reality it is running in another application domain. A proxy is established when an application instantiates the reference to the remote class. Once a proxy is established it will communicate with a peer by passing messages across a .NET remoting channel. We'll discuss remoting channels in more detail later in the chapter.

A major difference between marshal by value vs. marshal by reference is that marshal by value does not allow you to access remote properties and run remote methods. Instead, if you have a remote method (marshal by reference) that returns a class type, the class type must be marked with the *Serializable* attribute (marshal by value) so that the return type can be copied from a remote domain to your local domain.

Setting Up Remoting Communication

When your application is ready to access a class using marshal by reference and marshal by value across application domains, the remoting communication infrastructure must be prepared to handle the marshaling using the class *RemotingConfiguration*. The *RemotingConfiguration* class allows you to set up the communications for the remoting infrastructure programmatically or with configuration files. *RemotingConfiguration* also allows you to identify what class types are available for remoting. We'll first show how to set up remoting communications programmatically and then we'll show how to set up remoting communications using configuration files.

Programmatic Set Up

Remoting communications have two sides, which are the client side (message sender) and the server side (message receiver). For a client to cross application domain boundaries and access the remotable class, a server must be available to sponsor the remoting infrastructure and communications.

Server

On the server side, you'll need to select a remoting channel that will listen for communications from a client. The *ChannelServices* class allows you to select and register a channel programmatically by calling the *RegisterChannel* method. The *RegisterChannel* method accepts an instance of a remoting channel and registers the channel to the remoting infrastructure. Once a channel is registered, you'll need to register class types that can be accessed on the server. Registering class types on the server can be accomplished by calling either *RegisterActivatedServiceType* or *RegisterWellKnownServiceType*. Both methods make a class type available to a remoting client. *RegisterActivated-ServiceType* makes a class available as a simple class data type, while *Register-WellKnownServiceType* registers a class as a Uniform Resource Identifier (URI) where the client has to specify a URI to access the type.

When a server registers a class type using *RegisterWellKnownServiceType*, the class type becomes server-activated, which means that the server side of the channel publishes the remoted class and makes an instance available to a client. By comparison, when *RegisterActivatedServiceType* is used, the class type becomes client-activated, which means that the client has to tell the server when to instantiate the class. Remoted classes that are server-activated can run in either *singleton* or in *single-call* mode. In singleton mode, all client calls to the remoted class type are handled by one instance of that object. This means that all client calls share a single instance of the remoted class. In single-call mode, a new instance of the class is created every time a call from the client comes in. When a class is client-activated, a new instance of the remoted class is created each time a call from the client arrives.

The following code sample shows how to set up the .NET Framework Transmission Control Protocol (TCP) channel to listen for remoting communication on TCP port 5150. The code also shows how to register the *Demo.DemoClass* presented earlier as a client-activated service type.

C#

```
TcpChannel Channel = new TcpChannel(5150);
ChannelServices.RegisterChannel(Channel);

ActivatedServiceTypeEntry MyActivatedServiceTypeEntry =
    new ActivatedServiceTypeEntry(typeof(Demo.DemoClass));

RemotingConfiguration.RegisterActivatedServiceType(
    MyActivatedServiceTypeEntry);
```

Visual Basic .NET

```
Dim Channel As TcpChannel = New TcpChannel(5150)
ChannelServices.RegisterChannel(Channel)

Dim MyActivatedServiceTypeEntry As _
    ActivatedServiceTypeEntry = _
    New ActivatedServiceTypeEntry( _
    GetType(Demo.DemoClass))

RemotingConfiguration.RegisterActivatedServiceType( _
    MyActivatedServiceTypeEntry)
```

Once this code runs, the *TcpChannel* will begin listening for remoting requests to access the *DemoClass* type. This code can be run from almost any type of application; for example, you could develop a Windows application that will host the *TcpChannel*. Or you could develop a simple console-style application that runs this code and waits for the user to stop the console application. The choice is yours. As long as the server-side application is running, the *TcpChannel* will continue to process remote requests.

Client

Accessing a remote class from the client side requires that you identify a class type to the client side remoting infrastructure as being available as a remote type. Two methods allow you to inform the remoting infrastructure that a class type is available as a remote type. They are *RegisterActivatedClientType* and *RegisterWellKnownClientType*. The *RegisterActivatedClientType* method will identify a remote class by type, while *RegisterWellKnownClientType* will identify a remote class as a URI. As discussed earlier, remote types on a remote server can be identified as simple types or as a URI depending how they are registered.

Once a class type has been identified as a type or as a URI to the client remoting infrastructure, your client application can begin accessing the class across a remoting channel. When your client application creates an instance of a registered class using the new operator, the client remoting infrastructure will set up a transparent proxy on the client that will be used to access methods and properties of the remote class on the server. The following code sample shows how to register the *DemoClass* described earlier as a client-activated type that will connect to a server using *TcpChannel*.

C#

```
TcpChannel Channel = new TcpChannel();
ChannelServices.RegisterChannel(Channel);

ActivatedClientTypeEntry MyActivatedClientTypeEntry =
    new ActivatedClientTypeEntry(typeof(Demo.DemoClass),
    "tcp://MyServer:5150");

// Register DemoClass on the client end so that it
// can be activated on the server.
RemotingConfiguration.RegisterActivatedClientType(
    MyActivatedClientTypeEntry);

// Activate the DemoClass as a remote object
Demo.DemoClass TryDemo = new Demo.DemoClass();
```

Visual Basic .NET

```
Dim Channel As TcpChannel = New TcpChannel()
ChannelServices.RegisterChannel(Channel)
Dim MyActivatedClientTypeEntry As _
    ActivatedClientTypeEntry = _
    New ActivatedClientTypeEntry(GetType(DemoClass), _
    "tcp://MyServer:5150")
' Register DemoClass on the client end so that it
' can be activated on the server.
RemotingConfiguration.RegisterActivatedClientType( _
    MyActivatedClientTypeEntry)
' Activate the DemoClass as a remote object
Dim TryDemo As DemoClass = New DemoClass()
```

In this example, specific parameters such as remote channel port information and class type information are hard-coded for the remoting configuration. Hard-coded parameters do not make the application very flexible, especially if the application is designed to run in different operating environments. As an alternative, in this code we could have supported command-line parameters and set up the remoting communication. However, the *RemotingConfiguration* class offers a better way to configure the remoting infrastructure parameters by using configuration files.

Configuration File Setup

The most flexible way to set up communications in .NET remoting is by using XML configuration files on both the client and server to activate class types. A configuration file enables you to control every aspect of setting up remoting channels and object-activation activities without having to change your application directly. In this section we'll show how to set up a remoting channel that uses TCP to communicate over the network so a client can access the remotable class named *Demo.DemoClass* described earlier.

Setting up remoting communications on both the client side and server side requires calling the *RemotingConfiguration.Configure* method and passing an XML file that describes remoting settings for each side of a channel. An XML configuration file should have tags that describe specific remoting settings such as what classes you are remoting and what communications channel you plan to use. There are many tags—consult the .NET Framework software development kit (SDK) for a complete listing.

Client

Setting up a remoting client requires constructing a client-configuration XML file and passing the file name to *RemotingConfiguration.Configure*. The following code fragment demonstrates how to set up client remoting using an XML file named *client.config*.

C#

```
RemotingConfiguration.Configure("client.config");
```

Visual Basic .NET

```
RemotingConfiguration.Configure("client.config")
```

In the earlier discussion of programmatically configuring a remoting client, we configured the *Demo.DemoClass* to use the TCP remoting channel. The following XML script performs the same settings using an XML file.

```
<configuration>
  <system.runtime.remoting>
    <application name="DemoClient">

      <client url="tcp://localhost:5150">
        <activated type="Demo.DemoClass, Demo" />
      </client>

    </application>
  </system.runtime.remoting>
</configuration>
```

As this example shows, configuring settings such as channel information by means of XML configuration files allows you to make changes to your remoting application's behavior without changing any code.

Server

The server side is as easy to configure as the client side. In your application you also must invoke the *RemotingConfiguration.Configure* method and pass a server configuration XML file. Using the programmatic server configuration example described earlier, the following XML script shows how to register the demo class as an activated client type and use the TCP channel. The sample also tells the remoting server to listen for TCP communication on port 5150.

```
<configuration>
  <system.runtime.remoting>
    <application>
      <service>
        <activated type="Demo.DemoClass, demo"/>
        />
      </service>
      <channels>
```

```
          <channel
            ref="tcp"
            port="5150"
          />
        </channels>
      </application>
    </system.runtime.remoting>
</configuration>
```

In the configuration examples provided so far, we selected the TCP remoting channel to use across application domains. We also called out specific parameters such as port settings. The next section describes all the available remoting channels in the .NET Framework that are used to sponsor communications between application domains. As we describe each channel, we also will list its configuration properties.

In the downloadable book samples there is a sample named *Remoting-Example* that shows how to use marshal by reference and marshal by value as well as how to programmatically control remoting configurations.

Remoting Channels

Now that you have an understanding of how to set up and use .NET remoting, we'll discuss choosing an appropriate remoting channel for your applications needs. Two remoting channels are currently available in the .NET Framework—HTTP and TCP.

> **Note**   The next version of the .NET Framework is expected to include an interprocess communication (IPC) channel that will allow communication between application domains in different processes on the same computer in the most efficient manner possible.

HTTP Channel

The HTTP channel is designed to communicate over the HTTP protocol. The channel features both a client side and a server side to host HTTP-based remoting communication across application domains. The client side of the HTTP channel is also designed to work with Microsoft Internet Information Server (IIS). IIS can substitute for the server side of the HTTP channel. Using IIS as the server allows the HTTP channel to be more secure by using authentication and more scalable where IIS can more efficiently service thousands of HTTP requests per second. The HTTP channel provides two major features for hosting remoting communications—interoperability and security.

Interoperability

The HTTP channel by default uses SOAP serialization to encode class types for data transmission. Chapter 4 described SOAP serialization in more detail. The advantage of using SOAP is that the other end of communication can be practically any platform or device as long as it understands the SOAP format and understands how to respond to remoting messages accordingly. This makes communications portable. On the downside, however, SOAP requires more data bytes to be transmitted from the client and the server than other serialization formatters. If you do not want to use SOAP as the HTTP channel's default formatter, you can specify another formatter, such as binary serialization, using a remoting configuration file as described earlier.

Another major advantage of using the HTTP channel is that HTTP communications are usually allowed to pass across firewalls. As a result, you can build distributed applications that can run on both sides of a firewall without special protocol configurations. HTTP communication is sometimes by proxy, which means there is a server that makes HTTP requests on your behalf. Web browsers such as Microsoft Internet Explorer allow you to configure proxy settings that enable the browser to reach the Internet from an intranet environment. The HTTP channel also allows you to configure proxy settings through a remoting configuration file.

Security

An advantage of using the HTTP channel is that you can have IIS host the server side of the remoting communications channel. Using IIS to host remoting allows you to authenticate the user attempting to access a remoting class. IIS handles authentication security by allowing you to lock down the published URI that a client attempts to access. For example, we could expose a well-known object type URI of the *DemoClass* type described earlier and require that the client use Kerberos authentication to access the class. The authentication capability is only available when running IIS hosting. If you decide to provide direct HTTP channel hosting, then you will lose the authentication security functionality.

Properties

The HTTP channel features several channel properties that can control the behavior of both the HTTP server and the client side of the channel. Table 12-1 outlines the available properties that can be specifically configured on the client and the server.

Table 12-1   **HTTP Channel Properties**

Property	Availability	Description
allowAutoRedirect	Client	A Boolean value that determines whether the client will handle HTTP redirects.
bindTo	Server	A string representing an IP address for the server to bind to.
clientConnectionLimit	Client	An integer defining how many concurrent connections can be opened to the server.
connectionGroupName	Client	A string representing a group name if the *unsafeAuthenticatedConnectionSharing* property is set.
credentials	Client	An *ICredentials* instance that allows a client to pass credentials for password-based authentication schemes such as Kerberos authentication.
exclusiveAddressUse	Server	A Boolean value that forces the server to use the listening IP address and port exclusively so that another application cannot steal the listening TCP port.
listen	Server	A Boolean value that determines whether to allow activation to hook into the outside listener service.
machineName	Client and server	A string representing the machine name of the listening server.
name	Client and server	A string representing the name of the channel.
port	Server	An integer value that specifies what TCP port the server will listen on or what port the client will send TCP packets from. If the value 0 is selected, the infrastructure will choose a port automatically.
priority	Client and server	An integer value that defines the priority of the channel when multiple channels are available.
proxyName	Client	A string identifying a proxy if the client communication must pass through a proxy.
proxyPort	Client	An integer identifying the port on which a proxy is listening for communication from a client.

Table 12-1   **HTTP Channel Properties**   *(continued)*

Property	Availability	Description
suppressChannelData	Server	A Boolean value that prevents the server channel from returning channel properties.
timeout	Client	An integer that specifies how long the client channel will wait for a server response.
unsafeAuthenticatedConnectionSharing	Client	A Boolean value that indicates the client will supply credentials and a group name for the connection.
useAuthenticatedConnectionSharing	Client	A Boolean value that tells the server to reuse a connection from an authenticated user.
useIpAddress	Server	A Boolean value that forces the channel to use a specific IP address instead of using the *machineName* property.

In general, channel properties can be configured in an XML configuration file or they can be configured programmatically using a channel constructor when the channel is created. Values specified in a configuration file are represented as strings while values specified programmatically are configured with native data types.

For example, if you needed to configure proxy settings for an HTTP client channel to pass communications through a proxy server, you could do so by setting the *proxyName* and *proxyPort* parameters programmatically on the creation of the client side of the HTTP channel. You also could specify values in an XML client configuration file. The following XML configuration demonstrates how to configure proxy settings for the client side of an HTTP channel to remotely access the class *Demo.DemoClass*.

```
<configuration>
  <system.runtime.remoting>
    <application name="DemoClient">
      <client url="http://localhost:80">
        <activated type="Demo.DemoClass, Demo" />
      </client>
      <channels>
        <channel
          ref="http"
          proxyName="MyCorporateProxy"
          proxyPort="8080"
        />
```

```
      </channels>
    </application>
  </system.runtime.remoting>
</configuration>
```

TCP Channel

The TCP channel is a remoting channel that communicates directly over TCP. One of its advantages is that it handles remoting communications in the most efficient manner possible. On the downside, however, the channel does not offer security mechanisms to protect remoted resources.

By default, the TCP channel uses binary serialization to format messages to streams. In Chapter 4 you learned that the advantage of binary serialization is that the resulting serialized stream is compact, whereas the disadvantage is that a binary stream is not very portable. If the computers on both ends of a remoting channel have the same operating system, then using the TCP channel with binary serialization is the way to go. However, if your application needs to interoperate with a different type of computer, you can override the default binary formatter with the SOAP formatter.

A major disadvantage of the TCP channel is that it does not offer any security authentication solutions to protect the server from malicious clients; anyone can connect to the server and invoke remoted classes. This can be hazardous if you run a TCP channel server on the Internet and expose classes that can perform hazardous operations on your computer, such as adding or removing files.

> **Note**   The next version of the .NET Framework is expected to offer an authentication mechanism in the TCP channel. This should enable you to safely deploy TCP channel remoting solutions on the Internet.

Properties

The TCP channel features several channel properties that can control the behavior of both the server and the client side of the channel. Table 12-2 outlines the available properties that can be specifically configured on the client and the server.

Table 12-2   TCP Channel Properties

Property	Availability	Description
bindTo	Server	A string representing an IP address for the server to bind to.
exclusiveAddressUse	Server	A Boolean value that forces the server to use the listening IP address and port exclusively so that another application cannot steal the listening TCP port.
machineName	Client and server	A string representing the machine name of the listening server.
Name	Client and server	A string representing the name of the channel.
Port	Server	An integer value that specifies what TCP port the server will listen on or what port the client will send TCP packets from.
Priority	Client and server	An integer value that defines the priority of the channel when multiple channels are available. A larger value indicates greater priority.
rejectRemoteRequests	Server	A Boolean value that determines whether the server will only accept requests from the local host.
suppressChannelData	Server	A Boolean value that prevents the server channel from returning channel properties.
useIpAddress	Server	A Boolean value that forces the channel to use a specific IP address rather than the *machineName* property.

Developing a Custom Channel

The .NET Framework remoting architecture provides substantial extensibility that allows you to develop a custom channel. Developing a custom channel requires building a class that features both the sender side and the receiver side of a remoting channel. The work required for a custom channel is not trivial, but with a little perseverance the task is not too daunting.

Figure 12-2 shows a custom remoting channel. As with the built-in channels, a custom channel has two sides—client side and server side. The client side is responsible for sending out formatted (or serialized) messages when an application attempts to access a remoted class. The server side, on the other hand, is responsible for receiving the serialized client request that in turn will deserialize the message and access the remoted class. Once the remoted class has been accessed, a serialized response message is returned to the client indicating the status of accessing the remoted class. Chapter 4 examined the serialization process in greater detail.

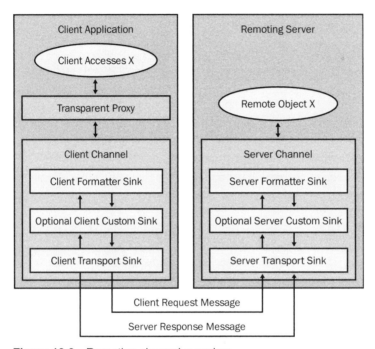

Figure 12-2   Remoting channel overview

The first step in developing a custom channel is to develop a class that implements the *IChannelSender* and *IChannelReceiver* interface classes. Inheriting these classes requires you to implement the abstract methods and properties of both interfaces and also the *IChannel* interface. Figure 12-3 outlines the methods and properties that must be implemented in the channel class. The *IChannelSender* interface represents the client (or sender) side of the channel, while *IChannelReceiver* represents the server (or receiver side). The basic idea is to have the channel class handle both sides of communication when .NET remoting communicates across application domains.

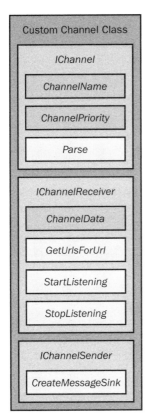

Figure 12-3   Abstract methods and properties required for implementing a custom channel

Channel Constructors

In addition to the abstract methods and properties that must be implemented, you also will need to provide several overloaded constructor methods that will respond to channel-creation activities. You should supply at least one constructor for handling client and server creation of the channel from a configuration file, as described earlier in this chapter. The following C# code demonstrates how to create multiple constructors for creating the server and client side of a User Datagram Protocol (UDP) custom channel.

```csharp
private int m_ChannelPriority = 1;
private string m_ChannelName = "udp";
private int m_ChannelPort = 5150; // default port

public UDPChannel()
{
```

```
        SetupClientSinkProviders(null);
    }


    // This constructor is used by a server application to
    // programmatically configure the server side of the
    // remoting channel.
    public UDPChannel(int Port) : this()
    {
        m_ChannelPort = Port;
        SetupServerSinkProviders(null);
    }


    // This constructor is used by the .NET remoting
    // infrastructure to configure the channel via a
    // configuration file.
    public UDPChannel(
        IDictionary Properties,
        IClientChannelSinkProvider ClientProviderChain,
        IServerChannelSinkProvider ServerProviderChain
        )
    {
        if (Properties != null)
        {
            foreach (DictionaryEntry entry in Properties)
            {
                switch ((string) entry.Key)
                {
                    case "name":
                        m_ChannelName =
                            (string) entry.Value;
                        break;

                    case "priority":
                        m_ChannelPriority =
                            Convert.ToInt32(entry.Value);
                        break;

                    case "port":
                        m_ChannelPort =
                            Convert.ToInt32(entry.Value);
                      break;
                }
            }
        }

        SetupClientSinkProviders(ClientProviderChain);
        SetupServerSinkProviders(ServerProviderChain);
    }
```

Since both sender and receiver functionality is handled in the main channel class, we recommend separating the client and server portions of the channel into two separate helper classes that work with channel sink providers. In the preceding constructors code, we demonstrated the idea of separating the client and server functionality by calling out *SetupClientSinkProviders* and *SetupServerSinkProviders* methods. These methods are responsible for setting up the channel sink providers needed on both sides of the channel to handle the sending and receiving of messages. Client and server channel sink providers are discussed in more detail later in this chapter.

Abstract Methods and Properties

As we discussed earlier, when a custom channel class inherits the *IChannelSender* and *IChannelReceiver* interface classes, the channel must provide implementation for the *IChannel*, *IChannelReceiver*, and *IChannelSender* abstract methods and properties, as shown in Figure 12-3. The following C# code demonstrates how to implement *IChannel* for a custom UDP channel.

```
public string ChannelName
{
    get
    {
        return m_ChannelName;
    }
}

public int ChannelPriority
{
    get
    {
        return m_ChannelPriority;
    }
}

public string Parse(string Url, out string ObjectUri)
{
    ObjectUri = null;
    string ChannelUri = null;

    try
    {
        System.Uri ParsedURI = new System.Uri(Url);

        ChannelUri = ParsedURI.Authority;
        ObjectUri = ParsedURI.AbsolutePath;
    }
```

```
catch(Exception)
{
    ObjectUri = null;
    ChannelUri = null;
}

return ChannelUri;
}
```

The *ChannelName* and *ChannelPriority* properties simply return the name and the priority for a channel. A channel name identifies the name of a channel to the remoting infrastructure and is useful when a client attempts to activate a remote class and specifies a channel URI using *ActivatedClientType-Entry*, as shown earlier. For example, a channel name for a UDP channel can be *udp*. The *ChannelPriority* helps the remoting system decide what channel to pick if a client and server have multiple channels registered on the client and server. The channel with the highest number will be picked first.

The *Parse* method is responsible for returning a channel URI and an object URI from an input URL. A channel URI is the authority component part of a URI that identifies the connection information for the server of the channel. The object URI identifies the path component part of a URI and identifies a remote class instance on the server. For example, given the URL *udp: //www.microsoft.com:5150/RemoteActivationService.rem*, the channel URI would be */www.microsoft.com:5150* and the object URI would be */RemoteActivation Service.rem*. See Chapter 5 to review URIs in more detail.

IChannelReceiver is the next interface that must be implemented. The *IChannelReceiver* interface is the starting point for running the server side of the channel and requires that you implement the *ChannelData* property and the *StartListening*, *StopListening* and *GetUrlsForUri* abstract methods. The goal of the interface is to start a listening server that handles requests from a client. When the server receives a request, the request is handed to the server provider's sink chain that is set up at the channel's initialization. Once the request is serviced by the remoting infrastructure on the server side, a response message can be generated and the server is responsible for sending the response message back to the client. The following C# code sample shows how to set up *IChannelReceiver* for a UDP custom channel.

```
private ChannelDataStore m_ChannelDataStore;
private Thread m_ServerThread = null;

public object ChannelData
{
    get
    {
```

```
            return m_ChannelDataStore;
    }
}


public void StartListening(object Data)
{
    m_ServerThread = new Thread(new
        ThreadStart(RunServer));
    m_ServerThread.IsBackground = true;
    m_ServerThread.Start();
}


public void StopListening(object Data)
{
    ServerChannel.StopServer();
    if (m_ServerThread != null)
    {
        m_ServerThread.Abort();
        m_ServerThread = null;
    }
}


public string[] GetUrlsForUri(string ObjectUri)
{
    string[] UrlArray = new string[1];

    if (!ObjectUri.StartsWith("/"))
        ObjectUri = "/" + ObjectUri;

    string MachineName = Dns.GetHostName();

    UrlArray[0] = m_ChannelName +
        "://" + MachineName + ":" +
        m_ChannelPort + ObjectUri;

    return UrlArray;
}
```

The *ChannelData* property is responsible for returning channel-specific data to the remoting infrastructure, such as the channel's URI. The *StartListening* and *StopListening* methods are responsible for starting and stopping the server channel from listening for client request messages. A server-side remoting application can freely start and stop the listening server by calling these methods. We'll describe how to implement a listening server later in this chapter. The *GetUrlsForUri* method takes a URI and returns an array of URLs that specifically represent the URI. See Chapter 5 for a review of how to derive URLs from a URI.

To complete the abstract methods and properties needed for a remoting channel, you'll have to implement the *IChannelSender* interface. *IChannelSender* only requires you to implement one method named *CreateMessageSink*. *CreateMessageSink* prepares the client side of the remoting infrastructure to communicate with the server side using a client provider sink chain set up during initialization of the client channel described earlier. The method should call *CreateSink* from the chain of client sink providers to set up communication to a remoting server for accessing a remote class. The method determines how to reach a listening server using either a passed-in URL or channel-specific connection information returned from the server side of the channel and passed in from *RemoteChannelData*. The following C# code describes how to develop *IChannelSender*.

```csharp
public IMessageSink CreateMessageSink(string Url,
    object RemoteChannelData, out string ObjectUri)
{
    // Set the out parameters
    ObjectUri = null;
    string ChannelUri = null;

    if (Url != null)
    {
        ChannelUri = Parse(Url, out ObjectUri);
    }
    else
    {
        if (RemoteChannelData != null)
        {
            IChannelDataStore DataStore =
                RemoteChannelData as IChannelDataStore;
            if (DataStore != null)
            {
                ChannelUri =
                    Parse(DataStore.ChannelUris[0],
                        out ObjectUri);

                if (ChannelUri != null)
                    Url = DataStore.ChannelUris[0];
            }
        }
    }

    if (ChannelUri != null)
    {
        if (Url == null)
            Url = ChannelUri;
```

```
      // Return the first sink of the newly formed
      // sink chain
      return (IMessageSink)
          m_ClientSinkProvidersChain.CreateSink(
              this, Url, RemoteChannelData);
   }
   return null;
}
```

In the preceding sections we presented an overview for the methods that are necessary to set up the server side of a remoting channel that receives communications from a client channel by starting a server application. We also discussed how to implement *CreateMessageSink*, which is used by the client side remoting infrastructure to establish communication to a remoting server to access a remote class. The methods described thus far depend on underlying methods that actually handle the client and server remoting communications. The next two sections describe how to implement the client and server sides of a custom channel.

Implementing the Client Channel

The role of the client channel is to set up a chain of channel sink providers that communicate with one another to handle the client-side communications of the remoting channel, as shown in Figure 12-2. On the client channel side, the .NET remoting infrastructure hands messages to a client channel sink chain that gets returned to the remoting infrastructure using *CreateMessageSink* described earlier. The first sink in the chain is a formatter that serializes messages into a request stream and passes the stream down to the chain of sink providers until the message reaches the end of the chain. At the end of the chain, a transport sink is responsible for transmitting the serialized request stream to the server side of the remoting channel. This is typically done over a network.

To set up a client chain of sink providers requires building your own transport sink provider that will end up at the end of a chain of client sink providers. We'll show how to set up a chain of sink providers later in this section; for now we'll build a client transport sink provider. Since our transport sink provider is at the end of the chain, it will handle the sending of remoting requests to the server and the receiving of responses from the server.

Creating a Client Sink Provider

Building your own client sink transport provider requires implementing the *IClientChannelSinkProvider* interface and applying the provider to the end of the chain of client sink providers for the remoting infrastructure. The following C# code demonstrates how to implement the client provider:

```
internal class ClientChannelSinkProvider :
    IClientChannelSinkProvider
{
    public IClientChannelSink CreateSink(IChannelSender channel,
        string url,
        object remoteChannelData)
    {
        return new ClientTransportSink(url);
    }

    public IClientChannelSinkProvider Next
    {
        get
        {
            // We are at the end of the sink chain in the client
            // so return null.
            return null;
        }
        set
        {
            throw new NotSupportedException();
        }
    }
}
```

As shown in the code, you must implement the *CreateSink* method and the *Next* property. The *Next* property is supposed to return the next provider in the sink chain, but since our client transport provider is at the end of the sink chain, it should return *null*. *CreateSink* is responsible for creating a channel sink that sends client requests and receives client responses. Recall from the earlier discussion that *CreateSink* gets called on each of the client channel sink providers in the chain when the client remoting infrastructure calls *CreateMessageSink*. *CreateMessageSink* sets up a connection to a remoting server to access a remote class. Therefore, in the code sample for the client transport sink provider, we create a new client transport sink that receives a URL that indicates where to access a remote class. The following C# code sample shows how to implement the client channel sink when *CreateSink* is called. To implement the sink requires inheriting the *IClientChannelSink* interface. Figure 12-4 shows the abstract methods and properties that must be implemented.

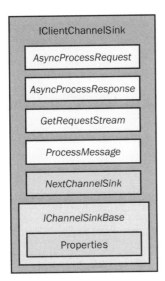

Figure 12-4   *IClientChannelSink* abstract methods and properties

The following C# code sample provides a code outline for how to develop a client transport sink for the client sink provider:

```
internal class MyClientTransportSink :
    IClientChannelSink
{
    internal MyClientTransportSink(string Url)
    {
        // This is a good place to set up communication
        // to the server by using the Url parameter to
        // determine where to connect.
    }
    public void AsyncProcessRequest(
        IClientChannelSinkStack SinkStack,
        IMessage Msg,
        ITransportHeaders RequestHeaders,
        System.IO.Stream RequestStream)
    {
        // Provide implementation to handle processing
        // requests asynchronously
    }

    public void AsyncProcessResponse(
        IClientResponseChannelSinkStack SinkStack,
        object State,
        ITransportHeaders Headers,
        System.IO.Stream Stream)
```

```
{
    // We are last in the chain - no need to
    // implement
    throw new NotSupportedException();
}

public System.IO.Stream GetRequestStream(
    IMessage Msg,
    ITransportHeaders Headers)
{
    // We don't do any serialization here.
    return null;
}

public void ProcessMessage(
    IMessage Msg,
    ITransportHeaders RequestHeaders,
    System.IO.Stream RequestStream,
    out ITransportHeaders ResponseHeaders,
    out System.IO.Stream ResponseStream)
{
    // Get the URI from the Msg parameter to send
    // to the server
    IMethodCallMessage MCM =
        (IMethodCallMessage) Msg;
    string Uri = MCM.Uri;

    // Send the Uri, RequestHeaders, and
    // RequestStream to the server

    byte [] RequestBuffer = null;

    PrepareOutboundMessage(Uri,
        RequestHeaders,
        RequestStream,
        out RequestBuffer);

    SendMessageToServer(RequestBuffer);

    // Wait for the server to respond with
    // ResponseHeaders and a ResponseStream to
    // return from this method.
    Byte [] ResponseBuffer = null;
    ReceiveResponseFromServer(out ResponseBuffer);

    PrepareInboundMessage(ResponseBuffer,
        out ResponseHeaders, out ResponseStream);
}
```

```
public IClientChannelSink NextChannelSink
{
    get
    {
        return null;
    }
}

public System.Collections.IDictionary Properties
{
    get
    {
        return null;
    }
}
}
```

The methods that need implementation are a constructor that accepts a URL, *AsyncProcessRequest*, and *ProcessMessage*. Since the sink is intended to be the last provider of the client sink provider chain, the rest of the methods and properties return *null* or raise exceptions,. The sink constructor is important because it lets you set up communication with the remoting server channel. For example, if you were creating a TCP channel, you could create a socket and make a connection to the server.

ProcessMessage is the core method that sends a client request message to the remoting server and awaits a response from the server. Sending a client request in *ProcessMessage* requires the following steps:

1. Package up the URI from the *Msg* parameter with the *RequestHeaders* and the *RequestStream* and send the information to the server. The URI identifies the remote class instance you are trying to access on the server.

2. Wait for the server to process the request information. Once the server has completed the request, it will respond with packaged *ResponseHeaders* and a *ResponseStream*.

3. Unpackage the *ResponseHeaders* and *ResponseStream* from the server and return the information up the sink chain.

The process of packaging up request headers and streams and unpackaging response headers and streams can be handled any way you like, depending on how your client sink communicates with the server. For example, if you are trying to send requests and receive responses over a socket, you'll want to bundle all the information as a stream of bytes and transmit the information over the socket. In the previous code example we called *PrepareOutboundMessage* to package up the request headers and the request stream. We called *Prepare-InboundMessage* to unpackage response headers and a response stream received from the server side of the channel. In our discussion to follow of the server transport channel, we'll reuse *PrepareOutboundMessage* and *Prepare-InboundMessage* to handle client requests and server responses on the server.

AsyncProcessRequest is an asynchronous version of *ProcessMessage*. The main difference is you do not return *ResponseHeaders* and *ResponseStreams* directly from the method call. Instead, you have to call *AsyncProcessResponse* from the sink stack when the server returns response headers.

You have now learned how to construct a client transport sink provider. This provider must be applied to the end of a client sink provider chain that is constructed during the client initialization of the channel.

Client Sink Provider Chain

Once you have established a client sink transport provider, you can set up a chain of client sink providers that will handle:

■   The client-side serialization for remoting calls

■   Data transmission for the serialized calls using the transport sink we just constructed

Setting up a chain of sink providers for the channel happens when a remoting channel is created. Earlier in the chapter we explained that remoting channels are created either programmatically or by using configuration files. Our channel constructor methods called either *SetupClientSinkProviders* or *SetupServerSinkProviders*, depending on whether the channel constructor was creating the client or server side of the channel. The following C# code shows how to implement *SetupClientSinkProviders* to set up a chain of sink providers for the client.

```
private IClientChannelSinkProvider
    m_ClientSinkProvidersChain = null;

internal void SetupClientSinkProviders(
    IClientChannelSinkProvider ClientProviderChain)
{
    if (ClientProviderChain == null)
    {
        // Install at least default formatter for
        // serialization
        m_ClientSinkProvidersChain =
            new BinaryClientFormatterSinkProvider();
    }
```

```
    else
    {
        // Get the provider chain from the outside
        m_ClientSinkProvidersChain =
            ClientProviderChain;
    }

    // Move to the end of the sink provider chain
    IClientChannelSinkProvider TempSinkProvider =
        m_ClientSinkProvidersChain;

    while (TempSinkProvider.Next != null)
        TempSinkProvider = TempSinkProvider.Next;

    // Append our new channel sink provider to the
    // end of the chain
    TempSinkProvider.Next = new
        MyClientChannelSinkProvider();
}
```

When setting up a chain of client sink providers, you are responsible for setting up a formatter sink that serializes messages from the remoting infrastructure and you must place a client transport sink provider at the end of the chain. The remoting infrastructure might hand you a formatter sink from a client configuration file. If you do not receive a formatter sink provider, you must provide a default formatter. In the preceding code sample we provided the binary serialization sink formatter from the .NET Framework.

You have now learned the basics for setting up a channel and implementing the client side of a custom channel. Next we'll look at how to implement the server side of a custom channel.

Implementing the Server Channel

Implementing the server side of a custom channel is the reverse of the client channel. On the server side, the server transport sink (the lowest sink in the chain) reads requests received from the client and passes the requests up the server sink chain as a stream. The server formatter sink (the sink at the top of the chain) will deserialize the request stream and hand the request up to the server remoting infrastructure. Once the server remoting infrastructure has processed the client request, a response is usually generated and sent down a chain of server sink providers where a server transport sink at the end of the chain is responsible for sending the response message back to the client. Therefore, on the server side you must implement a server transport sink provider.

Creating a Server Transport Sink Provider

To implement the server transport sink requires inheriting the *IServerChannel-Sink* interface. Figure 12-5 shows the abstract methods and properties that must be implemented.

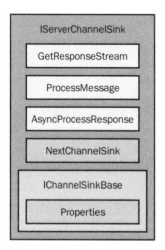

Figure 12-5 *IServerChannelSink* abstract methods and properties

The following C# code fragment provides a code outline for how to develop a server transport sink for the server sink provider described earlier.

```
internal class MyServerTransportSink : IServerChannelSink
{
    private IServerChannelSink m_Next;

    internal MyServerTransportSink(IServerChannelSink Next)
    {
        m_Next = Next;
    }

    public System.IO.Stream GetResponseStream(
        IServerResponseChannelSinkStack SinkStack,
        object State,
        IMessage Msg,
        ITransportHeaders Headers)
    {
        return null;
    }

    public ServerProcessing ProcessMessage(
        IServerChannelSinkStack SinkStack,
        IMessage RequestMsg,
```

```
        ITransportHeaders RequestHeaders,
        Stream RequestStream,
        out IMessage ResponseMsg,
        out ITransportHeaders ResponseHeaders,
        out Stream ResponseStream)
    {

        ResponseMsg = null;
        ResponseHeaders = null;
        ResponseStream = null;

        throw new NotSupportedException();
    }

    public void AsyncProcessResponse(
        IServerResponseChannelSinkStack SinkStack,
        object State,
        IMessage Msg,
        ITransportHeaders ResponseHeaders,
        Stream ResponseStream)
    {

        throw new NotSupportedException();
    }

    public IServerChannelSink NextChannelSink
    {
        get
        {
            return m_Next;
        }
    }

    public IDictionary Properties
    {
        get
        {
            return null;
        }
    }
}
}
```

Since a server transport sink provider is at the beginning of the receiving end of the server chain of sink providers, most of the methods and properties do not need implementation. The only method that needs implementation is *Next-ChannelSink*, which is responsible for returning the next server sink in the chain of sink providers. This method is needed when the server transport sink provider communicates up the chain of sink providers with client request messages.

At this point you might be wondering how the server provider transport sink handles servicing requests from the client channel. Recall the *IChannel-Receiver* abstract methods discussed during creation of the channel; at that time we mentioned that you have to implement *StartListening* and *StopListening*. In the *StartListening* method we asynchronously (using a thread) called a method named *RunServer* that handles the receiving of remoting requests from a client and returns responses back to the client after the server side has processed the request. The following C# code describes how to implement a listening server:

```csharp
public void RunServer()
{
    SetupCommunication();
    byte [] buffer = new byte[4096];

    for (;;)
    {
        // Let the server wait for a message to
        // arrive from a client
        ReceiveMessageFromClient(out buffer);

        ITransportHeaders RequestHeaders;
        Stream RequestStream;

        PrepareInboundMessage(buffer,
            out RequestHeaders, out RequestStream);


        // Setup a sink stack to pass to Process
        // message in the next sink

        ServerChannelSinkStack SinkStack =
            new ServerChannelSinkStack();

        SinkStack.Push(this, null);

        // Setup the response to hand back to
        // the client
        IMessage ResponseMessage;
        ITransportHeaders ResponseHeaders;
        Stream ResponseStream;

        // Call the upstream sinks process message
        ServerProcessing Processing =
            this.NextChannelSink.ProcessMessage(
                SinkStack,
                null,
                RequestHeaders,
```

```
                RequestStream,
                out ResponseMessage,
                out ResponseHeaders,
                out ResponseStream);

    // handle response
    switch (Processing)
    {
        case ServerProcessing.Complete:

            // Call completed synchronously send
            // the response immediately
            SinkStack.Pop(this);

            // Prepare response to send back to
            // client

            byte [] SendBuffer;

            Utility.PrepareOutboundMessage("",
                ResponseHeaders, ResponseStream,
                out SendBuffer);

            SendResponseToClient(SendBuffer);

            break;

        case ServerProcessing.OneWay:
            break;

        case ServerProcessing.Async:
            SinkStack.StoreAndDispatch(this, null);
            break;
    }
  }
}
```

The listening server is designed to wait for a client request to arrive. When it does, it will unpackage the *RequestHeaders* and *RequestStream* and send the information up a chain of server sink providers by calling *ProcessMessage* from the next sink provider on the chain. When *ProcessMessage* completes, the server has to determine if it needs to send back a response based on the return state of *ProcessMessage*. *ProcessMessage* can return one of three states: *Complete*, *Async*, and *OneWay*. If *ProcessMessage* returns *Complete*, a response must be sent back to the client. A response is not needed in the *OneWay* and *Async* state. Sending a response requires packaging up the *ResponseHeaders* and the *ResponseStream* and sending the response back to the client.

In the preceding sample, request headers and streams from the client were unpackaged using a custom *PrepareInboundMessage* method. Response headers and streams were packaged up to send to the client using a custom method called *PrepareOutboundMessage*. Earlier in the chapter, *PrepareOutboundMessage* was used to send requests from the client transport sink to the listening server and *PrepareInboundMessage* was used to receive responses from the listening server. These methods are designed to work together to prepare client requests and server responses for data transmission between the client and server side of the channel. It does not really matter how they are implemented as long as they are capable of packaging and unpackaging *ITransportHeaders* on a *Stream*.

Server Sink Provider Chain

Once you have established a server sink provider, you can set up a chain of server sink providers to handle:

- The receiving of request messages

- The server-side serialization of the remoting calls

A chain of server sink providers must be set up whenever the server channel is created directly by an application or is created by the remoting infrastructure from a configuration file. The following C# code shows how to set up sink providers for the server.

```
internal void SetupServerSinkProviders(
    IServerChannelSinkProvider InputSinkProvider)
{
    string MachineName = Dns.GetHostName();

    m_ChannelDataStore = new ChannelDataStore(null);
    m_ChannelDataStore.ChannelUris = new string[1];
    m_ChannelDataStore.ChannelUris[0] = m_ChannelName +
        "://" + MachineName + ":" +
        m_ChannelPort.ToString();

    IServerChannelSinkProvider
        ServerSinkProvidersChain;

    // Create a default sink provider if one was
    // not passed in
    if (InputSinkProvider == null)
    {
```

```
        ServerSinkProvidersChain = new
            BinaryServerFormatterSinkProvider();
    }
    else
    {
        ServerSinkProvidersChain = InputSinkProvider;
    }

    // Collect the rest of the channel data:
    IServerChannelSinkProvider provider =
        ServerSinkProvidersChain;
    while(provider != null)
    {
        provider.GetChannelData(m_ChannelDataStore);
        provider = provider.Next;
    }

    // Create a chain of sink providers

    IServerChannelSink next =
        ChannelServices.CreateServerChannelSinkChain(
            ServerSinkProvidersChain, this);

    // Put the transport sink at the receiving end
    // of the chain.
    m_transportSink = new UDPServerTransportSink(next);
}
```

When setting up a chain of server sink providers, you are responsible for setting up a formatter sink that deserializes messages sent from the client. The remoting infrastructure might hand you a formatter sink from a client configuration file. If you do not receive a formatter sink provider then you must provide a default formatter. Note that the formatter should match the formatter of the client sink; otherwise, deserialization of client messages will not work. Once the formatter sink provider is established, you'll need to place the server transport sink provider at the receiving end of the chain. After the server chain is established, the listening server can send request messages from the client up the server sink provider chain to access remote classes.

You now know the basics for developing your own custom remoting channel. In the downloadable samples that correspond to this chapter, a custom channel sample named *UDPChannel* is provided that uses the principles described here and will enable the .NET remoting infrastructure to communicate over UDP.

Summary

.NET remoting offers a relatively simple yet highly flexible way to develop distributed applications. This chapter introduced important remoting concepts that will help you select and use remoting channels. We also described the available remoting channels in the .NET Framework and reviewed their advantages and disadvantages, including security and interoperability, to help you select the best channel to use for remoting communications. We also showed how to develop your own custom remoting channel to allow you to make .NET remoting communicate over any data transmission medium.

13

.NET Framework Network Security

Security is critical in a networked world. When designing a networked application, developers must be constantly aware of security, because network programs can potentially expose data or users that interact through them. If the data or the users are compromised, then fewer people will use the application. The Microsoft .NET Framework and the underlying Common Language Runtime (CLR) were designed from the ground up with network security in mind.

In this chapter, we'll briefly describe security capabilities in the .NET Framework that can help you secure your networking application. We'll first present code access security that protects system resources from dangerous applications. After that, we'll present how you can tighten up security in a socket application, especially when it is connected to the Internet. Next, we'll look at the Hypertext Transfer Protocol (HTTP) and see how networking security can be improved in Web services and .NET remoting applications. Finally, we'll briefly describe other network security concepts, such as XML digital signatures, that can further protect your data when running network applications.

Code Access Security

Code access security (CAS) is a run-time security mechanism for managed code applications designed to help protect your computer resources using the .NET Framework. CAS is applied to applications based on the identity of running code instead of a user ID. For example, if a .NET application is downloaded from the Internet and executed from a Web browser, the .NET Framework can limit the application's ability to use operating system resources, including opening a file or using a network socket. CAS associates trust permissions to an assembly and enforces security when an assembly calls a protected resource.

Permissions

Table 13-1 outlines the available permission sets in the .NET Framework. Each permission set is a collection of multiple permissions for various resources on the computer. For example, the *Socket Access* permission set defines whether an application can use a socket to connect or accept a connection on a network. Permissions sets are managed and maintained by the .NET Framework's run-time security policy, which is defined in multiple security configuration XML files.

Table 13-1   .NET Framework Permissions

Permissions	Description
Directory Services	Grants assemblies access to directory service paths
DNS	Grants assemblies access to DNS queries
Environment	Grants assemblies access to event logs
Event Log	Grants assemblies access to environment variables
File IO	Grants assemblies access to files and directories
File Dialog	Grants assemblies access to file dialog boxes
Isolated Storage File	Grants assemblies access to file-based isolated storage where you can set disk quotas
Message Queue	Grants assemblies access to message queues
OLE DB	Grants assemblies access to OLE DB providers
Performance Counter	Grants assemblies access to performance counters
Printing	Grants assemblies access to printers
Reflection	Grants assemblies permission to discover information about other assemblies
Registry	Grants assemblies access to registry keys
Security	Grants assemblies specific security permissions
Service Controller	Grants assemblies access to control services
Socket Access	Grants assemblies access to sockets
SQL Client	Grants assemblies access to Microsoft SQL Servers
User Interface	Grants assemblies access to user-interface elements, such as windows, events, and the clipboard
Web Access	Grants assemblies access to specific Web sites

Most of the permissions have a limited number of actions they can do to enforce security on a resource. For example, the *Registry* permission set has one action, with which you list registry keys that assemblies can access. The *Security* permission set is larger. The following list outlines the many actions available for the *Security* permission set:

- Allow calls to unmanaged assemblies
- Allow domain policy control
- Allow evidence control
- Allow policy control
- Allow principle control
- Assert any permission that has been granted
- Create and control application domains
- Enable assembly execution
- Enable remoting configuration
- Enable serialization formatter
- Enable thread control
- Extend infrastructure
- Skip verification

As mentioned earlier, permissions are applied by the CLR based on a security policy when an assembly attempts to access a protected resource.

Policy Levels

The CLR references a security policy to determine what security permissions are applied to what assembly at run time. Security policy in the .NET Framework is managed by three configurable policy levels: *Enterprise, Machine,* and *User.* These three policy levels determine what permissions an assembly receives. *Enterprise* is the highest level, followed by *Machine* and then *User,* which is the lowest level. When security policy is evaluated by the CLR, the minimum permission allowed by all three levels is applied.

The highest policy level determines the most that all the other policies can do. Lower-level policies can only further restrict policies. For example, if your machine's *Enterprise* policy allows all assemblies running on the machine to use sockets freely, the *Machine* policy level can restrict the use of sockets by disallowing any assembly to accept socket connections. The *User* policy can further restrict socket use by disallowing any assembly to make connections from a socket.

The *User* policy level is special because it is unique to a user account that logs onto the machine, meaning there can be multiple *User* policies on a computer if multiple accounts log on to the computer. So security policy can vary for different *User* accounts on the same computer.

Security policy levels are managed in the following XML configuration files. *Enterprise* settings are managed in %SystemRoot%\Microsoft.NET\Framework\v1.1.4322\config\enterprisesec.config. *Machine* settings are managed in %SystemRoot%\Microsoft.NET\Framework\v1.1.4322\config\security.config. *User* settings are managed in %SystemDrive%\Documents and Settings\<user account name>\Application Data\Microsoft\CLR\Security Config\v1.1.4322\security.config.

A useful configuration tool named *Microsoft .NET Framework 1.1 Configuration* can be found in the Control Panel under Administrative Tools. This tool enables you to manage code access security permissions in the XML configuration files by presenting a graphical user interface that shows each policy level and allows the user to set up permissions by defining code groups.

Code Groups

Every security policy level configures specific security permissions by defining security code groups. Code groups enable you to associate specific security permissions with security conditions that an assembly must meet in order to run with permissions available in a code group. For example, you could define a code group named *MyCoolGroup* with a condition stipulating that any assembly downloaded and run from the Internet can only have the *File IO* permission to read certain files on the local computer. For every policy level, one or more code groups can be arranged in a hierarchy to define the level's security policy.

Conditions

When a code group is defined, it must specify a condition that an assembly must meet to use security permissions associated with the code group. Several condition types can be defined in a code group, as described in Table 13-2.

Table 13-2   Condition Types for Code Groups

Condition Type	Description
All Code	Identifies any assembly
Application Directory	Identifies the current directory of a running assembly and any child directory
Custom	Allows you to develop a custom method to identify assemblies
Hash	Identifies an assembly with a unique hash key
Publisher	Identifies an assembly using a certificate
Site	Identifies an assembly by the site portion of a URL
Strong Name	Identifies an assembly using a public security key
URL	Identifies an assembly by a URL
Zone	Identifies an assembly by a zone—Internet, Intranet, My Computer, Trusted, and Untrusted—where the assembly is running from

The .NET Framework 1.1 comes configured with Zone conditional access defined in code groups at the Machine policy level. The Enterprise and User policy levels allow full trust, so Zone conditional access is the default policy. Zone conditional access defines access for five security zones—Internet, Intranet and My Computer, Untrusted, and Trusted, as shown in Table 13-2. Each conditional zone identifies where an application comes from and what run-time restrictions are placed on the application.

Internet Zone

The Internet zone identifies applications that are downloaded and executed from the Internet. Applications downloaded from the Internet are generally considered unsafe to run on your computer. The .NET Framework places the highest level of restrictions on applications running in the Internet zone.

Intranet Zone

The Intranet zone is designed for running applications that are run from a local Intranet, such as a company's private networking infrastructure. For example, applications running in the Intranet zone are applications running from a company's private Web server or even applications running from mapped drives and UNC shares. Typically a company's private network runs behind a firewall and is protected from the Internet. Applications running in this zone generally have a higher level of trust as compared to applications running from the Internet and have fewer code access restrictions as compared to applications downloaded from the Internet.

My Computer Zone

The My Computer zone is designed for running applications originating from the local computer, such as an application running from your local hard drive on your computer. This does not include mapped drives or UNC shares, which are a part of the Intranet zone. Applications running in the My Computer zone are allowed access to all resources.

Untrusted Zone

The Untrusted zone identifies applications that come from the Microsoft Internet Explorer list of restricted Web sites. Internet Explorer allows a user to identify a list of restricted Web sites through the Internet Options menu Security tab. If an application is downloaded and matches one of these restricted Web sites, then it is considered unsafe and the application will not run on your computer.

Trusted Zone

The Trusted zone is a security zone controlled by the user. The user is responsible for identifying URLs that can run in this zone through the Internet Explorer list of trusted Web sites. This list can be found using the Internet Options menu and selecting the Security tab. Applications running in this zone can perform limited actions, such as open windows and create files.

Zone conditional security is a great way to protect resources from running assemblies. Table 13-2 outlines other conditional ways security permissions can be applied to running assemblies in the .NET Framework. Since the focus of this book is on networking, we will take a closer look at how CAS can be applied to sockets using Zone security.

Controlling Socket Applications

CAS can be applied to running socket applications. This is important because a socket application potentially can talk with any network application on the Internet. Fortunately, CAS allows you to control how applications use sockets and Domain Name System (DNS) on your computer.

Socket Permissions

As we have seen, the .NET Framework provides CAS for the *Socket* class. Running a server requires having the *Socket Access Accept* permission in order to create a listening socket that can receive connections from a network. Running a client application requires the *Socket Access Connect* permission to connect a remote socket. These permissions apply to all instances of the *Socket* class, including Transmission Control Protocol (TCP) and User Datagram Protocol (UDP). Having CAS on sockets helps prevent random applications from using network sockets.

In version 1.1 of the .NET Framework, both the *Socket Access Accept* and *Connect* permissions are granted only to applications run in the My Computer zone. Code executed from other zones will result in a *System.Security.SecurityException* being thrown.

DNS Permissions

Most socket applications require DNS service to resolve names to network addresses when setting up network communication. Since DNS is designed to communicate over a network, CAS permissions are also required to allow an application to query DNS. You can configure the .NET Framework to either allow or deny assemblies to query DNS using the *DNS* CAS permission.

DNS Spoofing

Using DNS to resolve host names in your application can be hazardous because names in DNS can be spoofed by an attacker. DNS spoofing is an attack on a DNS server where an attacker fools a DNS system into believing a domain name is something other than it really is. As a result, you should be aware that DNS spoofing can cause your application to connect to another host that you do not intend to connect to.

Securing Socket Data Communications

As we've seen so far, CAS provides good run-time security for controlling managed code running on your computer. But what about securing the data communications when network applications communicate with other applications over a network such as the Internet using a socket? Writing network applications using the *Socket* class can provide an application the greatest flexibility to communicate over a network. With flexibility, however, comes the potential for a socket application to be exposed to unintended network communications and a denial of communications. Fortunately, a socket application can defend itself with the following techniques:

■   Using socket options

■   Identifying connections and sessions

■   Handling idle connections

■   Handling data encryption

Using Socket Options

Beyond CAS mechanisms for socket communication, security in a socket application also can be improved using socket options. Listening server sockets should always use the *ExclusiveAddressUse* option to ensure no other socket can bind the same interface. Under certain circumstances, it is possible for socket applications to have several sockets bound to the same address and port on a machine. However, depending on the protocol, the effects of this can be undesirable. For TCP and UDP, if multiple sockets are bound to the same address, it is undetermined which socket will receive traffic. Normally, a *SocketException* occurs whenever an attempt is made to bind a socket to an interface and port already in use.

For all Windows operating systems prior to Windows Server 2003, sockets were shareable by default. This meant that if a second socket was created and the *SocketOptionName.ReuseAddress* was set via *SetSocketOption*, the socket could then be bound to an interface and port already in use by another socket. To prevent another socket from doing this, a new socket option—*SocketOptionName.ExclusiveAddressUse*—was introduced on Windows NT 4 SP4. It is also available on later versions, but not on Windows 9*x*. If a socket first sets this option before binding, no other sockets can reuse the same address and port after the socket is bound, regardless of whether the *ReuseAddress* option is set. The following code fragment demonstrates how to set the *ExclusiveAddressUse* option:

C#

```
Socket MySocket;
MySocket = new Socket(AddressFamily.InterNetwork, 0, 0);
try
{
    int          one = 1;
    MySocket.SetSocketOption(SocketOptionLevel.Socket,
        SocketOptionName.ExclusiveAddressUse, one);
}
catch(SocketException ex)
{
    Console.WriteLine("Set socket option failed: {0}",
        ex.Message);
}

IPEndPoint  bindEndPoint = new IPEndPoint(IPAddress.Any,
    5150);
MySocket.Bind(bindEndPoint);
```

Visual Basic .NET

```
Dim MySocket As Socket
MySocket = New Socket(AddressFamily.InterNetwork, 0, 0)
Try
    Dim one As Integer = 1
    MySocket.SetSocketOption(SocketOptionLevel.Socket, _
        SocketOptionName.ExclusiveAddressUse, one)
Catch ex As SocketException
    Console.WriteLine("Set socket option failed: {0}", _
        ex.Message)
End Try
Dim bindEndPoint As IPEndPoint = New IPEndPoint(IPAddress.Any, _
    5150)
MySocket.Bind(bindEndPoint)
```

On Windows Server 2003 and later, the default security model for sockets was changed so that sockets are not shareable. As a result of this change, the uses of the two socket options *ReuseAddress* and *ExclusiveAddressUse* have also changed somewhat. Now, when a socket wants to allow another socket to bind to the same address and port, the first socket must set the *ReuseAddress* option—which in effect sets the permission to allow others to steal the address and port. The second socket also must set the *ReuseAddress* option to bind to the same address and port.

The Winsock *IP_RECEIVE_BROADCAST* option is another useful socket option worth mentioning for securing UDP communications. This option is new to the Windows 2003 platform and can help reduce inbound traffic to your UDP socket by preventing UDP broadcast traffic from being received. This option is not defined in the .NET Framework *SocketOptionName* enumeration for the *SetSocketOption* method. To use this option, it is necessary to pass the actual Winsock value of 22 to the *SetSocketOption* method. This can be done by casting the value 22 to the *SocketOptionName* enumeration type. It is also necessary to pass the value 0 to the *OptionValue* parameter of *SetSocketOption*, which indicates the value is false and you do not want to receive broadcast UDP datagrams. The following code fragment demonstrates how to use the Winsock *IP_RECEIVE_BRODCAST* option:

C#

```
Socket mySock = new Socket(AddressFamily.InterNetwork,
    SocketType.Dgram, ProtocolType.Udp);
IPEndPoint  localEndpoint = new IPEndPoint(IPAddress.Any, 5150);

mySock.Bind(localEndpoint);

const int ReceiveBroadcast = 22;
mySock.SetSocketOption(SocketOptionLevel.IP,
    (SocketOptionName) ReceiveBroadcast, 0);
```

Visual Basic .NET

```
Dim mySock As Socket = New Socket(AddressFamily.InterNetwork, _
    SocketType.Dgram, ProtocolType.Udp)
Dim localEndpoint As IPEndPoint = New IPEndPoint(IPAddress.Any, 5150)

mySock.Bind(localEndpoint)

Const ReceiveBroadcast = 22
mySock.SetSocketOption(SocketOptionLevel.IP, CType( _
    ReceiveBroadcast, SocketOptionName), 0)
```

Identifying Connections and Sessions

When you use a socket connection over TCP, you can determine the connection peer by IP address and port. The *Socket* class maintains remote endpoint information that becomes populated with peer connection information after a socket has been successfully connected over TCP. The following code fragment demonstrates how you can determine that the connecting peer socket is connecting using the peer IPv4 address of 200.200.1.200:

C#

```
Socket MySocket = new Socket(
    AddressFamily.InterNetwork,
    SocketType.Stream,
    ProtocolType.IP);
IPEndPoint LocalEndPoint = new IPEndPoint(IPAddress.Any, 5150);

MySocket.Bind(LocalEndPoint);
MySocket.Listen(5);

Socket AcceptedSocket = MySocket.Accept();

IPEndPoint RetIP = (IPEndPoint) AcceptedSocket.RemoteEndPoint;
if (RetIP.Address.Equals(IPAddress.Parse("200.200.1.200")))
{
    Console.WriteLine(
        "We got a connection from IP address 200.200.1.200");
}
```

Visual Basic .NET

```
Dim MySocket As Socket
MySocket = New Socket( _
    AddressFamily.InterNetwork, _
    SocketType.Stream, _
    ProtocolType.IP)
Dim LocalEndPoint As IPEndPoint = New IPEndPoint(IPAddress.Any, 5150)

MySocket.Bind(LocalEndPoint)
MySocket.Listen(5)

Dim AcceptedSocket As Socket = MySocket.Accept()

Dim RetIP As IPEndPoint = CType(AcceptedSocket.RemoteEndPoint, _
    IPEndPoint)
If (RetIP.Address.Equals(IPAddress.Parse("200.200.1.200"))) Then
    Console.WriteLine( _
        "We got a connection from IP address 200.200.1.200")
End If
```

Conditional Accept in Winsock

In Winsock, a server application can conditionally accept connections on a listening socket. Conditional acceptance is enabled by using the Winsock *SO_CONDITIONAL_ACCEPT* option on the listening socket. The .NET Framework *Socket* class, however, does not expose this conditional acceptance of client connections. Typically, the TCP/IP stack automatically acknowledges an incoming TCP request before the application even makes a call to accept it. This behavior lets an attacker know that the destination machine is valid and is running a server to accept connections. By enabling conditional acceptance, an application can decide whether or not to acknowledge each incoming connection request. In Winsock, this is done by calling the *WSAAccept* function with a conditional callback.

There are several major drawbacks to using conditional acceptance. First, if an application is poorly architected and cannot keep up with the incoming connection requests, the client's connect request will time out (which is bad for other well-behaved clients). Secondly, enabling conditional acceptance disables the TCP/IP stack's SYN attack detection logic. By default, the TCP/IP stack looks for patterns indicating a denial of service attack and ignores connections from malicious source IPs. When an application enables conditional acceptance, the application has the burden of detecting attacks since it is in control of what connections are accepted or rejected.

Another useful technique for improving security on connected sockets is to place limits on how many connections are allowed to connect to a listening socket. When a socket connection arrives, your application can determine the connection peer by its IP address and simply close the socket if the peer is servicing too many connections. It is up to your application to decide how many connections are allowed.

On unconnected sockets such as UDP, your application cannot identify the communication peer until after it sends a datagram packet. Once a datagram is received, your application can decide whether to process the incoming datagram based on the communication peer IP endpoint information returned from a *ReceiveFrom* call. The following code fragment shows how to determine if a datagram has arrived from a communication peer with IPv4 address 200.200.1.50:

C#

```csharp
Socket ReceivingSocket = new Socket(
    AddressFamily.InterNetwork,
    SocketType.Dgram,
    ProtocolType.Udp);

IPEndPoint LocalEP = new IPEndPoint(IPAddress.Any, 5150);
ReceivingSocket.Bind(LocalEP);

IPEndPoint RemoteEP = new IPEndPoint(IPAddress.Any, 0);
SocketAddress RemoteAddress = new SocketAddress(
    AddressFamily.InterNetwork);
EndPoint RefRemoteEP = RemoteEP.Create(RemoteAddress);

byte [] buffer = new byte[2048];
int BytesReceived = ReceivingSocket.ReceiveFrom(buffer,
    ref RemoteEP);

IPEndPoint RetIP = (IPEndPoint) RemoteEP;

if (RetIP.Address.Equals(IPAddress.Parse("200.200.1.50")))
{
    Console.WriteLine("We got a packet from 200.200.1.50");
}
```

Visual Basic .NET

```vbnet
Dim ReceivingSocket As Socket = New Socket( _
    AddressFamily.InterNetwork, _
    SocketType.Dgram, _
    ProtocolType.Udp)
Dim LocalEP As IPEndPoint = New IPEndPoint(IPAddress.Any, 5150)
ReceivingSocket.Bind(LocalEP)

Dim RemoteEP As IPEndPoint = New IPEndPoint(IPAddress.Any, 0)
Dim RemoteAddress As SocketAddress = New SocketAddress( _
    AddressFamily.InterNetwork)
Dim RefRemoteEP As EndPoint = RemoteEP.Create(RemoteAddress)

Dim buffer(2048) As Byte
Dim BytesReceived As Integer = ReceivingSocket.ReceiveFrom(buffer, _
    RemoteEP)

Dim RetIP As IPEndPoint = CType(RemoteEP, IPEndPoint)

If (RetIP.Address.Equals(IPAddress.Parse("200.200.1.50"))) Then
    Console.WriteLine("We got a packet from 200.200.1.50")
End If
```

There is one caution to be aware of when identifying a communication peer by IP address in UDP. Because UDP is not connected, the communication peer application can spoof the source IP address and make it look like its communication is from another computer. Of course, if the communication peer application expects your application to send something back, it will have to supply a proper source IP address.

Handling Idle Connections

A server should guard against idle connections, which are often forms of attacks. Consider a request-response–based server that accepts client connections, waits for a request, and issues a response. If the client connects, but never sends the request, the server typically posts an asynchronous receive that will never complete. If enough malicious clients do this, valid clients can be prevented from connecting when the server runs out of resources. A defensive server should track how long each client is idle and close the connection if it exceeds a predefined limit.

Handling Data Encryption

So far, we have examined three ways to make running socket applications more secure on your computer. Another way to improve socket data communication security even more effectively is to encrypt the data that is transmitted over a socket at the application level.

Encrypting Application Data

Chapter 2 described the composable .NET Framework *CryptoStream*, used to encrypt and decrypt data over a stream and read or write encrypted data to a file. The *CryptoStream* can be used to send and receive data over a network using a *NetworkStream* that in turn requires TCP sockets to communicate over a network. Several data encryption schemes are available in the *CryptoStream*, such as Data Encryption Standard (DES) and RSA Security. See Table 2-3 in Chapter 2 for more details. Using the *CryptoStream* to secure communications only works over a TCP socket. There is no data encryption technique available at the application level for UDP. Instead, you can encrypt the data at the network layer using IPSec.

IPSec

Internet Protocol Security (IPSec) can be used to securely transmit data between two IP hosts by using data encryption at the network transport layer. IPSec can be transparently applied to any IP network communication without having to change your application. While IPSec can provide secure communication between two hosts, you should not consider it a complete replacement for application-level security. It is better to design your application securely and only encrypt the sensitive data at the application level.

HTTP Security

In .NET, network application communication happens not only with sockets over TCP and UDP, but also when communicating with HTTP. Chapter 10 showed that Web classes can be built around communicating over HTTP without worrying about the underlying network socket communication. And Chapter 11 demonstrated that Web services use HTTP to communicate with ASP.NET on a Web server. HTTP is a simple protocol that is request-response oriented. The client makes a request to the server to perform some action. The server receives the request and generates a response that is returned to the client. Following the response, the entity or content being requested is transmitted.

When clients attempt to request resources on an HTTP server, the server can optionally require a client to identify itself by using authentication mechanisms. The HTTP 1.1 specification defines optional challenge-response authentication mechanisms named Basic and Digest by which means a server can challenge a client request to provide authentication information when accessing resources. An HTTP server that supports the HTTP 1.1 specification must at least provide Basic and Digest authentication support. However, the server is free to implement additional authentication mechanisms such as Forms-based authentication. Microsoft Internet Information Server (IIS) is a Web server that offers secure communication through HTTP by providing authentication and authorization to Web resources.

Authentication Schemes in IIS

IIS version 6 features several forms of authentication to secure Web resources—Anonymous, Basic, Digest, Integrated, and Certificate. Working in conjunction with ASP.NET, IIS also provides Forms- and Passport-based authentication.

Anonymous

Anonymous authentication is not very secure because the client that is accessing a resource is not positively identified. Although Anonymous is not secure, it is needed for Web resources that are meant to be freely shared with clients, such as the launch page of a retail catalog Web site.

Basic

Basic authentication is a simple password-based authentication scheme supported by most Web browsers. When a Web resource is protected using basic authentication, IIS prompts users for a valid user account and password. The password information travels unencrypted over a network, however, which means that Basic authentication is not very secure even though it can identify a user. One way to make Basic more secure is to only use it over a Secure Sockets Layer (SSL) connection, which will be described later in this chapter.

Digest

Digest is another password-based authentication scheme similar to Basic authentication. User credentials are hashed and encrypted, however, typically using the MD5 message digest algorithm (see RFC 1321), when they are passed over the network during authentication, which makes the scheme more secure. The big advantage of Digest is that it can be easily deployed over the Internet to protect resources.

Integrated

Integrated authentication, also known as Windows authentication, is an authentication scheme that uses NTLM or Kerberos to authenticate users that are a part of a Windows domain. The nice thing about Integrated Windows authentication is that the authentication step is transparent to a client, such as a Web browser, because the user's domain logon credentials are used to perform authentication. Windows authentication operates well in an intranet scenario. It does not work well on the Internet, however, because Windows domains are normally managed at the business organizational level rather than across the Internet.

Certificates

Certificate authentication uses public and private key security technologies to identify clients. The .NET Framework supports the use of X.509 version 3 certificates, which are a mechanism for validating that the private and public keys used to access a resource are correct. Chapter 10 described certificates used with the *HttpWebRequest* class.

Forms

Forms authentication is a mechanism that causes a user logging on to a secure Web site to receive an encrypted cookie that is used to access secure resources at the Web site. When the user first attempts to access a secured resource, HTTP client-side redirection sends the user to a form for providing authentication credentials. If the credentials satisfy the secure Web site, the client receives a cookie that contains an authentication ticket. Typically, the redirected connection to the form runs over SSL to handle the authentication step. Once authenticated, the cookie is used to identify the client everytime a request is made to a secure resource. Forms-based authentication is only available in IIS from ASP.NET. Forms authentication allows you to develop a custom data store to manage credentials and authentication, which is usually handled by a Microsoft SQL Server database.

Passport

Passport authentication is similar to forms-based authentication where a client is redirected to an authentication server to receive a cookie containing an authentication ticket. The main difference is that the passport authentication service is centrally managed by Microsoft to authenticate HTTP clients. Passport is designed to standardize the authentication step by using one user account and password for all Web sites that support Passport authentication. The idea is to reduce a customer need to access Web sites with different logon credentials.

The .NET Framework Web class *HttpWebRequest* does not support forms-based authentication or Passport authentication, because the class does not handle the client-side redirection step needed to authenticate a client. For example, a request to a resource that is protected by forms-based authentication would be challenged by the server sending a redirect to a login page. This model works well for graphical clients such as a browser, but does not work well for clients that run as a service or contain no user interface. *HttpWebRequest* supports password-based authentication schemes, which are Basic, Digest, Integrated, and custom.

Choosing an Authentication Scheme

With so many authentication schemes available in IIS for HTTP communication, how do you decide which one to choose when designing an application? There are several factors to consider, such as browser type and accessibility of the authentication scheme. Table 13-3 provides a comparison overview for each scheme.

Table 13-3 Comparison of Authentication Schemes

Authentication Scheme	Advantages	Disadvantages
Basic	Used by most Web browsers. Far reach over the Internet.	Not a secure authentication scheme because passwords travel over a connection without encryption. Must use SSL to make authentication secure. Must maintain a user account database.
Digest	Used by Web browsers supporting HTTP 1.1. Passwords are encrypted over the wire. Far reach over the Internet.	Must maintain a user account database.
Integrated	User account management is handled by a Windows Domain.	Does not have far reach over the Internet and is useful only in intranet scenarios.
Certificate	Far reach over the Internet. Works with all Web browsers.	Clients must have X.509 certificates.
Forms	Far reach over the Internet. Works with all Web browsers. Easy to develop using ASP.NET.	Does not work with HTTP Web classes because it requires interaction with the user. Must use SSL to make authentication method secure. Must maintain a user account database.
Passport	Far reach over the Internet. Centralized single-user account to access Web sites supporting Passport. Works with all Web browsers.	Does not work with HTTP Web classes because Passport requires user interaction.

Choosing the correct authentication scheme really depends on the deployment scenario of your .NET application. For example, do you expect all your clients to use the same Web browser? Do you plan on deploying your application only in an intranet scenario where all your clients have a Windows account? Does you application work over the Internet? Knowing the answers to these questions will help you decide what authentication scheme is appropriate.

Preauthentication

Preauthentication is a method that allows an HTTP client to supply user credentials via an Authorization header so a Web server will not have to perform an authentication challenge using a *WWW-authenticate* header when a client application accesses a secure Web resource. The reason for it is to reduce the communications needed to set up and authenticate a client. Preauthentication is only supported by Basic and Digest authentication schemes. The *HttpWebRequest* class supports preauthentication by allowing a client application to supply authentication credentials.

Web Services

The ASP.NET Web service uses HTTP and HTTPS to communicate over a network. Once a client has been authenticated by IIS or by ASP.NET, the authenticated identity of the client is used by ASP.NET to authorize access to specific Web resources.

Authorization

In ASP.NET, authorization determines whether an authenticated client has been granted access to a given resource. ASP.NET handles authorization in two ways, which are URL authorization and File authorization.

URL Authorization   URL authorization determines which users have access to specific URL resources by defining access in the Web.config control file for ASP.NET. In the Web.config XML file, the <authorization> section allows you to allow or deny specific users or groups to a specific URL.

File Authorization   File authorization requires the use of Windows authentication to apply an access control list (ACL) on Web resources. ACLs on Web resources are supported only if the file system is formatted using NTFS. ASP.NET applications can use impersonation to control the security of Web file resources. In an ASP.NET application, the application can execute using client-authentication identification. For example, you can lock specific file resources for specific users or groups that have been authenticated by Windows authentication.

Web services offer good security control of Web resources using IIS when communicating over HTTP. .NET remoting also benefits from the authentication and authorization security mechanisms of IIS.

.NET Remoting

.NET remoting allows you to build highly distributed applications that can communicate securely over a network by using HTTP and IIS to host remoting. Using IIS to host remoting allows you to authenticate the user attempting to access a remoted class. It also allows you to securely transmit data over HTTPS (SSL). The HTTP channel offers most of the authentication schemes in IIS except for Forms or Passport authentication. The TCP channel for remoting currently does not offer the security mechanisms available in the HTTP channel. See Chapter 12 for more information on .NET remoting.

Secure Sockets Layer

SSL is a protocol that allows Web servers and Web clients to communicate securely by using data encryption for the HTTP communication. One of the great advantages of using SSL in the .NET Framework Web classes is that SSL support is nearly transparent. The only difference between a normal request and an SSL-encrypted request is that the URI scheme is *HTTPS* instead of *HTTP*. The SSL negotiation that occurs to establish the underlying connection, send the request, and retrieve the response is transparent and requires no intervention by the application.

XML Digital Signatures

XML digital signatures allow you to secure Web data by validating who sent the data and that the data is authentic. The *System.Security.Cryptography.Xml* namespace contains classes that support creation and validation of XML digital signatures. The *SignedXML* class enables you to create a signed XML document. Once an XML document is signed, it can be transmitted over a network and the receiver can validate that the XML is authentic by using security keys.

WS Security

Web Services Security (WS-Security) is an effort by Microsoft and IBM to help Web service developers secure SOAP messages by associating security tokens with the messages. Associating security tokens with SOAP messages provides message integrity, confidentiality, and authentication functionality in their transmission. The WS-Security architecture is designed with flexibility in mind enabling the application developer to associate any kind of security token with messages.

A Web Services Enhancements (WSE) download is available to help Web service developers take advantage of the latest WS-Security and other enhancements to Web services. The WSE download can be found at *www.microsoft.com/downloads*. Because WSE implements Web service standards that are still evolving, it might be inappropriate to use this download for projects that have a low tolerance for change.

Summary

Understanding security mechanisms in the .NET Framework can help you develop and run secure networking applications. In this chapter, we explored code access security, socket security, and HTTP security. Using the techniques described here will help you develop more secure and robust networking applications using the .NET Framework.

14

Network Performance and Scalability

The previous 13 chapters introduced a number of network classes, including streams, sockets, and Hypertext Transfer Protocol (HTTP). The complexities of these three fundamental classes can be overwhelming at first, and the prospect of writing scalable, high-performance applications might seem daunting. The good news is that it's less difficult than it seems. The secret to developing applications that offer high performance and scalability rests on understanding three things: the underlying protocol, the asynchronous I/O pattern, and resource management. In addition to these three basic considerations, the Microsoft .NET Framework Web classes require additional knowledge, since these classes hide many of the underlying operations.

First, let's define what we mean by high performance and scalability. High performance is the ability of an application to send and receive data in the most efficient way possible. Scalability is an application's ability to handle anywhere from one to thousands of connections or requests without significantly impacting client performance (such as starving a connection). As clients are added, the amount of required system resources follows a linear path. A scalable application should be able to handle an increasing number of connections or requests until system resources are exhausted—rather than failing at the point where the application design creates a bottleneck.

This chapter will cover several general principles for designing applications for performance and scalability, including how the underlying protocol affects performance, tips for using the asynchronous I/O pattern, and resource management. These principles apply to the .NET Framework *Socket* class and to the Web-related classes covered in Chapters 8, 9, and 10. We'll also cover issues specific to the Web classes, such as managing threads and connections, issues specific to the HTTP verbs *GET* and *POST*, and authentication, among other topics.

Underlying Protocols

A thorough understanding of the underlying transport protocol is necessary for writing a good network application. Many protocols were designed for the lowest common denominator—high-latency, low-bandwidth connections—perfect for connections over a 2400 baud modem or a satellite link. Unfortunately, this tends to cause problems on the fast Local Area Networks (LANs) of today, which is why it's important to have an understanding of the protocol's design. The most prevalent protocols in use are Transmission Control Protocol (TCP) and User Datagram Protocol (UDP).

Transmission Control Protocol (TCP)

TCP is the underlying transport for HTTP and is commonly used by socket-based applications. TCP offers several advantages such as being connection-based, reliable, and able to support flow control; however, it also has several possible disadvantages.

One of the most common mistakes using TCP occurs when applications serialize calls between sending and receiving. That is, an application will send data, wait for the send to complete, and then receive data. After data is received, another send is made. This practice is undesirable because TCP is a bidirectional protocol where the sending and receiving paths are independent of one another. Alternating between calls to send and calls to receive means an application cannot use bandwidth available for sending, as it is frequently blocked by a receive operation.

A good application should be receiving data at all times. This is because each side of a TCP connection advertises what is called a TCP *window* to the peer. The window is the number of bytes that the peer can send in such a way that the local side's receive buffers won't be overrun. If a peer is sending so much data that the receiving side can't keep up, the window size will go to 0, which tells the peer to stop sending data. If this occurs, your application will alternate between bursts of data and periods of no data being transmitted, which is an inefficient use of the network. An application should have separate send-and-receive operations so that it can receive data as fast as it can.

Another common problem with TCP is having many connections in the *TIME_WAIT* state. The TCP protocol defines several states for a connection, and when a connection is closed the peer receives indication of the closure. At this point, the side initiating the close waits for an acknowledgement of its close request by the peer. It then waits for the peer to send its own request to close the connection (since TCP is bidirectional, each side must close the connection), which must be acknowledged when it arrives. Whichever side initiates the close request goes into the *TIME_WAIT* state. The connection can remain in this state for minutes while it ensures that all outstanding data is properly acknowledged.

The *TIME_WAIT* state is important because the combination of a local IP address and port along with a remote IP address and port must be unique to successfully establish a connection. For example, if a client from 10.10.10.1:5000 makes a connection to a server address of 10.10.10.2:5150, then another connection from 10.10.10.1:5000 cannot be established because the identifier for the TCP connection would no longer be unique. This isn't a problem when the client connection is active; however, if the server actively initiates the close, the connection described by 10.10.10.1:5000,10.10.10.2:5150 goes into the *TIME_WAIT* state. The client receives notification that the connection was closed and can close its socket, but if the client attempts another connection to the server from the same address and port of the previous connection that is in *TIME_WAIT* on the server, it will be refused.

The solution to this problem is to have the client actively initiate the close so that the connection on the client side goes into *TIME_WAIT* state. This is less problematic since most client sockets do not bind to an explicit local port. By contrast, servers must bind to a well known port for clients to know how to reach them. In the example, the connection would succeed if the client actively initiated the close and then connected to the server from a different local port.

Implicit socket binding is another important issue many developers encounter with TCP. A server socket is always bound to a well-known port so that clients know how to reach it, but most clients either do not explicitly bind the socket before calling connect or they bind to the wildcard address and port zero. A client that does not call bind explicitly will have the socket bound implicitly to a local port in the range of 1024 to 5000 when a connection request is made.

A final issue that can be disadvantageous in TCP (and HTTP) applications is the Nagle algorithm. When data is sent on a connection, the Nagle algorithm causes network stack delays for a brief moment (up to 200 milliseconds) to see if the application will make another send call. It does this so that the data may be consolidated into a single TCP packet. If the stack were to send the data in its own TCP packet for every send by the application, the majority of the packets would contain a relatively small amount of data. This makes for a congested network as each TCP packet send adds 20 bytes for the IP header and 20 bytes for the TCP header.

Most applications never need to disable the Nagle algorithm, and doing so can degrade network performance, but there are certain classes of applications that do require data to be sent immediately. Applications that return user feedback sometimes need to disable Nagling to be responsive—extra delays in sending data that result in feedback to the user might be perceived as a hang. Applications that send small amounts of data infrequently also benefit from disabling Nagling as the network delay is unnecessary in these cases.

Using the *Socket* class, the Nagle algorithm is disabled by calling the *SetSocketOption* method with *SocketOptionLevel.Tcp* and *SocketOptionName.NoDelay*. For Web requests such as using the *WebRequest* or *HttpWebRequest* class, the *ServicePoint* object associated with a request exposes a Boolean property, *UseNagleAlgorithm*, which can be set to false.

User Datagram Protocol (UDP)

Unlike TCP, the UDP protocol is very basic with few or no restrictions on how to use it. UDP is connectionless, so there is no overhead associated with establishing a connection before data can be transmitted. UDP also makes no guarantee that data will be delivered, which greatly simplifies its design—just send and forget.

However, these freedoms can lead to problems. Because UDP is connectionless, a single UDP socket can be used to send datagrams to several endpoints, but each socket object within the networking stack possesses a lock that must be acquired to send data. No other send operations can be performed on the socket while the lock is held. Therefore, if data is being sent on a single socket to multiple destinations, the sends are serialized, which can degrade performance. A better solution is to use multiple UDP sockets to send datagrams to different endpoints.

UDP is also unreliable. If an application sends too many datagrams simultaneously, some datagrams can be dropped in the network stack before they are sent. The stack maintains a limited number of buffers to use for sending datagrams. Therefore, data can be dropped when the network stack runs out of buffer space. No error message is indicated to the sender when data loss occurs. This scenario typically happens when a *Socket* posts too many asynchronous *BeginSendTo* operations. If you use blocking *SendTo*, you'll rarely encounter this problem.

The Address Resolution Protocol (ARP) plays a part in UDP unreliability. When a UDP datagram is sent to a new destination that has not been sent to before, the network stack must determine whether the destination resides on the local network. The network stack must also determine whether the UDP packet must be sent to the default gateway, so that the packet is routed to its destination. The ARP protocol resolves the IP destination address into a physical Ethernet address. When the network stack determines that there is no ARP entry for a given IP destination, it makes an ARP request. As a result, the first UDP datagram is silently discarded while the ARP request is made. Developers should be aware of this behavior if their applications assume that the local network is quiet and the destination will receive all sent packets—applications should send the first packet twice or implement reliability on top of UDP.

Asynchronous I/O Pattern

Using the asynchronous I/O pattern whenever possible provides what is probably the single greatest performance boost. Asynchronous I/O is the only method that can efficiently manage hundreds or thousands of simultaneous operations on multiple resources. The only alternative is creating multiple threads and issuing blocking calls—but this solution doesn't scale well. Threads are an expensive resource and there is a cost associated with every context switch from one thread to another.

For example, consider a TCP server implemented using the *Socket* class. If the server is to handle 1000 client connections simultaneously, how will it do so? Many developers would create a thread to handle communication on each connection, but a process that spawns 1000 threads will quickly exhaust available resources and spend needless CPU cycles switching execution between the threads.

The more efficient method is to use the asynchronous I/O pattern, which typically utilizes the .NET Framework thread pool to handle requests. An application posts one or more asynchronous operations and specifies the delegate methods, which are invoked upon completion. These delegates are called from the thread pool maintained by the Framework. This thread pool is a constrained resource and it is important that it not spend too much time in the asynchronous completion routine. That is, the delegate should simply call the end routine for the initiated call (for example, calling *EndReceive* in response to the *BeginReceive*) and then return. If the application needs to perform any kind of processing upon completion, the completion routine should not compute in the completion routine—it should queue the operation to be handled by an application-spawned thread.

The following code sample illustrates this process. The *IoPacket* class is the context information associated with each asynchronous operation. In the sample, *IoPacket* contains the byte buffer that received the data, the TCP *Socket* object, and the number of bytes actually received into the buffer. The *HandleReceive* function is the asynchronous callback invoked when the receive completes. If the receive succeeded by receiving data, the *IoPacket* object is added to a list and an event is signaled. The *ReceiveThread* method is a spawned thread that waits for the event to be signaled and then walks the list of pending *IoPacket* objects and processes them. Note that access to the list is synchronized by using the *Monitor* class.

C#

```csharp
ArrayList           receiveList = new ArrayList();
ManualResetEvent    receiveEvent = new ManualResetEvent( false );

public class IoPacket
{
    public byte []  receiveBuffer = new byte [ 4096 ];
    public Socket   tcpSocket;
    public int      bytesRead;
    // Other state information
}

void HandleReceive( IAsyncResult ar )
{
    IoPacket    ioData = (IoPacket) ar.AsyncState;

    ioData.bytesRead = ioData.tcpSocket.EndReceive( ar );
    if ( ioData.bytesRead == 0 )
    {
        // Connection has closed
        ioData.tcpSocket.Close();
    }
    else
    {
        Monitor.Enter( receiveList );
        receiveList.Add( ioData );
        receiveEvent.Set();
        Monitor.Exit( receiveList );

        ioData = new IoPacket();
        // Post another BeginReceive with the new ioData object
    }
}

void ReceiveThread()
{
    IoPacket    ioData;
    bool        rc;
```

```
    while (true)
    {
        rc = receiveEvent.WaitOne();
        if ( rc == true )
        {
            receiveEvent.Reset();

            Monitor.Enter( receiveList );
            while ( receiveList.Count > 0 )
            {
                ioData = (IoPacket) receiveList[0];
                receiveList.RemoveAt( 0 );

                // Do something with data
            }
            Monitor.Exit( receiveList );
        }
    }
}
```

Visual Basic .NET

```
Dim receiveList As ArrayList = New ArrayList
Dim receiveEvent As ManualResetEvent = New ManualResetEvent(False)

Public Class IoPacket
    Public receiveBuffer(4096) As Byte
    Public tcpSocket As Socket
    Public bytesRead As Integer

    ' Other state information
End Class

Public Sub HandleReceive(ByVal ar As IAsyncResult)
    Dim ioData As IoPacket = ar.AsyncState

    ioData.bytesRead = ioData.tcpSocket.EndReceive(ar)
    If (ioData.bytesRead = 0) Then
        ' Connection has closed
        ioData.tcpSocket.Close()
    Else
        Monitor.Enter(receiveList)
        receiveList.Add(ioData)
        receiveEvent.Set()
        Monitor.Exit(receiveList)

        ioData = New IoPacket
```

```
            ' Post another BeginReceive with the new ioData object
        End If
End Sub

Public Sub ReceiveThread()
    Dim ioData As IoPacket
    Dim rc As Boolean

    While (True)
        rc = receiveEvent.WaitOne()
        If (rc = True) Then
            receiveEvent.Reset()
            Monitor.Enter(receiveList)
            While (receiveList.Count > 0)
                ioData = receiveList(0)
                receiveList.RemoveAt(0)

                ' Do something with data
            End While
            Monitor.Exit(receiveList)
        End If
    End While
End Sub
```

Consider an application that creates multiple connections to a server and receives data that must be written to local files. The application posts one or more asynchronous receive operations on each connection. When the completion routines fire, the application takes the receive buffer, which now contains data, and enqueues the data in some kind of array (such as an *ArrayList*). An event is then signaled to wake up an application thread to dequeue the buffer and then write the data to disk. The application avoids performing blocking operations in the asynchronous delegate. This prevents the Framework's thread pool from being blocked and it also disassociates the network operations from the disk operations, which allows data to be received at the fastest rate possible.

> **Note**   In versions 1.0 and 1.1 of the .NET Framework, the necessary code access security checks create considerable overhead in executing a callback function when an asynchronous method completes. This overhead results in significantly decreased performance when compared to native Winsock applications. Significant performance improvements for asynchronous callbacks are anticipated in the next major release of the .NET Framework.

Resource Management

When performing network operations, it is important to post multiple asynchronous receive operations to ensure that the application receives data as fast as possible. However, this practice can cause problems when the number of concurrent connections handled by a server increases. Additionally, as a server accepts more and more connections and performs send operations on each connection, the bandwidth of the local network also must be taken into consideration. For this reason, memory and bandwidth issues are important considerations when designing a scalable server. The following two sections will discuss these concepts in more detail.

Memory

Using the asynchronous I/O pattern is paramount for high performance, but rules still need to be followed to achieve scalability. For example, posting dozens rather than a few asynchronous receive operations on a *Socket* or *Stream* will not drastically increase performance, but it will increase the amount of memory used. The application can run out of resources, which will affect the number of connections an application can handle.

Consider a TCP *Socket*–based server application that maintains multiple connections and posts varying numbers of asynchronous receive operations. Each *BeginReceive* posted requires a buffer to receive the data, plus a small structure to maintain context information for the operation (including a reference to the receive buffer). If each receive operation uses a 16-KB receive buffer, plus a 200-byte context structure, then each *BeginReceive* uses 16,584 bytes. Table 14-1 calculates the memory requirements for various connection counts and operations per connection where each operation requires 16,584 bytes.

Table 14-1   Sample Memory Requirements for Asynchronous I/O

Total Connections	Operations Per Connection	Total Memory (Bytes)
10	10	1,658,400
1,000	10	165,840,000
50,000	10	8,292,000,000
10	2	331,680
1,000	2	33,168,000
50,000	2	1,658,400,000

Notice that the operations per connection field can be any combination of asynchronous send and receive operations—the basic idea is that each connection has the given number of operations outstanding. Posting 10 asynchronous operations for each connection limits a typical server to handling around 24,000 connections maximum—a typical server being defined as an architecture running a 32-bit operating system at the maximum memory configuration possible of 4 GB. If the application keeps the number of outstanding operations on each connection down to two, you'll notice a significant increase in the number of connections that can be handled.

OS Networking Limitations

The number of network connections the Microsoft Windows NT operating systems (Windows NT 4, Windows 2000, Windows XP, and Windows Server 2003) can establish is limited based on the memory resources available. The operating system reserves a portion of the total memory in what is known as non-paged memory. Non-paged memory contains information and data structures that are never paged out of memory. Usually, the system reserves one-quarter of the total memory for the non-paged pool, with a limit of 256 MB on Windows 2000 and later and 128 MB on Windows NT 4. These limits are for 32-bit versions of the operating system.

Operating system constructs, such as file handles, process information, networking connections, and so on, are examples of information that must always be resident in physical memory. Each TCP connection consumes approximately 2 KB of the non-paged memory. Because of this, a system with 256 MB of the non-paged pool can establish roughly 100,000 connections. Remember that a portion of the non-paged pool is being used by other system components, so networking cannot consume the entire amount. Also, the data buffers used to send and receive data must be locked into the non-paged pool while the network stack processes data.

Socket operations will start to fail if a server reaches a point where there is too little free memory. In this case, a *SocketException* is thrown where the *ErrorCode* property is the Winsock error code *WSAENOBUFS* (10055). The *Socket* should be closed when this occurs to free all associated resources and ensure other operations on different sockets don't also fail due to insufficient memory.

Lastly, a server should guard against idle connections, which are a form of attack. Consider a request-response–based server that accepts client connections, waits for a request, and issues a response. If a client connects but never sends the request, the server typically posts an asynchronous receive that never completes. If enough malicious clients do this, valid clients can be prevented from connecting as the server will run out of resources. A defensive server should keep track of how long each client is idle and close the connection if it exceeds a predefined limit.

Bandwidth

When performing network operations, the bandwidth of the network directly affects how well the application scales. For example, an FTP-like application that sends or receives large data in bulk is not going to scale well past a few hundred connections on a 10-MB network. When designing network-based applications, responsiveness is an important design goal. If the FTP server allowed 1,000 concurrent users, each connection would rate at 1,250 bytes/second. This isn't terrible unless the file being retrieved is several megabytes in size. Table 14-2 lists transfer rates for concurrent connections and local network bandwidths.

Table 14-2   Bandwidth Per Connection Statistics

Total Connections	Network Bandwidth (megabits)	Bytes/Second per Connection
100	10	12,500
1,000	10	1,250
50,000	10	25
100	100	125,000
1,000	100	12,500
50,000	100	250

The local bandwidth plays an important role in establishing limits on the number of concurrent asynchronous operations to allow per connection. For example, if a server is designed to handle 1,000 concurrent connections on a 100-MB network, each connection can send and receive at 12,500 bytes/second. Posting 10 asynchronous sends of 8 KB each is a waste of resources as there always will be eight operations waiting on the network to send the data. An efficient design limits two asynchronous sends per connection.

If a network becomes overly congested, packets will be lost or dropped and the TCP protocol will be forced to retransmit packets. This causes more congestion, and it's likely that TCP will timeout when the recipient fails to acknowledge it received the data, which causes the network stack to abort the connection. When this connection is dropped, any pending socket operation or a subsequently issued socket method will fail with a *SocketException*. The *ErrorCode* value will be the Winsock error *WSAECONNABORTED* (10053). If a server experiences an excessive number of aborted connections, it should disallow additional connections until the number of currently established clients drops below a threshold. Another option is for it to close valid connections to lower network congestion. If no action is taken, it's probable that other accepted connections will be aborted leading to many failed clients—many more than if the server preemptively closes a number of connections to bring the network congestion down so that the remaining clients can be successfully serviced.

If an application efficiently handles sending data, it also must efficiently handle receiving data. As we mentioned earlier, if an application does not receive data fast enough, the TCP window size shrinks, which throttles the sender from sending additional data until the receiver catches up. The rule of thumb for receiving is to ensure at least one asynchronous receive is posted at all times. To do this, an application should have three or four receive operations posted at any given time. This allows the application to process one operation while several are still outstanding and the network stack can fill those buffers as data arrives. Again, it is important that the receive callback does not take too long to process. Of course, this rule applies only to applications that receive data at a high rate. A single asynchronous receive is sufficient for applications that receive small chunks of data infrequently.

Optimizing Web Classes

The previous topics in this chapter apply when using the Web classes, but since the Web classes implement a higher level protocol, as well as offer more functionality such as authentication, there are additional considerations. In this section, we'll cover threading with the Web classes, connection management, performance considerations using the *GET* and *POST* verbs, asynchronous I/O, and authentication.

Managing Threads and Connections

Using the asynchronous I/O pattern offers the most bang for the buck in terms of increasing performance with the Web classes. However, it is important to understand how asynchronous calls are made as the process can influence application design. When an asynchronous call completes, a thread from the thread pool that runs the delegate associated with the operation is consumed. The thread pool is a limited resource that can be exhausted if you're not careful.

Recall from Chapter 10 that the *ServicePointManager* enforces a limit of two concurrent connections per application domain per host. This can cause a few problems. First, in the case of ASP.NET, the server can be underutilized as the front-end requests are bottlenecked on the two threads limit. Second, the application may become deadlocked because the ASP.NET worker threads are waiting for requests to complete, except those requests require additional threads for additional operations so they can complete.

> **Note**   In version 1.0 and 1.1 of the .NET Framework, blocking Web calls are implemented using asynchronous calls. The blocking call issues an asynchronous request and then waits until it completes, which means even blocking calls use the thread pool resource. In the next major release of the .NET Framework, blocking HTTP calls will be true blocking calls.

A couple of solutions prevent a deadlock situation. The first solution is to move the methods being called from ASP.NET into a local dynamic link library (DLL) so that they can be invoked directly. The second solution is to use the *ServicePointManager* to increase the number of allowed concurrent connections. The global defaults can be modified by changing the *DefaultNonPersistentConnectionLimit* and *DefaultPersistentConnectionLimit* properties on the *ServicePointManager* class. Or, if an application needs to change the connection limits for a specific destination, the *ServicePoint.ConnectionLimit* can be changed. Increasing the connection limit to 10 or 12 is usually sufficient for ASP.NET and other middle-tier scenarios. The following code sample creates a request and sets the connection limit to the given destination:

C#

```
HttpWebRequest request =
    HttpWebRequest)WebRequest.Create("http://www.foo.com");

request.ServicePoint.ConnectionLimit = 12;
request.BeginGetResponse(new AsyncCallback(ResponseCallback), request);
```

Visual Basic .NET

```
Dim request As HttpWebRequest = WebRequest.Create("http://www.foo.com")

request.ServicePoint.ConnectionLimit = 12
request.BeginGetResponse(AddressOf ResponseCallback, request)
```

The connection limit plays a significant role in HTTP performance, as shown in Table 14-3. The table lists performance results for different values of the *ServicePoint.ConnectionLimit* property when making Web *GET* requests. In addition to the connection limit, HTTP pipelining and the Nagle algorithm play roles in performance. The numbers in Table 14-3 were measured on a 2.4-GHz Pentium 4 client running Windows XP Service Pack 1 with 512-MB memory retrieving a 1-KB file. The server was a quad processor 1.4-GHz AMD 64 server with 2-GB memory running Windows Server 2003 Service Pack 1. Both computers were on an isolated 100-MB network.

The sample application used to measure these results is entitled fastget and is located in the downloadable samples under Chap14\fastget.

Table 14-3   Web Class Performance

Connection Limit	Pipelining	Nagle	Requests per Second	MB/Second
2	No	No	2277.697	2.332
10	No	No	2760.601	2.826
20	No	No	2822.945	2.890
10	Yes	No	3906.25	4.000
20	Yes	No	3881.988	3.975
10	No	Yes	2712.674	2.777
20	No	Yes	2741.288	2.807
10	Yes	Yes	3633.721	3.720
20	Yes	Yes	3633.721	3.720

The performance numbers clearly show that increasing the connection limit to 10 offers a significant performance increase of approximately 20 percent. The results also show that increasing the connection limit beyond 10 does not offer an additional increase. This is likely due to the fact that at 10 concurrent connections a single processor client's CPU is maxed out and additional concurrent connections are bottlenecked by the CPU.

Another significant performance increase occurs when pipelining is enabled on the client. As we've mentioned, pipelining a request results in one TCP connection being used to issue multiple requests.

> **Note**   Significantly poorer performance results when pipelining is enabled in Internet Information Services (IIS) 6 released with Windows Server 2003. This is a known problem that should be fixed in Service Pack 1.

Table 14-3 also shows numbers for when the Nagle algorithm is disabled. Notice that no significant performance increase is seen with Nagle disabled. This is because an HTTP *GET* request involves a single request being sent to the server followed by receiving the response and the data. The Nagle algorithm only affects data being sent. Disabling the Nagle algorithm will have a larger influence on HTTP *POST* requests. It also makes a difference whenever authentication is involved as authentication requires many more roundtrip request-responses.

Managing HTTP Verbs

Developers should be aware that the HTTP verb used can impact performance. When performing a *POST* operation, the server often responds with a 100 Continue after the request has been accepted. This response is typically sent to prevent the client from sending the entire request when the server rejects it. The 100 Continue logic saves network bandwidth and unneeded processing on the client side when a request is rejected; however, it can cause a bottleneck as an extra roundtrip is required to complete the *POST* request.

An application can explicitly override the 100 Continue behavior by using the *ServicePointManager.Expect100Continue* property. By default, when a *POST* is issued, the Framework waits 350 microseconds before the body is transmitted unless the server responds with a 100 Continue. This timeout is in place in the event that the server simply expects the client to transmit the body.

With the default behavior of waiting for a 100 Continue response, a *POST* operation incurs two roundtrips plus a possible 350-microsecond delay before the request can complete. Setting the *Expect100Continue* to false would cause the body to be transmitted immediately, bypassing the 350-microsecond delay.

The *GET* verb can also suffer from a performance roadblock: the Nagle algorithm. A roadblock is especially likely if authentication is involved. When an application posts multiple *GET* requests to a server, the Nagle algorithm introduces up to a 200-microsecond delay before sending the requests. As we mentioned earlier, Nagling reduces network load by lumping more data into a single packet; this behavior can introduce significant delays, however, since HTTP *GET* requests tend to be smaller than the Nagle threshold and therefore incur a delay.

Authentication

Authenticating a request is a powerful and often necessary task. Of course, this process adds extra overhead to the HTTP request that can significantly affect overall performance. The .NET Framework Web classes support several authentication methods, including basic, digest, NTLM, and Kerberos. Each method incurs its own overhead for authenticating a request depending on the efficiency of the underlying protocol. Table 14-4 compares the performance of different authentication types.

Table 14-4   HTTP Authentication Performance

Authentication Type	Preauthentication	Unsafe Connection Sharing	Requests per Second	CPU Usage
None	No	No	1,322	89
Basic	No	No	1,312	90
Basic	Yes	No	962	91
Digest	No	No	219	63
Digest	Yes	No	511	60
Kerberos	No	No	1,298	59
NTLM	No	No	95	66
NTLM	No	Yes	1,261	100

The table shows the number of requests per second when using a given authentication type to retrieve a 1-KB file along with the default connection limit of two. The CPU usage on the client is also listed. Notice how enabling preauthentication increases performance for those authentication types that support it (Basic and Digest). Also notice that enabling the *HttpWebRequest.UnsafeAuthenticatedConnectionSharing* increases NTLM performance.

As we mentioned in Chapter 10, NTLM authentication occurs on every request as the default behavior. This can lead to server performance penalties, as illustrated by the rate of 95 connections per second shown in Table 14-4. The reason for this performance degradation is in the middle-tier scenario, where a client is making a request to a back-end server while impersonating another user. If *UnsafeAuthenticatedConnectionSharing* is used carelessly, then the first connection can be established using the Administrators privileges. If the client later impersonates a regular user, subsequent requests are made with Administrator rights. A way to guard against this risk when unsafe connection sharing is enabled is to use the *ConnectionGroupName* property to associate all requests from one user together, as shown in the following code sample:

C#

```
HttpWebRequest request;
NetworkCredential userJoe, userMike;

request = (HttpWebRequest)WebRequest.Create("http://foo.com");
userJoe = new NetworkCredential( "Joe", "JoePassWord!" );
userMike = new NetworkCredential( "Mike", "MikePassWord!" );

request.Credentials  = userJoe;
request.ConnectionGroupName = userJoe.UserName;
request.UnsafeAuthenticatedConnectionSharing = true;
// Make request for Joe

request = (HttpWebRequest) WebRequest.Create("http://foo.com");
request.Credentials = userMike;
request.ConnectionGroupName = userMike.UserName;
request.UnsafeAuthenticatedConnectionSharing = true;
// Make request for Mike
```

Visual Basic .NET

```
Dim request As HttpWebRequest
Dim userJoe As NetworkCredential
Dim userMike As NetworkCredential

request = WebRequest.Create("http://foo.com")
userJoe = New NetworkCredential("Joe", "JoePassWord!")
userMike = New NetworkCredential("Mike", "MikePassWord!")
```

```
request.Credentials = userJoe
request.ConnectionGroupName = userJoe.UserName
request.UnsafeAuthenticatedConnectionSharing = True
' Make request for Joe

request = WebRequest.Create("http://foo.com")
request.Credentials = userMike
request.ConnectionGroupName = userMike.UserName
request.UnsafeAuthenticatedConnectionSharing = True
' Make request for Mike
```

The sample uses two user credentials for Joe and Mike. Joe's credentials should not be used when making Mike's request, so *ConnectionGroupName* is set to the user's name for each request. This prevents Mike's request from executing under Joe's user credentials.

A final note about NTLM authentication is that an extra TCP connection is used each time the client authenticates the supplied user credentials. With the default security (i.e., unsafe authentication disabled), the extra connection can exhaust the local port space causing subsequent HTTP requests to fail with a protocol error. Recall that when a socket is created and bound to port zero, it is actually randomly bound to a local port between 1024 and 5000. Each time a request is made with credentials, an extra TCP connection is created to the server that is bound to a port in this range. Once the credentials are verified, the connection is closed, but it goes into a *TIME_WAIT* state.

Summary

There are only a few basic principles to follow when designing high-performance applications, including resource management and using asynchronous I/O whenever possible. Also, understanding the underlying protocol reveals several possibilities for improving performance depending on the behavior of the application. These principles can be applied to any of the networking-related classes in the .NET Framework, including the *Socket* class and the Web classes. Additionally, understanding how the Web-related classes are built offers insight on how to maximize performance. Following these simple guidelines is straightforward and will result in better performance and more scalable applications.

15

Advancements in .NET Framework Networking

This chapter will talk about emerging trends in the world of distributed application development and related enhancements in the Microsoft .NET Framework. Reviewing these trends will illuminate steps that you can take today as you architect solutions to ensure they will be poised to take advantage of new technology when it becomes available. In most cases, the .NET Framework already provides significant support for each of these trends. However, it is useful to recognize where the key focal points will be in the future.

A Note About the FTP Protocol

Customers of the .NET Framework versions 1 and 1.1 said they wanted the framework to support the File Transfer Protocol (FTP). In response to this feedback, FTP support is planned for the framework's next major release.

A couple of options are available for those who need immediate support. First, sample FTP implementations are available free of charge on public user groups, such as *www.gotdotnet.com*. Second, a number of third parties provide FTP solutions for the .NET Framework. Specific examples include /n Software (*www.nsoftware.com*), Sax.net (*www.sax.net*), and Dart Communications (*www.dart.com*).

Protocol Independence

As discussed in Chapter 11, a specific protocol such as HTTP is not the optimal tool for every situation faced by today's distributed applications. Maintaining protocol independence while still achieving interoperability is an increasingly important and achievable aspect to distributed application development. Each protocol in use on the network today comes with its own set of strengths and weaknesses. Applications with the agility to switch from one transport to another will be in demand as user needs evolve. To take advantage of this trend, the core functionality of your applications should be independent of the underlying transport protocol. The .NET Framework helps developers design applications with greater protocol independence by providing common I/O models, such as the *System.IO.Stream* type. Going forward, you can expect to see further enhancements in the *System.Net* namespace and in other areas of the .NET Framework, such as Web services, that support this trend.

Network Awareness

Although applications have had to interact with the network for many years, few have done a good job of staying aware of the network and dynamically changing their behavior to best suit current conditions. For example, today's smart client applications are considered advanced if they simply support an online/offline mode. While being aware of online/offline status is an important part of unity with the network, applications can do much more. For example, an application that is aware of network characteristics, such as connection speed and throughput between local and remote endpoints, can provide a much richer experience than an application that simply goes "offline" when the network is slow. Imagine an application that is written in such a way that it works with minimal reliance on the network in low bandwidth conditions, but automatically senses increases in speed and throughput and reacts accordingly to improve the user experience. What's more, this application could use network "fingerprinting" techniques to recognize different network configurations and remember which services were available the last time it ran on them or even associate a geographical location with that network.

Developers building .NET applications should be aware of the potential for network awareness and plan for it in an application. For example, you should consider factoring protocol logic and business logic into the application in such a way that the network intensive protocols can be used in high bandwidth cases, but the application can have a fallback in lower bandwidth scenarios. If your application is rich in information that comes across a network,

consider factoring the way your application uses the network into different pro-
files or buckets and providing scaled-down experiences for your users. A
scaled-down experience is preferable to having a user wrestle with an application that was designed for a LAN from a dial-up connection. Today, the .NET
Framework enables applications to address network elements such as connection speed and network connectivity through the *System.Management* classes.
The following code sample demonstrates how to determine whether a machine
has one or more valid IP addresses assigned, which can indicate the machine's
network connectivity:

C#

```
using System;
using System.Management;

/// <summary>
/// This sample demonstrates the use of System.Management
/// to detect whether one or more valid network
/// connections are associated with the machine.
/// </summary>
class NetworkInformation
{
    [STAThread]
    static void Main(string[] args)
    {
        // Check to see whether one or more connections
        // are assigned to this machine (based on IP address)
        int numConnections = GetNumAvailableConnections();
        if(numConnections > 0)
        {
            if(numConnections == 1)
            {
                Console.WriteLine("1 connection on this machine with ");
                Console.WriteLine("at least 1 valid IP address assigned");
            }
            else
            {
                Console.WriteLine(numConnections + " connections on this ");
                Console.WriteLine("machine with at least 1 valid IP address");
            }
        }
        else
        {
            Console.WriteLine("No cards found with a valid IP address");
        }
    }
}
```

```
public static int GetNumAvailableConnections()
{
    // Query for the list of network adapters on the machine
    // For more detail on this type you can search
    // http://msdn.microsoft.com for "Win32_NetworkAdapterConfiguration"
    SelectQuery NAQuery = new SelectQuery("select * from " +
        "Win32_NetworkAdapterConfiguration");

    ManagementObjectSearcher NASearcher = new
        ManagementObjectSearcher(NAQuery);

    int availableConnections = 0;

    try
    {
        // Loop through each adapter returned from the query
        foreach (ManagementObject enumerate in NASearcher.Get())
        {
            // Find out whether IP is enabled on this adapter
            bool  IPEnabled = (bool)enumerate["IPEnabled"];
            // Get the adapter description
            Console.WriteLine((string)enumerate["Caption"]);

            // If the IP is enabled check for non-zero IP
            if(IPEnabled)
            {
                string[] IPAddress =
                    (string[])enumerate["IPAddress"];

                Console.WriteLine("IP Address: " + IPAddress[0]);
                if(IPAddress[0] != "0.0.0.0")
                {
                    availableConnections++;
                }
            }

            Console.WriteLine();
        }
    }
    catch(Exception e)
    {
        Console.WriteLine(e.ToString());
    }
    return availableConnections;
}
```

Visual Basic .NET

```
Imports System
Imports System.Management
'This sample demonstrates the use of System.Management
'to detect whether one or more valid network
'connections are associated with the machine.
Module NetworkInformation
    Sub Main()
        ' Check to see whether one or more connections
        ' are assigned to this machine (based on IP address)
        Dim numConnections As Integer
        numConnections = GetNumAvailableConnections()

        If numConnections > 0 Then
            If (numConnections = 1) Then
                Console.WriteLine("1 connection on this machine with")
                Console.WriteLine("at least 1 valid IP address assigned")
            Else
                Console.WriteLine(numConnections & " connections on this ")
                Console.WriteLine("machine with at least 1 valid IP address")
            End If
        Else
            Console.WriteLine("No cards found with a valid IP address")
        End If
    End Sub
    Function GetNumAvailableConnections() As Integer
        ' Query for the list of network adapters on the machine
        ' For more detail on this type you can search
        ' http://msdn.microsoft.com for "Win32_NetworkAdapterConfiguration"
        Dim NAQuery As SelectQuery
        NAQuery = New SelectQuery("select * from " & _
            "Win32_NetworkAdapterConfiguration")

        Dim NASearcher As ManagementObjectSearcher
        NASearcher = New ManagementObjectSearcher(NAQuery)
        Dim availableConnections As Integer

        Try
            ' Loop through each adapter returned from the query
            Dim enumerate As ManagementObject

            For Each enumerate In NASearcher.Get()

                ' Find out whether IP is enabled on this adapter
                Dim IPEnabled As Boolean
                IPEnabled = enumerate("IPEnabled")
```

```
                    ' Get the adapter description
                    Console.WriteLine(enumerate("Caption"))

                    ' If IP is enabled then check for a non-zero IP
                    If IPEnabled Then
                        Dim IPAddress As String()
                        IPAddress = enumerate("IPAddress")
                        Console.WriteLine("IP Address: " & IPAddress(0))
                        If IPAddress(0) <> "0.0.0.0" Then
                            availableConnections = availableConnections + 1
                        End If
                    End If

                    Console.WriteLine()
                Next

            Catch e As Exception
                Console.WriteLine(e.ToString())
            End Try

            Return availableConnections

        End Function
    End Module
```

This code uses the *System.Management* classes to query the system for installed network adapters and then inspect each adapter for associated IP addresses. This behavior is expected to be improved with richer and easier to find information in future releases of the .NET Framework.

Interoperability and Web Services

You never know when the interoperability requirements on your application are going to change dramatically. For example, when business groups, divisions, and even companies reorganize or merge, it's not uncommon for applications to see requirements for interoperability shift overnight. Web services are the solution for interoperability in the .NET Framework. While the other distributed application technologies discussed in this book have specific benefits, the cost of interoperability must be carefully weighed when deciding to go with a solution that might not interoperate well with disparate systems. To achieve its vision for Web services, Microsoft is expected to advance the technology in the .NET Framework so that most applications will have no need to go beyond Web services for distributed application functionality.

Security

It should come as no surprise that security will continue to play a critical role in distributed application development. Security is a top priority for distributed applications being created today, and this will not change anytime soon. Therefore, you can expect to see the .NET Framework evolve with security features at all levels of network communication, ranging from raw packets to application-level messages. Security enhancements will come in up and down the stack, but some will be more compelling than others. Applications that work to maintain a clean separation between business logic and the nuts and bolts of security will be best positioned to take advantage of the most important security features as they evolve.

Productivity

Increasing developer productivity with distributed applications was a core reason for inventing the .NET Framework. Microsoft will continue to focus on developer productivity for many years to come by simplifying key scenarios in the framework and making it easier to achieve new ones. However, keep in mind that "increased productivity" doesn't always mean that you get a higher layer of indirection. Productivity is also achieved through extensibility where appropriate across all layers of the stack. Well-factored applications will be able to take advantage of productivity enhancements as they are introduced into the Framework.

Summary

This chapter reviewed emerging trends in the world of distributed applications. Developers are advised to take these advancements into consideration as they design new .NET applications. The FTP protocol was discussed along with options available to developers until it is included in the .NET Framework. In addition, we covered the importance of building protocol independence into your application. We talked about how network awareness and interoperability can play an important part in building a compelling and agile application. Finally, we looked at the evolving role of security and productivity as core tenets of the .NET Framework.

Index

Symbols and Numerics

(crosshatch), 89

/ (slash marks), 127

100 Continue

  Nagle algorithm with, 248

  overriding, 333

  performance issues, 333–334

  Web services using, 247

A

Accept property, 205

advantages of .NET Framework, 6–7

Anonymous authentication, 311

APIs, class-based model for, 6

application domains, 262–263

application protocols layer, System.Net, 102, 112–116

architecture of .NET model, 7

ARP (Address Resolution Protocol), 322–323

ASP.NET

  classes for, 10–13

  purpose of, 10

  threading, 237

  Weather Service sample application, 10–13

asynchronous HTTP model

  aborting requests, 226–228

  BeginGetRequestStream method, 221–224

  BeginGetResponse method, 224–226

  purpose of, 220

asynchronous programming pattern

  application model for, 18

  AsyncNetworkIO sample program, 66

  bandwidth requirements, 329

  BeginXXX methods, 62–65

  calling methods, 63

  class design, 62

  delegate callback methods for, 63–65

  ending tasks, 63

  EndXXX methods, 62–65

  HTTP. *See* asynchronous HTTP model

  IAsyncResult, 63–65

  memory requirements for, 327

  network streams with, 63–65

  optimizing Web classes, 331–333

  performance of, 323–326

  purpose of, 47, 62

  sockets. *See* asynchronous sockets

  state parameters, 65

  streams, 27

  synchronous calls, mixing with, 63

asynchronous sockets

  accepting requests, 195–197

  byte array preservation, 199

  canceling operations, 197, 201

  clients, 153, 159

  closing, 201

  connections, 197

  data transfer, 198–200

  methods for, 192–193

  Monitor.Enter calls, 199–200

  multiple accept operations, 197

  multiple callbacks, 199–200

  posting operations, 193–195

  purpose of, 192

  tracking operations, 201

attachments, 258–259

authentication

  Anonymous, 311

  Authenticate method, 232–233

  AuthenticationManager class, 231–232

  Authorization objects, 233

  Basic, 312, 314

  Certificate, 312, 314

  certificates, 234–237

  ConnectionGroupName property, 335–336

  connections, HTTP, 230–234

  CredentialCache objects, 233

  dangers of, 234

  Default Credentials, 233

  Digest, 312, 314

  escalation attacks, 335

  Forms, 312, 314

  HTTP, schemes for, 311–315

  IAuthenticationModule class, 232–233

  IIS schemes for, 311–315

  impersonation, 234

  Integrated, 312, 314

  .NET remoting, 271

  NetworkCredential class, 104–105, 230–231

  NTLM, 336

  Passport, 313, 314

  performance issues, 334–336

  pre-authentication, 232–233, 247–248, 315, 334

  TCP channels, 274

  Web services using, 247–248

  X.509 certificates, 234–237

X-Z

About the Authors

Anthony Jones

Anthony Jones was born in San Antonio, Texas, and graduated with honors from the University of Texas at San Antonio in 1996 with a bachelor's degree in computer science. His undergraduate thesis was based upon optimizing the Icon compiler. After graduation, Anthony worked for Southwest Research Institute, a nonprofit contract research company in San Antonio. There he worked on a variety of projects, including real-time embedded control systems and visualization and simulation software, for customers ranging from the U.S. Air Force to the Weather Channel. In 1997, he moved to Washington State to work for Microsoft Developer Support. Anthony is currently the test lead for the Winsock API in the Windows division. He is also the coauthor of Network Programming for Microsoft Windows.

In his spare time, Anthony enjoys mountain biking, skiing, hiking, photography, and traveling with his wife, Genevieve.

Jim Ohlund

Jim Ohlund works as a software design engineer for Microsoft's Security Business Unit in Redmond, Washington. Jim's focus is on future security technologies for Microsoft products. He has worked in many areas of the computer industry, from systems programming to developer support to software testing.

In 1990, Jim received a bachelor's degree in computer science from the University of Texas at San Antonio. Jim began his computer career while still in college by developing personnel systems for the United States Department of Defense. He expanded his working knowledge of computer networks and network programming in 1994 by developing terminal emulation software for Windows platforms. In 1996, Jim joined Microsoft's Developer Support Networking API team, helping software developers get the most out of networking APIs in all Windows platforms. By 1998, Jim joined Microsoft's Proxy Server team and helped deliver Microsoft's first network firewall solution—Microsoft Internet Security and Acceleration (ISA) Server 2000.

When Jim is not working with computers, he likes to ski, snowboard, bicycle, and hike in the beautiful Pacific Northwest.

Lance Olson

Lance Olson was born and raised in Salt Lake City, Utah. He holds a master's degree in business administration from the University of Washington and a bachelor's degree in information systems and technology from Weber State University.

Lance works as a lead program manager in Microsoft's Developer Division. He joined Microsoft in 1997 and has worked on the .NET Framework since its inception. While working on the .NET Framework, Lance has been actively involved in the developer community. He has presented in Microsoft's Professional Developers Conferences (PDC), published articles on the Microsoft Developer Network (MSDN), and contributed to various development newsgroups and mailing lists.

When he is not working, Lance enjoys fishing, camping, pottery, playing soccer, and spending time with his children and his wife, Julie.

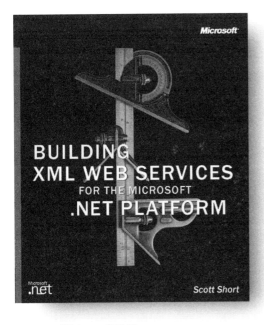

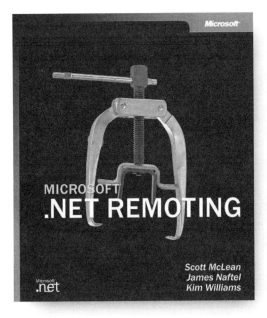

Get a **Free**
e-mail newsletter, updates,
special offers, links to related books,
and more when you
register online!

Register your Microsoft Press® title on our Web site and you'll get a FREE subscription to our e-mail newsletter, *Microsoft Press Book Connections.* You'll find out about newly released and upcoming books and learning tools, online events, software downloads, special offers and coupons for Microsoft Press customers, and information about major Microsoft® product releases. You can also read useful additional information about all the titles we publish, such as detailed book descriptions, tables of contents and indexes, sample chapters, links to related books and book series, author biographies, and reviews by other customers.

Registration is easy. Just visit this Web page and fill in your information:

http://www.microsoft.com/mspress/register

Microsoft

Proof of Purchase

Use this page as proof of purchase if participating in a promotion or rebate offer on this title. Proof of purchase must be used in conjunction with other proof(s) of payment such as your dated sales receipt—see offer details.

Network Programming for the Microsoft® .NET Framework
0-7356-1959-X

CUSTOMER NAME

Microsoft Press, PO Box 97017, Redmond, WA 98073-9830